CW01249654

PRINCE AND PRINCESS CHICHIBU
TWO LIVES LIVED ABOVE AND BELOW THE CLOUDS

In the garden of the Chichibu mansion in Omote-cho, Tokyo, 22 October 1939. *From left to right*: Prince Takamatsu, Prince Mikasa, Princess Chichibu, Princess Takamatsu, the Empress Dowager, Prince Chichibu.

PRINCE AND PRINCESS CHICHIBU

TWO LIVES LIVED ABOVE AND BELOW THE CLOUDS

INCLUDING A COMPLETE TRANSLATION OF SETSUKO, PRINCESS CHICHIBU'S MEMOIR *THE SILVER DRUM*

◆

DOROTHY BRITTON

GLOBAL ORIENTAL

PRINCE AND PRINCESS CHICHIBU
TWO LIVES LIVED ABOVE AND BELOW THE CLOUDS
By Dorothy Britton and Princess Chichibu

Part 2 first published in Japanese:
Gin No Bonbonnière by Shufunotomo Co. Ltd.
© 1991 by H.I.H. Setsuko, Princess Chichibu

First English edition 1996 by
GLOBAL ORIENTAL

Revised and expanded 2nd Edition 2010 by
GLOBAL ORIENTAL LTD
PO Box 219
Folkestone
Kent CT20 2WP

English Translation © Dorothy Britton 2010

ISBN 978-1-905246-24-3

All rights reserved. No part of this publication
may be reproduced or transmitted in any form or by any
electronic, mechanical or other means, now known
or hereafter invented, including photocopying and
recording, or in any information storage or retrieval
system, without prior permission in writing from
the publishers.

British Library Cataloguing in Publication Data
A CIP catalogue entry for this book is available
from the British Library

Set in Stone 9.5 on 12.5 point by Bookman, Langley, Berkshire
Printed and bound in Great Britain by CPI Antony Rowe, Chippenham, Wiltshire

Contents

◆

Preface						xi
Foreword by Tsunetada Matsudaira			xv
Preface by H.I.H. Princess Chichibu to First Edition of The Silver Drum		xix
Foreword by Kazuko Azo to First Edition of The Silver Drum		xxi
Introduction by Carmen Blacker to First Edition of The Silver Drum		xxiii
Chronology of Events in the Life of Prince and Princess Chichibu		xxix
Glossary of Japanese Words			xxxiii

PART 1
The Prince: A Vindication				3

PART 2
The Princess's Story – *The Silver Drum* (complete version)		23

1. BORN IN ENGLAND				25
   My Childhood Friend				25
   The Thread of Fate				27
   'Name: Setsuko'				29
   The Name-Father				31
   The Aizu Clan				33
   The Single Photograph			37
   The Flowered Bonnet				39

2. CHILDHOOD					43
   The Beijing Legation				43
   Heatstroke					45
   Taka's Room					48

3. GROWING UP					53
   The Peeresses' School				53
   The Great Kanto Earthquake			55
   The Aizu Spirit				58

	Summer in Nikko	60
	The Day I First Met Prince Chichibu	62
4.	AMERICA	65
	The Reunion	65
	The Friends School	69
	Brass Bands and Chewing Gum	71
	The Lindbergh Song	75
	Prince Chichibu's Visit	77
	Waltzing with Daddy	81
	The *furoshiki* and the Hole-in-one	84
	The Emissary	86
5.	UNTIL MY WEDDING DAY	93
	The Memory Book	93
	Right and Proper	97
	Learning to be a Princess	100
	The Last Few Days	103
6.	IMPERIAL BRIDE	107
	The Twelve-layered Robe	107
	'Pinetrees Twain'	109
	The Chrysanthemum and I	114
7.	THE SILVER BOX	119
	A Brotherly Chat	119
	A Young Pine and a Star	122
	Staff College Homework	126
	Hiking in the Summer Holidays	130
8.	OUR DAILY LIFE	133
	A Visit to the Chichibu Mountains	133
	The Temporary Imperial Residence, Hirosaki	136
	Attending the Coronation	141
9.	UP TO THE OUTBREAK OF WAR	148
	Papier Mâché String	148
	The Anti-Tuberculosis Association	150
	The Prince Falls Ill	153
	A Room with a View of Mount Fuji	155
10.	IMPERIAL VILLA, GOTEMBA	159
	Fuji's Four Seasons	159
	Artificial Pneumothorax	163
	15 August 1945	167
11.	THE POST-WAR YEARS	171
	The Shmoo	171
	The Prince Chichibu Farm	173

'I envy the weeds'	176
The Promise	179
The Oxford Rugby Team	183
Last Will and Testament	186
The Mitsumine Kiln	190
12. INTERNATIONAL FRIENDSHIP	198
The 'Little House'	198
Tea with the Queen Mother	202
'Do as you please more'	205
The Poems	208
APPENDIX Introductory Remarks by Dorothy Britton	213
A Critique of the Occupation by HIH Yasuhito, Prince Chichibu	215
Index	*219*

To the Memory
of
Geraldine Ward
with love and gratitude

Preface

◆

I suppose I have always felt close to Prince and Princess Chichibu because they were our neighbours when I was a child. Their imposing Victorian-style villa in Hayama on the other side of the shore road was no more than a hundred yards from our seaside home. Nowadays, as I walk along the lane that leads up the hill behind it, the few remaining oaks lining the wall at the back of the property hide the modern scene and make it easy to imagine the way it was in the old days, when down on the beach there stood a boathouse containing Prince Chichibu's racing sculls from Oxford. I often watched him row out to sea when the water was sufficiently calm. Sometimes his young cousin, Princess Sawa, would accompany him in another scull. Prince Kitashirakawa's lively and spirited daughter – my beach playmate – though little more than a child, never lacked enterprise.

Growing up, I was fascinated to hear about Prince Chichibu's rowing, skiing and other sports leading to his great popularity as the 'Sports Prince', and his fondness for England after being at Oxford. My parents had met the Princess when she was a schoolgirl in Washington where her father was ambassador, and later met them both at Japan-British Society gatherings in Tokyo, for the Prince was the Society's Honorary Patron. When I returned to Japan after the war, the Princess succeeded him as Patron, and the gracious royal lady took a warm interest in the Society's Elizabeth-kai, a club for its women members which my old friend Kazuko Asō, DBE, and I started together in 1958.

It was Dame Kazuko who came all the way down to Hayama one

day on behalf of her son-in-law, Prince Tomohito of Mikasa, to ask me to translate into English the memoirs of his favourite aunt by marriage, Princess Chichibu. Prince Tomohito is the son of Prince Chichibu's youngest brother, Prince Mikasa.

Kazuko suggested I leave out large portions of the autobiography so an English version could come out soon, because the Princess's health was deteriorating. Sadly, she died just before the book appeared, but fortunately I had taken her a copy of the typescript when about half of my translation was done. Her Imperial Highness very kindly invited me to tea, and while I was there she showed me the charming little silver sweet-container, in the hourglass shape of an ancient Japanese hand-held drum, mentioned in her memoir. I asked for a photograph of it, and it appears on the cover of the book, which I called *The Silver Drum*.

The memoir first came out in Japanese in 1991, entitled *gin* (hard 'g'!) *no bonbonnière* (*The Silver Sweet-box*). It has on the cover an illustration of a large and ornate receptacle made by Mappin and Webb, which the publishers photographed at a department store in Tokyo, possibly thinking it would be more eye-catchingly descriptive of the French word *bonbonnière* than a tiny drum!

But the miniature drum-shaped silver container has great significance in her story. The Princess explains about the custom in court circles of giving specially designed silver sweet-containers to commemorate certain occasions, and how it was the Prince's mother, a lady of great imagination and flair, with a lively interest in the world, who personally designed that particular little silver *tsuzumi* drum embellished with motifs representing England and America – countries connected with the Prince and the Princess – and gave one to each of them at the time of their betrothal to symbolize international friendship – a concept she held dear.

The sweet-boxes contain comfits – old-fashioned European sweets consisting of a tiny sugar-coated nut or seed. The fact that the Japanese word for comfit is *konpeitō*, from the Portuguese word *confeito*, suggests that the custom was introduced by the Portuguese traders and missionaries who came to Japan in the 16th century.

My Concise Oxford Dictionary calls the word 'comfit' archaic, but here in Japan, the *konpeitō* can still be found in traditional confectionaries. The custom of the silver *bonbonnière* continues in royal and upper class circles, and there is a shop in Kyoto which still makes very superior comfits. It was featured in the news in 2006 in connection with the wedding of the Emperor's daughter.

The Silver Drum has been out of print now, for some time, and I had been dearly wanting to complete the translation, and throw more light on the life and times of the girl who became a princess in that faraway country Japan in those far-off pre-war days, providing lots more insights – and humorous episodes, too, such as her mother's hilarious faux pas in a London bus as a young diplomat's bride at the turn of the previous century!

I have translated almost all of Princess Chichibu's many poems, which have a depth of feeling and an accomplished yet artless charm that merits a slim volume of their own. However, I did take the liberty of leaving out the chapter entitled 'Tears in the rainy season' consisting almost entirely of poems expressing sorrow at losing her beloved Prince.

She was devoted to him. But her marriage did not begin happily, and she tells in her afterword how she had decided to publish an autobiography because of all the untruths written about her, and she 'wanted to set the record straight'.

I have long yearned to set the record straight about the Prince, so I began this book with a short biography, to celebrate the recent vindication of Yasuhito, Prince Chichibu, Japan's once popular royal, of collaboration in the attempted army coups of the 1930s. Exhaustive research has found that the Prince was innocent, in spite of the persistent rumours that would not go away. It seems to me high time that the truth about this friendly, gregarious, intellectual, and ardently altruistic Prince should be better known.

During his long convalescence from TB at the foot of Mount Fuji the Prince took up writing. His articles and essays appeared in magazines and newspapers, and collections of his essays were published in book form as well. The latest collection came out in 2005, edited by his nephew – the son of the Princess's elder brother – entitled Born Into The Imperial Family. I am much indebted to Tsunetada Matsudaira for his kindness in allowing me to quote many of the Prince's autobiographical passages and views in those essays, as well as letting me use many of the photographs, and for so kindly agreeing to write a Foreword.

I have translated the Prince's last essay – which only recently came to light – as an Appendix. It is a thought-provoking evaluation written in 1949 after four years observing the American Occupation and the Japanese reaction.

The Japan-British Society's help with the publication of *The Silver Drum* in 1991 was invaluable. Mineo Yamaguchi, formerly Secretary to Her Highness, and Lady-in-Waiting Tsuyako Hattori kindly went through the original typescript making some corrections and many helpful suggestions. For this book, Hojo Nakajima, former Deputy Grand Master of Ceremonies, very kindly explained some of the ancient rites described in the additional chapters. My very special thanks go to Yoshiko Tanaka whose mellifluous audiotape of Princess Chichibu's memoirs in Japanese was not only helpful but a joy to listen to. Years of use by the visually impaired had taken its toll on the tapes, but she patiently re-recorded the additional chapters I translated for this book – elucidating the Prince's essay for me too – as well as helping me understand court customs, the imperial vocabulary, and many of the poems. I am, of course, much indebted to the works of historians Hosaka, Hata, and Shillony, and finally I would like to express my thanks to Prince Tomohito of Mikasa for choosing me to carry out his inspired wish to see Princess Chichibu's life story in English.

DOROTHY BRITTON
Hayama, October 2009

Foreword

BY

TSUNETADA MATSUDAIRA

CHAIRMAN OF THE ENGLISH SPEAKING UNION, JAPAN

◆

It was more than half a century ago that I first came to know Prince Chichibu and my aunt Setsuko, Princess Chichibu. The war was worsening and we had been evacuated to Gotemba. I was in my second year of primary school. My mother, my younger brother and I were living in a house in a small village near the Chichibu's Villa where the Prince was recuperating from tuberculosis. Where our house used to be on a small road in the midst of paddy fields, there is now a motorway interchange. The road led to the local school about a couple of miles away, to which we used to walk, gazing at Mount Fuji as we went along.

Princess Chichibu was kept busy from dawn to dusk looking after the Prince. It was a time of scarcity, and even royalty had to be self-sufficient. My brother and I often used to play in the garden near the Prince's sickroom. When the weather was fine, the glass doors would be slid way back to let in fresh air and we could see his smiling face as he lay in bed. They grew sweet corn on their large property as well as other crops, and at the bottom of the hill they kept a few sheep. The Princess was often clad in work pants, wearing a straw hat on her head. I always think of my aunt and the Prince whenever I eat an ear of corn.

The Prince and Princess both treated my brother and me with great affection, probably because they had no children of their own. Once some troops were billeted at the school and the soldiers ordered us pupils to collect edible wild plants for them to eat. We evacuees could not hold a candle to the local country children, and were totally at a loss as to how to go about it. Aunt Setsuko took pity on us and showed us a spot in the Villa grounds where some wild *fuki* (bog rhubarb) grew. I picked a huge bundle of it which I strapped to my back and carried to school feeling as proud as punch!

Bombing raids became frequent; some bombs even fell on Gotemba which was on the flight path of the B29s who used Mount Fuji as a navigation marker. A large concrete air-raid shelter was constructed at the foot of the garden outside the prince's sickroom, with rails laid so he could be rushed there in his wheeled bed. I remember watching with excitement as first the Princess and then members of the staff tried it out. Fortunately, the Prince never had to use it.

Besides the occasional bomb dropped in the Gotemba area, there was a curious habit the B29s had of scattering bits of silver tape over a broad area. Perhaps it was intended to confuse Japanese radar. As we watched the pieces drifting down like sparkling snow flakes, children would tear off into the woods and meadows to collect them. Especially prized were the rare rolls of tinfoil still intact. I gave one to the Prince and the Princess. I still remember how thrilled I was as I watched the Prince put on his glasses and study it with great interest. It was not until years later that I learned how worried they had both been about the Prince's elder brother, the Emperor, in regard to the worsening of the war and the possible reaction of the military.

Prince Takamatsu, Prince Chichibu's slightly younger brother and his wife drove to Gotemba on 15 August 1945, so that both families could listen together to the Emperor's radio broadcast proclaiming the end of the war. Aware of their brother's innermost feelings, they wondered what lay in store for the future of Japan. But I was too young to understand things like that.

Thanks to post-war streptomycin Prince Chichibu's health was partially restored, enabling him to resume some of his activities and to move to balmy Kugenuma, nearer Tokyo. But he died eight years later, in January 1953, at just fifty years of age. Heartbroken I rushed to his bedside, where my Aunt Setsuko said to her husband, speaking just as if he were still alive: 'Here's Tsunetada! He was always such a darling in Gotemba.'

The doctors had nothing but praise for Prince Chichibu, an ideal patient who never uttered a word of complaint or bitterness, and was always overflowing with gratitude for his wife's wonderful nursing.

She outlived him by forty-two years. Besides passionately supporting the Anti-Tuberculosis Association, Princess Chichibu indefatigably worked towards Anglo-Japanese friendship and made five visits to Prince Chichibu's beloved England. She visited other countries too, and all in all lived the kind of life the Prince would have wanted her to live and did the things he would have wanted her to do. She died in 1995.

Recently during a brief stay in hospital, the head doctor happened to mention to me how much he liked the song of their affiliated School of Nursing, the words of which were by Princess Chichibu. He said he found himself singing it to himself quite often:

> Trying to feel
> The way the invalid feels
> That is true nursing.
> Love is all important too,
> Each one helping the other.
>
> Day in and day out,
> Trying hard to nurse better;
> Hearts in unison
> Tirelessly striving for health,
> Each learning from the other.

The song was written in 1958 five years after the death of the Prince, when I often used to visit my aunt at the small part left after their palace was burned in the fire-bombing of Tokyo. Prince Charles called it 'The Little House'. We used to reminisce about the Gotemba days, and I got the impression she wished her nursing had been better. Superficially this song has all the trappings of the usual sort of school song, but it marvellously expresses the true soul and spirit of what nursing should ideally be. The poem was obviously based upon her own experience.

I hope this book will widen people's knowledge and understanding of two wonderful people – my aunt Setsuko, Princess Chichibu, and HIH Prince Chichibu.

Preface by H.I.H. Princess Chichibu to First Edition of *The Silver Drum*

◆

This book records my recollections of eighty-odd years. As they passed by in my mind like the images on a revolving lantern, there were fond, nostalgic memories, joyful ones and amusing ones, and painful and sad ones too. As I tried to recall them, it was as if I were living those 80 years all over again. Some things I could not even bring myself to recount. Every now and again a recollection would break off in the middle as if it had been erased. Some, I would find I had misremembered, and would have to go back and rack my brains again.

At times like that, it was my equerry Mr Mizoguchi, my private secretary Mr Yamaguchi, and my chief lady-in-waiting Mrs Shimizu who encouraged me to go on and painstakingly helped me look through old diaries, letters, drafts of poems, and photographs. In particular, I am most grateful to Mr Yamaguchi and Mrs Shimizu for their tireless attendance during the past six months when I have not been well. It is only because of their help that I have been able to follow the sequence of these old recollections. All I had to do was talk while others put it all together, but I often wondered what use there was in recording my memoirs at this late date, and there are some things I have not touched upon at all.

I decided to publish these memoirs because there has been so much written about me that was not true, and I wanted to set the record straight. It was generally believed that the Prince and I were involved in a great romance. The truth of the matter is that if it had not been for the sudden death of Emperor Taishō, the Prince was intending to return to Oxford University, while as for me, an immature and busy high school student in America, romance was the last thing I would have had time for. But wherever I go, that is all people ask me about.

The facts are as set down in this book, which I hope will give readers some idea of what the Prince was like in the brief time allotted to him on this earth. No-one would have been happier than the Prince to see how things have changed and how open and modern the life of the Imperial Family has become. If only he were alive and well now, so that I could know what he thought about it all, and about these memoirs of mine!

My childhood friend Masako Shirasu has been a tower of strength to me in preparing this book. I want to thank her not only for that, but for her long and steadfast friendship.

I am very grateful to Dorothy Britton (Lady Bouchier) for translating these memoirs and to Dr Carmen Blacker for providing the Introduction. I hope that this little book will bring my old friends nearer, and that it may help to further understanding between our countries.

Setsuko
PRINCESS CHICHIBU

Foreword by Kazuko Aso to First Edition of *The Silver Drum*

◆

Ever since Princess Chichibu's book appeared in Japanese in 1991, her nephew, Prince Tomohito of Mikasa, and I have felt that these unusual memoirs, with their fascinating insights into life in the Imperial Family, should be translated into English so that people abroad could enjoy them too.

Here in Japan, readers have enjoyed Her Highness's memoirs so much that it has not only been issued on cassette for the vision impaired, but has been released in paperback in the popular Kodansha Library series.

Her Imperial Highness and I managed to persuade Japan-born author and poet Dorothy Britton (Lady Bouchier) to undertake the task of translation into English, since we felt she had the necessary sensitivity and understanding of things Japanese.

Her Imperial Highness, alas, died on 25 August, and sadly did not live to see the translation of her book in print, but I know that Princess Chichibu's many international friends and admirers will welcome the appearance of this English edition, partly made possible by the generous support of the Japan-British Society.

Kazuko Asō, DBE
SEPTEMBER, 1995

Introduction by Carmen Blacker to First Edition of *The Silver Drum*

◆

Here is an unusual and remarkable book. Never before has a member of the Japanese Imperial Family written a complete autobiography, and never before have any such memoirs been made available to English readers. But here we have Princess Chichibu, born in 1909, telling of her childhood, her famous grandfather who was a feudal lord, her three years in Washington when her father was Japanese Ambassador to the United States, and eventually her marriage, utterly unexpected, to the Emperor's younger brother in 1928. We are further told of her difficulties of finding herself, untrained in any Court etiquette, suddenly thrown into a world which she had always regarded as inaccessibly remote and 'other', removed 'above the clouds' from ordinary human avocations.

Princess Chichibu was born in Walton-on-Thames while her father, Matsudaira Tsuneo, was an attaché at the Japanese Embassy in London. She returned to Japan after only eight months, however, so that her lifelong regard for England can stem from no conscious memories of an idyllic Edwardian childhood. Perhaps, however, some memory lingered in her subconscious mind, for with her excellent command of English, she has always proved a warm and staunch friend of this country. Indeed, the title of her book, *The Silver Drum*, symbolizes this feeling for Britain. The silver drum in question, a small *bonbonnière* or sweetbox in the shape of a Japanese hand-drum (illustrated on the book jacket), was a present to her from the Empress Dowager, the widow of the Emperor Taishō. Such silver mementoes were given by the Japanese Court to mark certain special occasions, much as Fabergé eggs were distributed by the Russian Court at Easter.

But this particular silver box was decorated with motifs which symbolized the friendship of Japan with Britain and America. And all her life, she tells us, it has proved a special treasure, a magic talisman which gave her courage and comfort in moments of difficulty and stress.

Princess Chichibu's grandfather was Matsudaira Katamori, the *daimyō* or feudal lord of the Aizu domain, whose unwavering support of the tottering Shogunate during the war preceding the Restoration of 1868 marked one of the most dramatic incidents of the whole momentous change. The castle town of Aizu Wakamatsu was besieged by the forces of the new government, and only by dint of the celebrated *Aizu-damashii*, the peculiar tenacious courage on which the samurai class of the Aizu clan prided itself, did the castle hold out for a month against overwhelming odds. The horrors of the campaign and its aftermath were vividly recalled by Dr Willis, the English doctor sent by the new government to render what medical aid he could to the wounded. He heard many tales of the bravery of the Aizu women in the castle during the siege; they cut off their hair, nursed the wounded, and often took a turn with a rifle at the defences of the castle. He saw the *daimyō*, a dirty and dejected prisoner, leaving for Edo under heavy guard with scarcely a dozen people to witness his departure.

On arrival in Edo he was branded a traitor to the Throne. In the complex web of loyalties of that turbulent time, Princess Chichibu assures us, Katamori was never disloyal to the Emperor, though he opposed tooth and nail the Satsuma and Chōshū clans who engineered the revolutionary change. So devoted was he to the Imperial house, indeed, that he always carried next to his skin, even in a hot bath, the letters written to him by the Emperor Kōmei, sealed in a bamboo tube. The fact that he was branded as a traitor after the fall of the castle was a cause of misery to him for the rest of his life, and he counselled his descendants not to rest until the stain on the honour of the Aizu clan was wiped out.

Accordingly, through her childhood, Princess Chichibu was never allowed to forget the *Aizu-damashii*. She was constantly reminded of the special spirit of the samurai members of her family, and of the wrong done to its honour. She must never waste a grain of rice, for example, but bear in mind the sufferings of the Aizu people in exile.

In 1925 her father was appointed Japanese Ambassador in Washington and she was sent to a much respected Quaker school in the city. She was getting on well with her English and algebra, and during the school holidays she enjoyed waltzing with her father, who liked Caruso and who sang arias from *La Traviata*.

But this happy period was interrupted by the arrival in Washington of Count Kabayama, with a proposal from the Empress Dowager that she should marry Prince Chichibu. The proposal came as a total surprise, not to say a bombshell. She had only met the Prince a couple of times and then their meetings had been marked by no special attention. The first reaction of both her parents and herself was to say no; she was untrained in Court etiquette, unsuitable in every way to take on the responsibilities of consort to an Imperial Prince. The prospect was daunting and terrifying, for to her, as to all Japanese outside it, the Court was an 'other world', remote and discontinuous with all that she was accustomed to.

The Empress Dowager, however, refused to take no for an answer. Back came Count Kabayama on the next boat, with even more pressing proposals. It was only when she remembered the *Aizu-damashii*, and realised that by accepting the proposal she might redeem the honour of the Aizu clan, that she reluctantly gave her consent.

She then found herself thrust, virtually from the schoolroom, into the vortex of a royal network of obligations and behaviour, in which every movement, every minute detail of clothing, every phrase and nuance of language, was almost ritually prescribed. And in which the evening diversion of the Court was not waltzing and singing Verdi, but playing the solemn game of *Nō-karuta*, Nō cards, on which passages from medieval Nō plays were written in difficult calligraphy.

It was not until three months after her wedding that she was able to dine with her parents again *en famille*. She found herself treated as royalty, and addressed with all the correct honorific complexities of the Japanese language. Her old nanny Taka, who had been in the family since she was a child, would not raise her eyes to look at her.

But her marriage with Prince Chichibu proved to be a very happy one, and they quickly became devoted to each other. He had many endearing qualities which she soon came to love and admire. Her life, accordingly, was largely focused on her husband and his work during the 1930s at the staff college. He worked so hard that he was often up all night, while she naturally sat up for him in the next room, listening in silence to the calls of the owls.

But historians will learn nothing from her on the vexed question of the part he actually played in the army during the years leading up to the war. Short of making clear that her husband was shocked and angry with the young officers behind the February 26th incident of 1936, in which a fanatical military faction occupied the centre of Tokyo and murdered three government ministers, we hear little from Princess Chichibu of the ominous signals of growing militarism in Japan.

Her account of the war years is resolutely personal.

We can gather from her narrative, however, that the Prince had little sympathy with the army's fatal policy of war with Britain and America. He received the news of the outbreak of war in silence, and thereafter refused to make any mention of the catastrophe. Now an invalid, he spent much of his time in their mountain villa in Gotemba gazing at Mt Fuji. She, for her part, cultivated a vegetable garden.

Those English readers who might expect more on this subject from the staunch friend of England and America that Princess Chichibu had undoubtedly been all her life, should remember that the book was initially written for Japanese readers, for whom the Imperial Family has always been outside the turmoil of politics, in the 'world above the clouds' indeed that Princess Chichibu mentions earlier in the book as seeming so remote and inaccessible. That she should make no mention of the broader issues, terrible though they were and terrible though they must have been for herself, is a matter of Court protocol. We know that there are many restrictions on the members of the Imperial Family; among them was the rule that required her when she wrote the book to stick to the purely personal account of their lives during those fateful years.

In her Preface she tells us that there is much more that she could have written, but that she did not choose to do so. We must read between the lines, and remember that special quality of the Japanese language so prized through the centuries: *honomekashi*, or the power of suggesting concentric circles of meaning radiating from the central nucleus of the word. Unfortunately, not even so excellent a translation as Dorothy Britton's can reproduce this quality in English. We might recall, perhaps, that in September 1941 the Emperor was confronted with a group of officers who, in the grip of their powerful and terrifying myth, believed that they knew 'the emperor's mind' better than he did himself. He chose to quote them a poem composed by his grandfather, the Emperor Meiji:

Yomo no umi/Mina harakara to/Omou yo ni
Nado namikaze no/Tachisawaguramu.

*In a world where all within the four seas
are brothers, why should the wind and
waves so furiously rage?*

Prince Chichibu's illness sadly proved incurable, and he died in 1953. Princess Chichibu's life since his death has been a busy one of charitable works, and travel to promote friendship between Japan and Britain. She has been several times to this country, and visited Magdalen College Oxford where Prince Chichibu studied in the autumn of 1926 before having to return to Japan on account of the illness of his father (Emperor Taishō).

Not long ago I was sorting some old papers and came across what seemed to be an old exercise book compiled in the year 1937. In it were stories and poems and cuttings from the newspapers. There on the first couple of pages were five pictures cut from the *Daily Mail*, of Prince and Princess Chichibu, who had come to England to attend the Coronation of King George VI. I must have been a fan of Princess Chichibu at the age of twelve. It is a special happiness therefore to write these words of Introduction for Dorothy Britton's translation, *The Silver Drum*. May it bring to English and American readers something of the fascination that Japanese have found in this account of a world from which legends and rumours spring galore, but few such authentic and intriguing recollections.

Chronology of Events in the Lives of Yasuhito, Prince Chichibu and Setsuko, Princess Chichibu

◆

1902	25 June: Yasuhito born in Tokyo.
1909	9 September: Setsuko born in Walton-on-Thames, England.
1910	Returns to Japan in April.
1913	Enters Japanese kindergarten, Peking.
1916	Enters primary school in Japanese Concession, Tientsin.
1917	Yasuhito graduates from Gakushuin Middle School.
1918	Setsuko returns to Japan. Enters Peeresses' School in September. Yasuhito enters Military Academy.
1920	Graduates as cadet 3rd Infantry Regiment 1st Division.
1921	Yasuhito comes of age and becomes Prince Chichibu.
1922	Commisioned 2nd Lieutenant.
1925	17 February: Setsuko leaves for USA, to which father appointed Ambassador. Enters Friends School in Washington in September. 7 July: Yasuhito arrives in London.

1926	October: Yasuhito enters Oxford University.
1927	25 December: His father Emperor Taisho dies.
1928	13 January: Setsuko's name moved to family register of uncle, Viscount Morio Matsudaira. 17 January: Yasuhito arrives in Yokohama. 18 May: Setsuko graduates from Friends School. 1 June: Leaves Washington, sailing from San Francisco on board the *Shunyo Maru*. 22 June: Arrives in Yokohama. 14 September: *Nōsai-no-gi*, betrothal ceremony, at Viscount Matsudaira's house. 17 September: Chinese characters for 'Setsuko' changed. 28 September: Wedding ceremony and Setsuko invested with Order of the Sacred Crown, First Class. 17-25 October: Visit Ise Grand Shrine and Imperial tombs in Nara and Kyoto. 31 October: Visit Tama Imperial Mausoleum. 6-27 November: Attend Enthronement ceremonies of Shōwa Emperor Hirohito. Prince Chichibu enters Staff College.
1931	Prince Chichibu graduates from Staff College.
1935	9 August: Prince Chichibu posted to Hirosaki as Commanding Officer, 31st Infantry Regiment.
1936	9 December: Prince Chichibu posted to General Staff, Tokyo.
1937	18 March: Leave Yokohama aboard *Heian Maru* for Canada, en route to England to attend Coronation of King George VI. 12 May: Prince Chichibu receives medal from the King commemorating the Coronation of Their Majesties. 14 July: Leave for Switzerland and the Netherlands, later returning to Japan from London via Canada. 15 October: Arrive in Yokohama.
1939	22 May: Princess Chichibu becomes Honorary President, Japan Anti-Tuberculosis Association.
1940	21 June: Prince Chichibu becomes ill.
1941	16 September: Move to Gotemba.
1952	20 January: Move to Kugenuma.
1953	4 January: Death of Prince Chichibu. 24 March: Princess Chichibu becomes Honorary Vice-President,

Japan Red Cross.
13 August: Becomes Honorary Patron, Japan-British Society.
6 October: Becomes Honorary Patron, Japan-Sweden Society.

1954 15 November: Moves to Tokyo.

1962 21 July-7 August: Visits Britain and Sweden as Honorary Patron, Japan-British and Japan-Sweden Societies. Also visits Paris.
23 July: Created Honorary Dame Grand Cross of the Order of the British Empire.

1967 27 January-7 February: As Honorary Patron, Japan-British Society, visits Britain to attend 75th anniversary celebration in London of the Japan Society.

1969 8 April: Invested by the King of Sweden with the Grand Cordon of the Order of the Seraphim.
1 October: Becomes Honorary President of the Association for Traffic Accident Orphans.

1970 8-9 May: Visits Korea together with Prince and Princess Takamatsu to attend the funeral of Princess Li of the former Royal House.

1974 7-19 June: Visits Britain at the invitation of the British Government.

1978 9 October: Invested by Princess Margaret at the British Embassy on behalf of Her Majesty the Queen as Honorary Dame Grand Cross of the Order of St Michael and St George.

1979 4-18 June: Visits Britain at the invitation of the British Government, returning via the USA.

1980 19 February: Is made an Honorary Fellow of the Royal Horticultural Society.

1981 17-18 October: Visits Britain at the invitation of the British Government to attend the opening of the Great Japan Exhibition in London, and also visits Switzerland.

1985 4-11 March: Visits Nepal at the invitation of the Nepalese Government, returning via Thailand.

Glossary of Japanese Words

◆

anpan	Soft bread rolls with sweetened *azuki*-paste centre. From *an*, bean-jam, and *pan*, bread, from Portuguese *paõ*.
azuki	Tiny reddish-brown beans. Adzuki or aduki in English.
banzai	Hurrah! May you (he, she, etc.) live long!
chōyō	Alternative name, meaning 'Double Yang', for The Chrysanthemum Festival on the 9th day of the 9th month of the lunar calendar.
daijōsai	The ancient mystical rite of all-night communion with the spirits of his ancestors observed by a new emperor on his enthronement.
daimyō	Feudal lord.
dan	Grade.
doma	Large earth-floored room in old farmhouses, traditionally used for farming tasks, cooking, storage, etc.
eikoku	Britain.
engawa	A veranda-like wooden-floored strip about 3 feet wide on the outdoor edge of a tatami-matted room, protected by both wood and glass sliding doors and separated from the room by wood-framed paper sliding partitions.
furisode	Brightly coloured formal kimono with long sleeves worn by young unmarried women.

furoshiki	Square cloth used for wrapping things.
gin	Silver.
gishigishi	Creak.
go	Intricate game for two played with black and white stones on a board, competing for territory. Also called *igo*.
hakama	Ankle-length pleated divided-skirt worn over kimono by men or women.
hamon	Temper-pattern on the blade of a Japanese sword.
haori-hakama	Men's full-dress formal wear of, say, grey silk *hakama* and black silk kimono-type jacket (*haori*) bearing family crest.
hiragana	The cursive form of Japanese syllabic writing or kana (cf. katakana, the angular form).
hitoe	Unlined.
honomekashi	Hint; suggestion; illusion.
hori-gotatsu	*Kotatsu* (see below) having a sunken pit under it which enables sitter to put his or her feet down upon the warming device, while sitting on the tatami floor.
ichi	One.
itsutsuginu	Five silken robes. Nowadays just one simulating five.
jūnihitoe	Ancient costume originally comprising twelve robes.
kamadashi	Taking the finished pottery out of a kiln.
karaginu	Brocade jacket worn over the 'Twelve-layered robe'.
kashiko-dokoro	Sanctuary in the Imperial Palace grounds.
keikaku	Plan; project; scheme.
kempeitai	The former dreaded military police whose reputation for cruelty and injustice is still a byword.
kijo	On a desk; on paper; in theory.
kogin	Traditional handcrafted fabric made in Hirosaki. Dark blue homespun linen with patterns worked into weave in white yarn.
konpeitō	Tiny spiky sweet made of poppy seeds, flour, and sugar syrup.
kosode	Short-sleeved kimono.
kotatsu	Quilt-covered, table-topped framework holding a heat source for warming the knees as one sits on the tatami floor.
kumidashi	'Drawn-water cups' for serving hot water samples to demonstrate its quality to the guests before the

Glossary of Japanese Words xxxv

	tea-ceremony begins.
kunen-shu	A ceremonial thick black *sake* made by boiling black soybeans, ordinary *sake* and *mirin* (sweet *sake*).
manga	Japanese comics.
miai, o-miai	Formal meeting with a view to marriage.
mikagura	Sacred Shintō music and dances performed at shrines.
mirin	A sweet *sake*, mostly used in cooking.
mitsumine	Three peaks.
monbushō	Ministry of Education.
monpe	Jacket and baggy pants of splash-patterned indigo cloth worn over kimono for farm work.
naga-bakama	Full and very long *hakama* (see above) worn with ancient 'Twelve-layered robe'.
nōsai-no-gi	Ceremonial exchange of betrothal gifts.
o-shiruko	Thick sweet warm drink made with *azuki*-bean paste and served with rice cakes (*mochi*).
obi	Sash.
odoriko	Dancing girl.
rakugo	Traditional art of comic story-telling.
ryūnōgiku	Wild daisy. *Pyrethrum sinense*, var. *japonicum*.
sake	Alcoholic beverage brewed from fermented rice.
sembei	Rice crackers.
setsu	Season.
shichiriki	Ancient flute.
shō	The second character in the reign name Taishō (1912-1926) meaning 'great righteousness' is read *sei* or *shō* in its Chinese-based pronunciations, and *masa* or *tada* in the vernacular versions.
shō	Ancient mouth-organ.
shōgi	Japanese chess.
sukiyaki	Paper-thin slices of beef cooked with vegetables, *tōfu*, etc., and soy sauce and sweet *sake*, in a chafing dish at table.
sushi	Vinegared rice with fish, vegetables, seaweed, etc.
susuki	*Miscanthus sinensis*, a kind of pampas grass.
tabi	Foot mittens.
tanka	Literally 'short poem', and also called *waka*, 'Japanese poem', 31 syllables in five lines of 5,7,3,7,7 – in effect a triplet and a couplet. The triplet led to the three-line haiku.

tatami	Cloth-bordered mat of thick straw covered with woven rush about 3 by 6 feet and 2.4 inches thick. Room size is described by the number of mats, i.e. an 8-mat room, a 6-mat room.
tokonoma	Ornamental recess in sitting/dining-room designed for display of hanging scroll, single art object and flower arrangement.
tsuzumi	Hourglass-shaped hand-drum.
uchiginu, uchiki	Two of the many robes of the *jūnihitoe* court costume.
uwagi	Outer garment; coat.
waka	See *tanka* above.
washi	Japanese handmade paper.

PART 1

THE PRINCE : A VINDICATION

THE PRINCE: A VINDICATION

◆

Masayasu Hosaka's biography, published in 2000,[1] makes clear once and for all that Prince Chichibu, Japan's popular 'Sports Prince', was not an *éminence grise* behind the famous '2/26 Incident' – the 26 February 1936 uprising led by young army officers. After consulting available sources, the author discounts the various theories and rumours that have persisted over the years. In his Postscript, Hosaka deplores 'the groundless fabrications which have been circulated so extensively'. He writes that it made his blood boil with rage time and time again as he conducted his exhaustive research.

In addition, the eminent historian Professor Ikuhiko Hata writes in his *Hirohito: the Showa Emperor in War and Peace* published in 2007: 'There is little evidence to suggest that the rebel forces actively tried to enlist the prince' and that 'one can even detect a conscious effort on the part of the rebels to avoid causing problems for the prince'.[2]

Hata also brilliantly explains the intricate factional manoeuvring that led to the attempted coup, and reveals how it was the high-ranking army brass who were the real instigators. The army was becoming a law unto itself, acting against the wishes of the Emperor and the government. Finally, making use of idealistic young officers, they managed to get rid of most of the old conservative government, to make way for unrestrained military campaigns. One of those assassinated was Korekiyo Takahashi, the Finance Minister, who had kept on refusing the army's request for a budget with which to wage war in China. His daughter was one of my mother's closest friends, and when we came back to Japan after the Second World War she told my mother it was worth losing the war in order to 'get rid of those dreadful militarists'.

The Prince was serving in the army, following the tradition of young Western royalty, after the Meiji Restoration of 1868 when Japan came out of isolation and took her place in the world. His younger brother, Prince Takamatsu, served in the navy. Prince Chichibu was by nature friendly and sociable, like his father Emperor Taishō, from whom he inherited the 'common touch'. In the army, he was delighted to find himself in close proximity with people from all walks of life. He soon made friends with some of the young cadets. Learning about the poor homes from which many of the recruits came, he was filled with sympathy and a tremendous desire to do something to help alleviate the poverty among the working class. Like Britain's Edward, Prince of Wales, regarding the plight of Welsh miners, he felt 'something must be done'. So he did do something. He tried hard to persuade his brother, Emperor Hirohito, to contravene his position as a constitutional monarch and take control of the government and force them to make conditions better for the masses.

That is as far as Prince Chichibu went, while unbeknownst to him he was becoming a symbol and rallying cry for the insurgents. He was shocked when his reformist friends went as far as murdering cabinet ministers. In a post-war essay he writes:

> It was at the end of the Taishō era. Our country was in the midst of a colourful period when social problems, and various ideologies – including liberalism – were much to the fore. I was in my twenties, impressionable, and highly sensitive to the general feeling at that time. I was easily influenced by the current trends, and not a little dissatisfied with conditions in Japan. So I took quite a bit of interest in the ideas being circulated of reform and revolution.[3]

A year before the outbreak of the Second World War the Prince succumbed to tuberculosis and spent the war years convalescing near the foot of Mount Fuji. There, he discovered his considerable talent as an essayist, and so some of the following short biography will be expressed in my translation of the Prince's own words.

☐

Chichibu-no-miya, literally Prince of Chichibu, was born 25 June 1902, his mother's birthday. But it was not until he came of age at twenty that he received that title. Seven days after his birth, his grandfather, Emperor Meiji, named him Yasuhito, chosen from a list of suggestions. In Japan, parents suggest possible names, and a respected relative or friend makes the ultimate choice. In the name Yasuhito, the Chinese character yasu means 'to be kind, to ease and alleviate' and had been among those suggested for Hirohito, born fourteen months earlier. Emperor Meiji also gave him his initial title Atsu-no-miya, (again literally Prince of Atsu, although the 'of' is not used in the conventional Anglicization of imperial titles). *Atsu*, purity, comes from a line in the Chinese classics, 'Thro' purity and harmony one reaches truth'.

The palace was full of talk about Britain at the time. On the day of Yasuhito, Prince Atsu's, birth, King Edward VII fell ill with appendicitis and his coronation on the following day had to be postponed and Emperor Meiji sent an appropriate message through his ambassador in London. Friendship with Britain was much on people's lips, since the Anglo-Japanese Alliance was in the process of being formed. The little prince who grew up to be an Anglophile was of course unaware then of these historic connections with Britain, but an English nanny's advice did apparently exert a more direct influence.

According to an ancient custom, the sons of emperors were taken away from their parents when they were seventy days old and brought up in the home of a trusted aristocrat for their early years. Together with his elder brother Hirohito, Prince Atsu was brought up in the home of Count Sumiyoshi Kawamura, a retired admiral and member of the privy council who was well known as a family man of noble character. Breaking down the count's initial hesitance, Crown Prince Yoshihito, their father, had said to the count: 'Don't take it too seriously. Think of them as your own grandchildren and raise them any way you like.'

The count consulted books and asked the advice of various people. He said the most valuable instruction he received was from a Miss Ethel Howard, an English governess employed by the feudal lord of the Satsuma clan. Miss Howard had taught some of the future kings and emperors of Europe, and she told the count that her basic principles were the fostering of an independent spirit, a sympathetic heart and gratefulness.[4] In addition to these, Count Kawamura determined to foster a sound mind, a healthy body, a dauntless spirit and respect for others in the boys, as well as the ability to withstand hardship. He would also discourage arrogance and egotism while at the same time preserving their innate character. Both the Emperor and Empress, their grandparents, as well as the Crown Prince and Princess, their father and mother, heartily approved the Count's objectives, and all of the Kawamura family proceeded to concentrate on bringing up the two little princes.

The boys had only been with the Kawamuras three years when the count died, bringing, as it happened, that old custom to its end. The boys' father, Crown Prince Yoshihito, decided he would rather have his sons nearby, so he moved them into a house he had specially built in his own compound, where they were tutored, together with a few other selected boys, prior to entering the Gakushūin, formerly known as the Peer's School.

The Crown Prince, who later became Emperor Taishō, was an enterprising young man, and may have been encouraged in his iconoclastic decision by Dr Irwin von Baelz, the German physician whose services Emperor Meiji had obtained when his son was ailing as a child, thereby introducing Western medicine to the imperial court for the first time. When Prince Yoshihito brought his two boys back from the foster family, Dr Baelz wrote in his diary: 'The crown prince's family is now enjoying a genuinely happy domestic life in the European sense, father, mother and children associating without restraint in a way hitherto unknown for an heir to the throne. It is a pleasure to see such a happy family.'[5] Prince Chichibu, describes his childhood vividly in a post-war essay:[6]

> Being in the same compound with our parents made our lives much more like that of ordinary people. You could say we lived next door, but we were a little over a five-minute child-walk away. And anyway, our parents were busy with various chores, appointments, and courses, so we couldn't just go over there to play any time we felt like it. It boiled down to about twice in three weeks. In between, Father used to come over to see us, and sometimes we'd meet in the gardens. There were even times when we went backwards and forwards every day. Father was in excellent health then, and he would often suddenly stop in the middle of some activity and casually come over and play with us. He visited us more often than Mother did. He used to join us in raucous games of tag and blindman's buff. Father would come and see us too when we had gone to bed, and we loved to talk

with him until we fell asleep. Once, when Father took us to call upon an aunt, I remember she gave us green tea and when I complained that it was bitter, he whispered to me to shut up. He came to see us when we were summering in Nikko, and joined us in our fun in Hayama. Readers may think it strange I should take such pains to describe such ordinary activities, but they were not ordinary to us, since our situation was far from ordinary.

The first time I ate with my father was in Hayama when I was five. And having meals with our parents at the Togu Palace in Tokyo began when I was six. The dining room had a parquet floor and a very large table. Our parents sat on one side, and we brothers sat facing them on the opposite side. Sometimes a few chamberlains and ladies-in-waiting might be at a separate table. Father would make us take turns in serving him wine. If there were others there we would have to serve them too. We were still quite small, and never handled bottles at any other time, so we were not very good at pouring. We would spill the wine and our hands would get sticky, and we objected to the smell, so we didn't particularly enjoy that job. But there was the curiosity element of doing something we didn't normally do, and it was gratifying to see how happy it made Father to ask us to pour wine for this person or that person. After the meal we would often go into the room beyond the dining room where there was a piano, and sing songs. Mother played the piano and all of us, including the chamberlains and ladies in waiting, would join together and sing all sorts of songs, including military songs. The song we always sang was called the World Tour Song (*Sekai manyu no uta*) and began:

> In the wide, wide world, every country
> Differs from another, so let's go and see!

I shall never forget how much we enjoyed those evenings. I think Father must have liked the World Tour Song because he had wanted so much to travel abroad, and it served as an outlet for his frustration at not being able to do so. Besides that, although the period of fascination with things foreign was over, in various ways there was an eagerness for the culture of the advanced nations and Father's interest in conditions in foreign countries probably reflected that as well. I don't think there were many people in those days who had been abroad, even among the chamberlains. Whenever they did, they would bring us presents, so we had the opportunity from time to time of seeing foreign things. I received toys from abroad and had several albums of postcards, so I was an armchair traveller. In Father's living room there were three folding frames containing many photographs, half of which were of foreigners (mainly royalty and celebrities) giving rise to much conversation about foreign countries and the foreign royals who had visited us.

Father liked to smoke, and on his desk there were always boxes of rare brands of cigars and cigarettes from various countries. We children were terribly impressed by the beauty of the gorgeous cigar-bands decorated with gold, scarlet and vermillion designs, and Mother would save them for us. We filled many albums with them, in spite of the lack of variety as collections go!

And I shall never forget all the different kinds of dogs I saw. Father, like my grandfather Emperor Meiji was also fond of dogs, which he kept in the inner garden outside the living room. He always took several with him when he went for a walk. There were countless breeds such as pointers, setters, greyhounds, collies, terriers and bulldogs, and they were usually kept in kennels at what is now Meiji Shrine. Mother was at first terrified of dogs, but as far back as I can remember I never minded stroking the fiercest of them, and I had a pet Pekinese which I adored.

One of my most unforgettable memories is of my game of *shōgi* (Japanese chess) with my father. I think it was not long after I had begun to learn how to play. My father challenged me to a game and I accepted, cheekily refusing any handicap. But I was so overwhelmed by the impressive pieces and the handsome board and all the unfamiliar etiquette that I became terribly nervous, and before I knew what was happening, I lost piece after piece, and was quickly and utterly defeated. Lacking the courage to accept my father's offer of a revenge, I withdrew. But now, when I think of my one and only game of chess with my father, I cherish it as a most precious memory.

His father, Crown Prince Yoshihito, was a man of many interests. He was fond of reading, had studied English, French and German, as well as Chinese and Korean, and was an admirer of Kaiser Wilhelm. He paid a visit to Korea, and was due to visit Taiwan also if his father, Emperor Meiji, had not died; but plans for a visit to Europe had to be abandoned for health reasons. Not only a linguist, Yoshihito was a fine poet and calligrapher. Historian Ben Ami Shillony tells of his immense popularity, both as Crown Prince and then as Emperor Taishō. He was convivial, often went bicycle riding with friends, and enjoyed a smoke and conversation with all sorts of people, just like his second son, Prince Chichibu, later on, was to do. He was fun-loving and, as we have seen, a wonderful father. Shillony quotes a former chamberlain who wrote that Emperor Taishō 'was a very beloved man'.[7]

On the death of Emperor Meiji in 1912, Yoshihito moved to the main palace. But 'becoming Emperor' writes Prince Chichibu, 'I think shortened my father's life. During his Togu Palace days he seemed so lively to us children, the way he rode his horse, and his bearing and deportment in the palace. But after a few years as Emperor Taishō, he seemed quite a different person.'[8]

Affairs of state began to wear Yoshihito down, both physically and mentally, and in 1921 his elder son and heir, Crown Prince Hirohito, was made Prince Regent. Emperor Taishō's inability to cope gave rise to insinuations of mental problems, but in his *Enigma of the Emperors* Ben-Ami Shillony explodes that myth. It turns out that what the Emperor suffered from was the lingering effects of childhood meningitis.[9] It finally caused his memory to fail, and he had difficulty speaking. He spent the last five years of his fifteen-year reign in lovely, quiet, restful Hayama. It was Dr Baelz who 'discovered' that healthy seaside village and recommended that Emperor Meiji build a villa there. I was living quite nearby as a small child when Emperor Taishō died in 1926, and I remember how we were not allowed to sound our motor car horn because of His Majesty's grave illness.

After graduating from the Gakushūin middle school in 1917, Prince Atsu (not yet called Chichibu) was sent to the military preparatory school, entering the main military academy the following year, from which he graduated in 1920 and was assigned as a probationary officer, or cadet, to the Third Infantry Regiment's First Division.

It was at the First Division's big autumn military exercises in 1921, that Prince Atsu was 'discovered' by the media. In one of the manoeuvres there were two forces, 'East' and 'West', and cadet Prince Atsu was commanding an East platoon. East and West had spent several days trying to attack each other in the area around the Tama River in the outskirts of Tokyo. Eventually, Prince Atsu's platoon managed to attack West's artillery position in Futago-Tamagawa , but were met by a shower of 'bullets'. So he decided to attack them on their weak, unguarded side, from across the river, although he knew its waters would be very cold and the current swift. His attack was a success and he was awarded a victory. It had not occurred to most of the others to try to cross the river at that spot where there was such a current. A classmate, Etsusaburo Kobi, leading a different platoon, had considered doing so, but hesitated. He writes: 'The Prince jumped into the river. I was staggered, and just followed him, regardless, and so did the others, and we splashed our way across, up to our chests against the current.'

Pebbles had been collected near the spot where the Prince went in and there were suddenly places so deep the Prince was obliged to swim as he waved his sword in the air, leading his men. In addition to the cadets, the Prince's platoon included the company commander and an officer who was there to judge tactics and leadership, and they both rushed into the water after the Prince's platoon in a panic.

A newspaper cameraman just happened to be nearby, and his photograph of the Prince leading his men across the Tama River, waving his sword, was distributed nationwide. From that time on Prince Chichibu became known more and more as *wareware no kōzoku*, 'our very own royal'. The people's popular prince. It all started with that photograph.[10]

That was also the year the Prince came of age, at twenty, when his title was changed to *Chichibu-no-Miya*, Prince Chichibu. Regarding the new name, Masao Ōtani. Head of the Imperial Household's General Affairs department, is said to have considered various alternative proposals, and finally settled on Chichibu, the name of a mountain range near Tokyo. Ōtani wrote that it was epoch-making, because theretofore place names for royal titles had been chosen from areas around Kyoto. He implies that the late Emperor Meiji may have influenced the decision, and that the Household may have taken the Prince's fondness for mountaineering into consideration as well. The Prince's entry in the who's who of Japanese royalty states that Emperor Meiji had recommended that name for use when the time came, giving among many reasons the fact that the Chichibu peaks dominate the old province of Musashi in which Tokyo lies, and has connections with the legendary hero Prince Yamato-Takeru.

When the cadets were asked to write their thoughts on graduation from the military academy, the Prince's piece was not run-of-the-mill. Instead of the usual platitudes based on hopes for advancement, Prince Chichibu had simply expressed a desire to do everything in his power to set a good example to the masses. And now, as an officer on probation in the Third Infantry Regiment, he came in contact for the first time with conscripted soldiers from ordinary walks of life, mostly from the prefectures surrounding Tokyo.

In the assembly rooms, where officers could meet for various purposes or just to chat, Prince Chichibu made friends with a young cadet by the name of Toshihachi Morita, who was two terms junior to himself. A middle school graduate from Hachiōji on the outskirts of Tokyo, he had successfully passed the military academy entrance exams and decided to become a soldier. A serious student, he was a man of few words, not given to joking, and rather straitlaced. He had been assigned to the same company as the Prince, and although at first he seemed a bit nervous in the presence of a royal, he was never obsequious, which appealed to the Prince. One day in the assembly rooms the Prince asked him if he was getting used to army work. 'Yes, Sir,' he replied simply, 'I'm working hard at it every day.'

After that the Prince made a regular habit of speaking to Morita. They mostly talked about the weather, or about their army work. One day he invited Morita to the palace for tea. Morita seemed nervous and tense as the Prince showed him all around and described his daily life with his father, Emperor Taishō. The Prince then asked him about *his* father. Morita told the Prince that his father was just an ordinary simple farm worker, and described the sort of work he did. 'That's just the sort of man I like,' said the Prince.

Another friend the Prince made was Teruzō Andō, who had arrived as a cadet for a six-month training course. Andō was a similarly serious, ruggedly honest type of man, who besides that had the additional trait of never losing his poise no matter who he might be speaking to. Prince Chichibu also liked Andō for his enthusiasm for tackling things, and his thirst for knowledge. If there was something Andō did not understand, he never hesitated to ask questions. This appealed to the Prince immensely. He also invited Andō to the palace.

Both Andō and Morita shared the quality of incorruptible rectitude and refusal to flatter or play up to anyone, no matter who they might be. Officers who did so were not scarce in the Third Infantry Regiment. Nor were those who simply nodded in agreement to whatever opinion the Prince might express. Andō and Morita, however, never treated the Prince as different, addressing him as Second Lieutenant Chichibu, as if he were any other officer, which made the Prince extremely happy. He opened his heart to those two men, with whom he could talk frankly about anything.

Prince Chichibu was commissioned as a second lieutenant in 1922, after three months as a provisionary officer. A palace had been built for him in Akasaka's Omote-cho, and he moved into it that same year. It was a little over a mile from his office, and he insisted on walking the distance. As people he passed bowed to him, he never failed to return the courtesy. And he was so punctual that people on his route said they could set their watches by him! A private office had been made ready for him, but again, with his typical modesty, he insisted on being in the same room as everyone else of his rank.

Among the new recruits in No. 6 Company Prince Chichibu discovered poverty up close for the first time in his life. There were many men from poor families, some of whom were the sole support of their elderly parents and siblings. The Prince wanted badly to help them, but there seemed to be nothing he could do except ask his aide to try and find some way to help them indirectly. Royals do not carry cash, so he could do little personally besides sharing with them his water and riceballs whenever possible during a manoeuvre.

In 1923, in connection with plans to send him to study at Oxford, it was decided to have a professor from the Imperial University (now Tokyo University) arrange a special course of lectures for the Prince, to make sure he was well-grounded in his national cultural traditions. The courses would cover the following subjects: the Imperial Constitution, moral philosophy, comparative religion, Shinto and classical Chinese. Tuition in French was also included, and while he dreaded having to cope with the Analects of Confucius, he enjoyed learning French, and it enabled him to converse with comparative ease with the crown prince of Czechoslovakia who came on a royal visit! The Prince was not an academic, but he liked to read and to learn. Photography was his hobby and he had a darkroom installed in his palace. Yasuhito was above all a sportsman who loved mountaineering and almost every kind of sport, and he revelled in the way being an army officer brought him into close contact with members of the general public, unlike most of the royals, and consequently learning about ordinary lives.

Also, unlike his elder brother Hirohito, now Prince Regent, he was free to read newspapers and magazines, so naturally he formed impressions about society, which he then discussed with his friends Morita and Andō. They talked about things like the Kotoku incident of 1910 when an anarchist of that name who had picked up socialist ideas in America tried to assassinate Emperor Meiji. Although there is no record of them doing so, they also must have talked about the attempt on the life of the Prince Regent in December, 1923, when he was attacked by a discontented socialist while on his way to the Opening of the Diet in a State carriage. Prince Chichibu was in the carriage behind.

That incident probably served to encourage conservatives in the Palace to deplore the visibility of the two princes and they tried to discourage the plan to send Prince Chichibu to Oxford University. His elder brother's visit to England in 1921, against much opposition, had already given Hirohito an enticing glimpse of the greater openness of the British monarchy compared with its Japanese equivalent, and many people were worried about its possible influence on his younger brother. They tried their best to discourage the scheme with all sorts of arguments, even including: 'What if he falls in love with an English girl?'

Prince Chichibu sailed from Yokohama in the cruiser *Izumo*, 24 May 1925. He went by train from Marseilles to Paris, crossed the channel by ferry from Calais, took a train from Dover to London, arriving at Victoria Station at 7.20 p.m. on 7 July. It had taken him forty-five days.

He was met by the Duke of York (who later became King George VI), Foreign Minister Chamberlain and retired Major-General Laurence Drummond with whom he was to stay while studying English. A group of Japanese residents gave him a rousing *'Banzai!'* The friendly welcome of the British there to meet him belied his expectation that the people of that nation tended to be rather pompous and arrogant. In one of his essays he writes of how hazy his image of the country had been before coming. He knew Britain was conservative, and that its monarchy was democratic, and he had always loved the way they boasted that the sun never set upon their empire, but he soon realized how vague his preconceptions had been.

The Drummonds lived in a large, old-fashioned house in spacious grounds, surrounded by green hills, about twelve miles outside of London. While there he had to speak only English, which was at first quite a trial for the young Prince. But the couple who came daily to the Drummonds were excellent tutors, and he soon became reasonably fluent, besides learning a great deal about the country and the people, discovering many things that impressed him during his year-and-a-half stay and sadly interrupted time at Oxford University.

In his essay 'The British Monarchy' written in 1952,[11] he describes the deep impression made upon him 'by the strong relationship between the sovereign and the people':

> This relationship is partly like that between the closest of friends, but mixed with respect. It is true affection and fellow feeling, and not just form. It is expressed appropriately according to the place and the time, and is always perfectly natural and spontaneous. All I can say is that I feel envious. This beautiful relationship in which the feelings of the monarchy and the people are mutual, is not something that is one-sided or a pretence on either side. It is a feeling the people have learned to expect regarding the monarchy, and the royals understand that and never disappoint them. They have won each other's trust and formed a firm bond.
>
> What I had previously known of England was of the picture postcard variety, and limited in depth. I had heard the people were conservative and the monarchy democratic, but I knew little about such things as to how much the Great War had changed the country, or that a cabinet had been formed by the Labour Party.
>
> Settling down in the outskirts of London, my life was a stream of daily novelties, and as I gradually learned to know Britain and deepen my understanding of British people I discovered many unexpected things about them. Among these was the image of sumptuous grandeur – quite unimaginable to a Japanese – projected by the lives of the nobility – including of course the royal family. Granted the difference between our social set-ups, I could not help but think how odd that the British public never raised their voices in complaint – especially when the royal family were so central to British society and not something set apart. It was interesting, for instance, when Princess Elizabeth (the present Queen) was married in 1947, the way the people took a public interest in how it ought to be done. Some argued that her wedding should be kept simple because of the post-war austerities, while others demanded a brilliant show to cheer the country up. You could say it all boiled down to the people's love of pageantry, but I think it was because people felt that what concerned the monarchy concerned the people too.
>
> The reason the British people feel so friendly towards the monarchy is because they see them so often, at the multifarious

events which the royal family attend, as well as reading about them in the newspapers. If they were hidden away in the palace they would hardly become popular. Moreover, the British, who have long experience of social living make a clear distinction between what is public and what is private and do not interfere in people's private lives, so the king is able to have a large private life, which I think helps to make the people feel kindly towards him. It makes the king human for instance to think of him enjoying the life of a country gentleman at Sandringham. In comparison, our national character is such that people intrude on privacy to the extent that lives can be made miserable. Private lives and public lives are so confused that in Japan one intrudes upon the other.

The Prince goes on to praise the British police for their skill in bringing the people and the royals together, whereas in pre-war Japan the police did just the opposite, and isolated them. He tells how when he went on trips to the provinces he could not stop complaining about them, while in Britain he was constantly amazed by the mutual trust the police have built up with the populace.

When the funeral rites for his father were over, Prince Chichibu had every intention of going back to Oxford. He had left his aide in London, and his rooms at Magdalen College just the way they were, ready for his return to take up his studies from where he had been obliged to leave them off after just one term.

But now there was more opposition than ever to his going back. For one thing, he had become the heir apparent now that his brother Hirohito was Emperor, with three daughters and as yet no son. Besides that, the voices of those previously opposing his going, fearing his being influenced by the openness of the British monarchy, became ever more strident. Courtiers finally made him feel it was unthinkable for him to be going abroad during the extended period of mourning for his father and more or less forced him to give up the idea.

Prince Chichibu until the end of his days never ceased to regret not having been able to spend at least one whole year at the British university.[12] He mentioned it more than once in his essays, and he made the study in his palace a replica of his rooms at Magdalen College, as well as sending for a couple of sculls to row in Hayama to remind him of happy, carefree afternoons on the Cherwell and the Thames.

Back in Japan in the army and the company of his young officer friends, he tried to put Oxford out of his mind and concentrate on the plight of the working class soldiers, wanting so badly to help them, and feeling that something must be done to remedy the unfairness of society in Japan. Prince Chichibu's officer friends were greatly influenced by a book written by the fervent socialist Ikki Kita entitled *A General Outline for the Reorganization of Japan*. It advocated a reform, centred on an authoritarian 'people's emperor', to form a new cabinet free of what Kita described as 'corrupt politicians and businessmen'.[13] The book was banned, but his friends obtained a hand-written copy for the Prince.[14]

Knowing that his brother Hirohito, the Shōwa Emperor, was, like himself wholeheartedly dedicated to the welfare of the people of Japan, and similarly humble about having so much more than they, the 'something' that Prince Chichibu did was to go to his brother and tell him about the dire straits of the working class and try to persuade him to exert his influence with the government on their behalf.

It must have been sometime between the end of 1931 and the spring of 1932 – the year of the 15 May incident in which the prime minister was assassinated. Prince Chichibu's impassioned diatribe is referred to in the published diary of General Shigeru Honjo, who became the Emperor's aide-de-camp in 1933. These jotted notes have no indication as to when the information was obtained, or how:

> One day Prince Chichibu visits Palace. Speaks to His Majesty. Keeps vehemently advocating necessity of direct Imperial rule even if it means suspending Constitution. Argument becomes heated. Afterwards HM says to Chief Chamberlain: 'I cannot possibly consent to anything like direct rule, which would violate the virtue and dignity of my ancestors. I am ordered by the Constitution to embrace and oversee its principles. That is all I am allowed to do.'[15]

Although described as 'Head of the Empire' in the Meiji Constitution, the emperor was virtually the organ of the state and not the state itself, although historians claim there has always been a debate as to which it should be – maybe something in between.[16] Hirohito revered what he believed was his grandfather Emperor Meiji's emphasis on the constitutional aspect of the monarchy, and conscientiously acted accordingly.

Prince Chichibu apparently hectored the Emperor a second time,[17] urging him to prevail upon the government to do something to make life better for the masses. He is said to have had a bit of a temper and tended to forcefully 'thunder' his opinions when he felt strongly about anything,[18] so it is not surprising that it made the Emperor extremely unhappy and created a temporary rift between them.[19] The prince also must have said there was no telling what extremists might get up to if measures were not taken to try to rectify social inequity, for on the morning of the 2/26 uprising, chamberlain Osanaga Kanroji, who woke the Emperor with the bad news, tells how the monarch's first words were a sad and horrified: 'So they've finally done it,' then how after a moment or two he muttered to himself: 'It's all my fault.' In his book of reminiscences Kanroji writes: 'Those words struck me like an electric shock.'[20]

Prince Chichibu was in Aomori at the time, in the far north where he had been posted – possibly as an attempt by the elder statesmen to distance him from extremist influence. He first heard about the action from his younger brother Prince Takamatsu who telephoned him at 7 a.m. He had no foreknowledge of the attack plan and was appalled that the young officers had murdered some of Japan's finest statesmen claiming, moreover, that they had done it for the Emperor 'to rid him of bad counsellors'.

After getting permission to leave for Tokyo as soon as possible, Prince Chichibu called the officers of his battalion together and told them that 'the regrettable action was completely opposed to His Majesty's wishes', and ordered them not to align themselves with the rebels under any circumstances, and to refrain from doing anything rash.[21] He then set off on the fourteen-hour train journey to Tokyo to join his two younger brothers in protecting their elder brother the Emperor and giving him support. That it was appreciated is evident in Hirohito's remark to Marquis Kido: 'Prince Chichibu is acting so much more correctly now than at the time of the May 15 incident.'[22]

Unbeknownst to the Prince – for apparently he had no way of knowing – he had become the rebels' rallying symbol.[23] His friend Ando made a speech of unwarranted optimism at the Sanno Hotel: 'Prince Chichibu has returned to Tokyo! He understands our cause and sympathizes with us! The Shōwa Restoration is at hand!' That speech may have fuelled a lot of the rumours about the Prince's involvement in the attempted coup.

Three years after the Second World War ended Emperor Hirohito drafted a remarkable Apology – which, unfortunately, was never released. It only came to light in 2003 when author Kyoko Kato, biographer of the Emperor's chief chamberlain, Michiji Tajima, found it among Tajima's papers.[24] The Emperor was so deeply opposed to war that when someone asked him when he had first come to the conclusion that the Second World War should be ended, he is said to have replied: '8 December 1941' – which was the day it began![25]

He had made his disapproval clear at the Imperial Conference on 6 September 1941,[26] but should he have tried to veto their war plan? Should he have done as his brother wanted in 1932 and ordered a social reformation? Hating war, and yet not having been able to stop the militarists from pursuing it; the countless lives sacrificed in his name; and the memory of his brother Prince Chichibu's impassioned entreaties – all this may have weighed on his mind so heavily that in 1948 he had his chief chamberlain, Grand Steward Michiji Tajima draft the apology on his behalf for the enormous devastation and suffering caused by the tragic war for which he felt a deep personal responsibility. Using the imperial singular pronoun *chin* (the royal 'we') his statement included the solemn words *chin no futoku naru fukaku tenka ni hazu* (it was our fault, and we apologize with profound shame to all beneath heaven). *Tenka* (all beneath heaven) can either mean 'the whole nation' or 'the world'.

His words *futoku naru* could also be translated as: 'a failing on our part'; or: 'our lack of moral courage'. The Emperor used the same *futoku naru* when he heard about the 1936 uprising.

The Apology was not released because of doubts expressed in various quarters about the wisdom of such a declaration at that time. But it surely would have given the Emperor peace of mind, as well as gratifying a great many people – not least Prince Chichibu.

It is ironic, that the war, which the Prince hated as much as did the Emperor, should turn out to have been an ill wind that blew Japan quite a lot of good. Prince Chichibu would have rejoiced to see the egalitarian prosperity of Japan today, and the many reforms, and the internationalization. An enormous public relations windfall resulted from all those enemy scholars who learned Japanese and invariably became devotees of the culture, which they subsequently introduced to the world!

Other reforms are hopefully on the way. In his post-war essays,

Prince Chichibu aired bold opinions never before expressed by a member of the Imperial Family, and one of the things he advocated was an ever greater opening up of the monarchy.[27] The Imperial Family seem always to have longed for greater freedom. They do not appear to have 'been amused' by the rampant pre-war royal super-deificationism pursued by the militarists. It irritated Emperor Taishō's widow, the Empress Dowager, to think of the sovereign being raised up arbitrarily to such a divine state, and she complained in no uncertain terms regarding her annoyance at the increase of the guard around the royal family.[28] In an essay about his mother the Prince wrote that the guards were so thick about her that she couldn't see the people and so she finally gave up going out – which was something she had enjoyed so much, 'always wanting to add any little bit to her knowledge, and even one more person to her acquaintance, always hoping that her friendship could be a help to people'.[29]

Prince Chichibu's mother Masako, daughter of Prince Nashimoto, was a remarkable woman. Until Hirohito was named Regent on account of his father's deteriorating health, she had been a tower of strength in the Palace dealing with things for her husband. She had always taken a lively interest in everything, from promoting international friendship to conserving the national culture. Western dress was officially required by the new Meiji Era custom in the palace, but she made sure the kimono was not forgotten. She was convinced the imperial line could do with fresh new blood, so she busied herself in searching for congenial wives for her four sons not necessarily from the traditionally prescribed few families. To this end she regularly visited classes of the peer's school for girls. She was a wise and percipient go-between and a wonderfully kind and considerate mother-in-law.

It was she who first spotted the perfect bride for her son Prince Chichibu when visiting the school, and even managed to have a closer look when she invited the young lady's mother to the palace and said bring your daughter along. The Prince, aged twenty-three, happened to be there so she made sure he caught a glimpse too of the sixteen-year-old. And it was she who contrived that on his return journey from Oxford he spend a night with the girl's family in Washington. But none of that family had any inkling then of her plan.

The fantastic story of their engagement is far from romantic, but the press tried to make it appear as if they were revealing 'a great secret romance' when the Prince arrived back from abroad – and when soon afterwards so did she! It was just what the media wanted with which to follow up their own love affair with the people's popular 'sports prince'.

As the years went by, Princess Chichibu was more and more anxious to make it clear that it had not been like that at all. So some years after the decease of the Prince, she went against the wishes of hidebound members of the Court, and published a complete account of her life: there had been no secret romance, and she and her family had agonized and fought tooth and nail to avoid her becoming a virtual prisoner in the remoteness of the world 'above the clouds'.

But as readers will discover, it was not long before she was smitten by the charming Prince's caring consideration. She wrote: 'I knew that I would do anything in the world for him, and that nothing would be too hard.' Her marriage did, in fact, turn out to be a real love story after all!

NOTES

1. Hosaka, Masayasu, *Chichibu no Miya: Shōwa Tennō otōto-miya no shōgai* (The Life of Prince Chichibu, the Younger Brother of Emperor Shōwa) Tokyo, Chuō Kōron Shinsha, Inc. in Chuō Bunko paperback series, 2000.
2. Hata, Ikuhiko, *Hirohito: The Shōwa Emperor in War and Peace*, (Folkestone, Global Oriental, 2007) p.29 (first published in 1987 as *Hirohito Tennō itsutsu no ketsudan* (Five Decisions by Emperor Hirohito).
3. Yasuhito, Prince Chichibu, *Kōzoku ni umarete* (Born into the Imperial Family) (*Collected Essays*), Watanabe Shuppan, Tokyo, 2005) p.97.
4. Kanroji, Osanaga, *Hirohito: An Intimate Portrait of the Japanese Emperor*, Los Angeles, Gateway, 1975. p.18.
5. Baelz, Erwin, *Awakening Japan: The Diary of a German Doctor* (Indiana University Press, 1974) p.364, quoted by Ben-Ami Shillony in *Enigma of the Emperors*, (Folkestone, Global Oriental, 2005) p. 177.
6. Yasuhito, Prince Chichibu, *Collected Essays*, p.20.
7. Shillony, Ben-Ami, *Enigma*, p.175.
8. Hosaka, *Chichibu no miya*, p.58.
9. Shillony, *Enigma*, p.175.
10. Hosaka, *Chichibu no miya*, p.114-16 *passim*.
11. Yasuhito, Prince Chichibu, *Collected Essays*, p.98.
12. Hosaka, *Chichibu no miya*, p.194.

13. Shillony, *Prince Chichibu and the February 1936 Rebellion*, (Princeton Papers in East Asian Studies, August 1972) p.111.
14. Hata, *Hirohito*, p.12,
15. Hosaka, *Chichibu no miya*, p.260.
16. Hata, *Hirohito*, p.4.
17. Hosaka, *Chichibu no miya*, p.268.
18. Kikuko, Princess Takamatsu in *Omoide no Chichibu-sama*, (Prince Chichibu as I remember Him), p.52 in Chuō Kōron magazine, November 1996.
19. Hosaka, *Chichibu no miya*, p.269.
20. Kanroji, *Hirohito*, p.125.
21. Hosaka, *Chichibu no miya*, p.309.
22. Ibid. p.268.
23. Shillony, *Prince Chichibu and the February 1936 Rebellion*, pp.119-20.
24. Katō, Kyōko, *Shōwa Tennō shazai shōchoku sōkō no hakken*, (Tokyo, Bungei Shunjū magazine, July 2003).
25. Kanroji, *Hirohito*, p.128.
26. Hata, *Hirohito*, p.47.
27. Hosaka, *Chichibu no miya*, p.599 passim.
28. Ibid. p.193.
29. Yasuhito, Prince Chichibu, *Collected Essays*, p.83.

PART 2

THE PRINCESS'S STORY
THE SILVER DRUM
(complete version)

CHAPTER ONE

BORN IN ENGLAND

◆

MY CHILDHOOD FRIEND

It was on a beautiful autumn day, when the green maple leaves had only just started to turn red, that Masako Shirasu most recently came to see me at our palace in the Akasaka imperial compound. She is still a busy essayist, so we are able to meet no more than three or four times a year, and five at the most, but whenever we do, it is as if we had left each other's company only the day before, we are so compatible.

But that is not all. There has always seemed to be a special thread that binds us. Mrs Shirasu referred to it in something she wrote as a 'curious karma'. We first met when we were third formers at the Primary School of the Gakushūin, (formerly known as the Peers and Peeresses School) and our frank and openhearted friendship has continued all these years. And it wasn't even as if we were in the same class. My father had been transferred back to Japan from Tianjin and though I was the same year as Masako, we were in different classes, and we really only saw each other in the summer holidays. There was also the fact that Masako's father Count Aisuke Kabayama and my father were good friends, and I used to spend two weeks of my summer holidays every year with the Kabayamas at their villa in the foothills of Mount Fuji.

There we played together to our hearts' content from morning till a reluctant bedtime. Masako was lively and brilliantly resourceful, while I, though somewhat of a tomboy, was slow and not nearly so quick-witted as she. But in spite of our characters and personality being radically different, we greatly enjoyed each other's company. 'Perhaps it's because we're complete opposites that we never clashed!' we often say. Whatever the reason, we have always been the closest of chums.

The Kabayama villa was a spacious manor situated in a superb spot below Takigahara, the plain that stretches straight up to Mount Fuji. To us children it was another world. Neglecting our school work we did things like riding ponies to the Fuji foothills. Masako had her own pony and was a fine rider and could do things like gallop, and she helped me as I started out nervously. I think by the following year I managed to ride properly at a walking pace. We were children, so we didn't bother about riding habits and just wore our ordinary dresses.

My encounters with wild flowers mostly took place there. I liked the reddish purple summer thistle and the evening primrose with its yellow flowers, but I loved best the ones with amusing names, such as the pale-green-tipped white blossoms that hung down and were called 'wolf's lanterns'; the *odoriko-so* ('dancing-girl flowers') that resembled geisha doing the parasol dance; 'the mosquito-net flower' whose stems would split open and burst out like fireworks making yellowy-brown sprays of blossom that resembled mosquito-nets; and *gishigishi* ('creaky weed') covered with tiny pale green florets. Be it the Japanese knotweed with its tiny white flowers in sprays shaped like ears of grain, or the pink-tipped tail-like plumes of the young miscanthus, wild flowers seemed to me to have a charm quite different from that of cultivated blossoms. I could not have expressed it in my childish vocabulary, but their gentleness had for me a profound appeal. Perhaps to me, brought up until third form in Beijing and Tianjin, they meant Japan to me.

It was, of course, Masako who taught me the names of the wild flowers: 'Creaky weed is called that because when the flowers have withered and only the pods are left they make a creaky sound when you shake a spray.' She always provided an explanation. Decades later, as Masako Shirasu, she published several superb books of her own flower arrangements accompanied by essays filled with thoughts about flowers, no doubt germinated in the days when she was Masako Kabayama.

The days were never long enough for us as we played together, and what we enjoyed the most was playing fishmonger in the spacious bathroom, with its enormous square bathtub made of Japanese cypress. There were lovely tin toys in those days made in the shape of gaily coloured goldfish, and we used to display them and pretend to buy and sell.

We always played to our heart's content and were so tired by the time night came we'd fall exhausted into bed. Masako's parents, unlike the so-called 'education mamas and papas' of today, just left us alone. As for me, I felt so much more carefree than at home. Count Kabayama was a wonderful father, and the countess was a lovely lady – although somewhat frail – and highly literary.

One summer, while we were enjoying our holiday to the hilt, we neglected our school assignments to such an extent that we got in an awful panic and had to stay up a whole night to get them done. Now it's a fond memory!

THE THREAD OF FATE

Years later, after I had married into the Imperial Family, I looked back on my summer holidays in Gotemba, and it occurred to me that something which happened there must have been fate. For two consecutive summers, Masako and I were sent to either her imperial villa at Odawara or the one at Oiso in order to escort our Gakushūin classmate Hanako, Princess Kan'in, to the Katayama villa. It was because Count Kabayama was familiar with European royalty and knew what a great difference there was between them and Japanese royalty, that he felt our Japanese royalty should widen their outlook and learn to mix with international society. He hoped at least this one princess could benefit.

People abroad make friends with royalty, are invited to their homes, and enjoy learning to know them. In addition to respect, they are also able to feel true friendship towards them and covet the honour of the connection. So in order to help one imperial person become able to deal with such a situation, Count Kabayama, in a most progressive way of thinking for someone in those days, thought a stay with ordinary people such as ourselves would be beneficial.

Although my mother's elder sister was Itsuko, Princess Nashimoto, I had been born and brought up abroad and knew hardly anything at that stage about royals, little knowing that one day I should be one myself. So I had no preconceived ideas as I tagged along with Masako to fetch the young princess, and simply felt rather sorry for the poor girl, thinking how bored and lonely she must be having to spend her summer vacations in such great big empty villas. To my childish mind I had no idea what it meant to live the special kind of existence, isolated from the world, that Japanese royalty lived. Princess Hanako only stayed with us in Gotemba for two days, and she may have felt freer than she did in her palace at home, but she was very quiet, for she probably had never stayed overnight in a strange house before, and she did not react to anything, so Masako and I just played by ourselves. The second year, she was more used to it all, and came with us into the foothills of Mount Fuji, and even joined us for tennis.

But we heaved sighs of relief after we took Princess Hanako back to her villa and no longer had to mind our Ps and Qs, and threw ourselves into our own games with abandon for the rest of the summer.

But in spite of our intimacy, when we got back to school and were separated into our respective 'north' and 'south' class groupings, I do not remember playing with Masako much. But we are still such great chums there is no doubt about our close and special affinity.

When Masako Kabayama was fourteen, she went off alone to school in America. It was, of course, her father's plan. He himself had gone to study abroad at the age of fourteen. It would not be surprising today, but in 1924, my parents admired his courage in sending his only daughter off alone. Count Kabayama used to say: 'The stage has been reached when the people of the world should know about each other. Just because Japan is a far-off island nation we must not be left behind and now is the time to teach our young people how to get along in the international community.'

And by the strangest coincidence, only half a year later, in February 1925, my father was appointed ambassador to the United States and our family moved to America. My friendship with Masako continued there, and this time it was Masako's turn to spend part of her holidays with us at our ambassadorial residence in Washington.

I will write about that later, but right now I most certainly cannot refrain from thinking about another example of the hand of fate. Count Kabayama, who was not only the father of my best friend, but also a good friend of my father's, received from Empress Teimei, when she was Empress Dowager, private instructions to arrange a marriage between Prince Chichibu and me. That he would be faced with such a serious task was beyond the wildest dreams of both the persuader and the persuaded in those carefree days in Gotemba. How strong the thread that bound us! One never knows when fate will touch one's life.

There have been many speculations as to what it was that decided my life's destiny, and the things that led up to it, and I should like to set the record straight, but first I want to go back to the beginning.

'NAME: SETSUKO'

My birth in the London suburb of Walton-on-Thames took place on the ninth hour of the ninth day of the ninth month of the year 1909 – a date full of nines, with even one more thrown in, for I was born just before nine o'clock. I had an elder brother, Ichirō, who was going on for two years old.

My father often used to say to me, 'You were the only one born when I was at home!' He was a very busy diplomat and often away on official trips. At the time my brother and I were born, he was Third Secretary at the Japanese Embassy in London. As it just happened he was home when my mother felt labour pains in the middle of the night, and so he went out in the rain to call the midwife.

The ninth dawned fine and was apparently a lovely day. Intending to ask Mr Enjiro Yamaza, the acting Minister, to choose one, my father left home with a list he had made of some suitable names for his newly born daughter, and went in to see Mr Yamaza, who had already agreed to be my *nazuke-oya* (name-father). My father wanted me to have a plain, ordinary name like my brother's Ichirō (First-born).

'A daughter was born to us this morning, Sir', he said, 'and I should be grateful if you would be good enough to pick one of these when you have a free moment in the next two or three days.'

My father handed him the list, but after giving it no more than a glance, the Minister replied: 'I should think either Setsuko (festival child) or Kikuko (chrysanthemum child) would be good.'

Having to cope with a difficult diplomatic situation left by Ambassador Jūtarō Komura, the last thing Acting Minister Yamaza would have wanted to bother about was a name for the daughter of a junior member of staff.

When he got home, my father chose Setsuko. The ninth day of the ninth month is one of the five original festivals in the lunar calendar, and was called the 'Chrysanthemum Festival', which he must have thought was an appropriate day for a girl to be born. Moreover, it was also called the festival of *chōyō*, 'Double Yang' – yang symbolizing the sun, brightness, and the positive principle in Chinese philosophy – for there was yang in the number Nine, of which the day comprised two. At the court in ancient times it is said they fêted that day as being particularly auspicious, and held a banquet at which chrysanthemum wine was bestowed upon the guests. The custom most probably originated in China.

The next day was a holiday, but the day after that my father reported to the Minister that he had chosen 'Setsuko', whereupon Mr Yamaza said: 'So Setsuko it shall be,' and getting out a sheet of high quality hand-made paper he inscribed the words 'Name: Setsuko' in calligraphy with brush and Indian ink and gave it to my father. Beside the Chinese character for Setsu, he thoughtfully indicated the pronunciation in *hiragana* syllabary because the name of the then Crown Princess (later known as Empress Teimei) was written with the same characters as mine but pronounced Sadako. Years later, the characters in my name to read Setsuko would be changed, but no one was to have known that then.

No sooner had the Minister handed the 'Name: Setsuko' inscription to my father than he busily sent for the First Secretary regarding some sort of conference or other, as if he had completely forgotten having just acted as a 'name-father' for Tsuneo Matsudaira's daughter. While a moment later, said my father, he himself dashed out of the room, inscription in hand, his own mind similarly flying towards the conference.

It was the time when the Japanese government had a Resident-General in Korea and a policy of annexation was steadily being carried out, so Britain, with whom we had a treaty, had to be informed of its progress, making it an extremely busy time for the embassy, which was in effect a branch office of the Foreign Ministry. I was born in a time of crisis and named in a fearful hurry, but I liked the name. My father had wanted us all to have ordinary everyday names, and as we grew up, my brother and sister and I at first agreed with him, but as time went by we began to feel that our names were too dull. My elder brother was Ichirō (first son), then there was Jirō (second son), then the Chrysanthemum Festival's Setsuko (season child), and Masako born in the new Taishō reign whose second character *shō* can also be read *masa*.

Much later on, in my father's twilight years, when it came to naming my elder brother's children, Father chose grandiose ones for his grandsons. He named Ichirō's boys Tsunetada, Tsunenari and Tsunekazu, giving each the first character of his own name Tsuneo. 'Good heavens!' thought we, his plain-named offspring.

Once when I had to go up to Tokyo from our villa in Gotemba I have a happy memory of stopping by the Matsudaira house in Senzoku. My father was in such a good mood, my brothers and sister and I jokingly protested about our commonplace names, accusing him of having obviously despised us, and we definitely scored a point with our conclusion: 'Father's older now and sees things in a different light'! We all enjoyed a good laugh.

In about 1923 as I remember, soon after my younger brother was born, there was a magazine for girls with humorous illustrations rather like today's *manga* that was serializing a novel about a happy group of village children whose names by coincidence happened to be just the same as ours – Ichirō, Jirō, Setchan (short for Setsuko) and Ma-chan, (short for Masako) and I loved reading about them.

As if we weren't content with having scored a point regarding our names, we dredged up the story of our father's dreadful *faux pas* at the naming of brother Ichirō, and had another big laugh. We gave Father a hard time, but judging by his wry smile I think he rather enjoyed it.

THE NAME-FATHER

The *faux pas* mentioned above happened at the time of Ichirō's birth in London, when my father was so thrilled at the firstborn being a boy that he asked Ambassador Komura to be the name-father. After serving successively as Minister in Korea, America, and Russia, Mr Komura had been Foreign Minister in the first Katsura cabinet when he was instrumental in concluding the Anglo-Japanese Alliance. In 1905, he was sent to Portsmouth as Foreign Minister Plenipotentiary at the peace negotiations with Russia after the Russo-Japanese War. His signing of a peace treaty there which gave Japan only half of Sakhalin caused an uproar in the government and public opinion over what they considered his weak-kneed stance, and an angry mob even tried to set fire to his house. All of which caused his health to suffer, forcing him to resign his post as Foreign Minister. It was partly as a measure to help things cool down that Mr Komura was appointed Ambassador to Britain.

It was while serving under Ambassador Komura in London that my father married Nobuko Nabeshima and asked the ambassador to act as the official go-between. And when my elder brother was born, the name the ambassador suggested for the third secretary's baby was 'Ei-ichi', signifying 'first son born in Britain' from *ichi* (first) and *ei*, the first character in *eikoku* (Britain).

At this point when courtesy called for a little bow and a 'thank you, Sir', my father did not even smile.

'It's kind of Your Excellency,' he replied, 'but...'

'But what?!' said Mr Komura, and my father continued: 'Putting an *ichi* at the end of the name makes one think of Sawa-ichi in the puppet play *The Tsubosaka Miracle*.'

The ambassador seemed quite put out by this complaint and raised his voice uncharacteristically: 'How rude of you to ask me to be name-father and then be so fussy. Call him anything you like. Call him Tarō. Or just number them, beginning with Ichirō.'

With that the ambassador rose to indicate the meeting was over, and my terribly flustered father blurted out: 'Well then, Sir, I shall name him Ichirō.'

Although aware he had done something inexcusable, my father could not understand why the ambassador's mood should have soured so suddenly. A colleague to whom he mentioned it said: 'Well, you did put up a frightful black, because his eldest son is called Kin-ichi!' Moreover, my young father was understandably shaken to learn that this very same Kin-ichi was also in the Ministry of Foreign Affairs.

However, his scolding by Ambassador Komura truly brought home to my father how carefully diplomats should always think before they speak, and refrain from making careless remarks.

When she heard about it from my father when he got home, my mother, too, was mortified and all she could say was: 'Darling, what a dreadful *faux pas*! My heart aches for you.' My father referred to it once in something he wrote as his life's greatest blunder.

But the story somehow makes me smile to think how young and inexperienced my parents were those days in London as they strove to do their best.

THE AIZU CLAN

As I have already written, my father and mother's wedding was held in London, with Ambassador Jūtarō Komura acting as go-between. The couple had not even had a formal meeting, or *o-miai*. in the usual way. What with one of them in Tokyo and one in London, it is possible that they were shown photographs of each other, but I think it was probably settled before that by the two families.

'It often happened in the old days, didn't it?' we used to say when we children discussed our parents' marriage. 'It was just like those "picture weddings" among emigrants to Brazil!' And we wondered how anyone could choose a lifetime partner that way. We thought it was absurd, but in the old feudal times they didn't even use photographs and marriages were apparently arranged between families, and traces of that must have still remained. Our parents, however, had both had a modern education and were not the sort of people to let themselves be coerced into marrying someone they did not fancy, so I think they must have liked what they saw in those photographs.

Before writing about my parents' marriage and newly-wedded life, I began with the births of myself and my brother. I am afraid the story has been going backwards and forwards. And now I must go backwards again because I want readers to know how my family's former Aizu clan were thought to be rebels, and how they languished for a while in disgrace.

My father, Tsuneo Matsudaira, was the fourth son of Katamori Matsudaira, Lord of the former feudal domain of Aizu, who had been unjustly accused of being a traitor to the Emperor.

'Might is right', as the saying goes, and my grandfather was on the wrong side: a victim of circumstance in the struggle for the overthrow of the Tokugawa Shogunate – the military government of Japan that lasted from 1600 to 1868.

Far from being a traitor, my grandfather's loyalty to the Emperor was beyond question, and the Emperor held him in high regard. My grandfather, in the service of the Shōgun, was in charge of the defence of Kyoto, where the Emperor resided, and we have a long, confidential letter that he once received from Emperor Kōmei himself.

'Thou hast exerted thyself mightily on our behalf and we are well pleased', begins part of the missive, and goes on:

'Thy loyalty is such that even our most secret and confidential thoughts may be safely entrusted to thee, and moreover we have asked thee to undertake this matter because we are confident that whatsoever we desire can be brought to pass by thy skilful manoeuvring in the art of bringing about the agreement of many.'

In order to maintain secrecy, the Emperor composed his letter in the form of an Imperial poem in classical Chinese and sent it to my grandfather by special messenger in a ceremonial lacquer scroll box to make it appear as if he were merely bestowing an Imperial gift of a poem.

To Katamori, who had been held in such a position of deep trust, the sudden death in 1866 of the young, thirty-six-year-old Emperor Kōmei, must have been a bitter blow in that time of great upheaval, with its plots and counter-plots and divergent opinions regarding the future of Japan.

The overthrow of the Shōgunate and the restoration of power to the Emperor had been planned by men of the far-flung domains of Satsuma and Chōshū. The Lord of Satsuma was well aware of my grandfather Katamori's unswerving loyalty to the Emperor, but he also knew that the Lord of Aizu owed allegiance to the Shōgun, in his capacity as the Defender of Imperial Kyoto.

There was, therefore, no way for my grandfather to escape being considered an enemy. In the civil war that followed, the Aizu clan came under heavy attack by the Imperial Restoration forces, made up largely of Satsuma and Chōshū men, under the command of Taruhito, Prince Arisugawa.

The heroism of the Byakkotai – the White Tiger Brigade – is legendary. Of that band of several hundred young sons of Aizu samurai, twenty survivors saw in the distance their castle in flames, and committed suicide.

Women and children fought side by side with the men in the desperate, month-long defence of Wakamatsu Castle until finally the white flag of surrender was carried out through the North Gate. From that time on, there was nothing but hardship and humiliation for the Aizu Clan. After surrendering Wakamatsu Castle, my grandfather, whose initial death penalty was commuted to life imprisonment, was taken to Tokyo to be held prisoner in the manor of the Lord of Tottori, and all of his lands were confiscated.

The new Imperial government, however, lifted the sentence in less than a year. Then, as well as recognising Katamori's eldest son Katahiro as the head of the house of Matsudaira, they bestowed on him the fief of Tonami on the Shimokita peninsula in the province of Mutsu (present-day Aomori Prefecture).

It was a poor fief in undeveloped country that could only produce 150,000 bushels of rice a year at best – a shabby exchange for a major domain that produced 400,000 bushels! It was tantamount to exile. Some of the clansmen, including my uncle Kataharu, travelled there by boat from Niigata, while others made their way north by road. The members of the Aizu clan were obliged to lead a harsh life there for five years before they were allowed, in 1873, to return to Aizu and earn a proper living.

Although my grandfather Katamori was pardoned in 1870, he stubbornly refused to accept public office again. In November 1874, Emperor Meiji personally requested that he be made a courtier of the fifth rank, from which he was promoted subsequently to the senior grade of the third court rank, but while he had the greatest respect for Emperor Meiji, he continued to harbour a deep resentment against those whose might had made them right.

My father, Tsuneo, was born in a suburb of Tokyo in April, 1875. By that time, although the tragedy suffered by the Aizu clan had left a deep hurt that remained in the people's hearts, most of the former clansmen went along with the times and were beginning to make a new life for themselves.

Tsuneo was about seven when his parents took him back to live in their ancestral home, the old castle town of Wakamatsu in their former Aizu domain. His younger brother Morio went too. His three elder brothers, Kataharu, Takeo and Hideo, who had experienced all the hardships of Tonami, were farmed out to various members of the former clan who lived in Tokyo, in order to pursue their education.

The journey to Wakamatsu from Tokyo was made in a procession of twenty rickshaws. Their destination was the Herb Garden. It was a sort of country villa belonging to His Lordship, with a magnificent kitchen garden where many herbs were grown. The property had been sadly neglected, but repairs were made and the family took up residence there.

The local primary school was about half a mile from the Herb Garden, and my father used to tell of the ordeal it had been in winter, walking there over the frozen snow on the footpaths between the rice paddies, wearing only wooden clogs on their bare feet. Sometimes there were blizzards, too. The school was an old-fashioned institution of the temple school variety, with tatami-matted floors, and father often made us laugh about how the first thing the teacher taught them was the fact that *'T'soon rises in t' East, and gaws dahn in t' West'*, spoken in a rich local dialect.

My father spent about three years in Aizu, after which he was to rejoin his parents in Tokyo, but during his primary school days there, the scars of the Battle of Aizu were still far from healed, and mixing freely as he did with the local children, he heard from them of the suffering their families had endured. It was learning about it at first hand, I think, that gave him his spiritual strength and the deep love for his ancestral province, which in due course he passed on to us children.

The day they left Aizu behind to move to Tokyo, my grandfather's former retainers followed the cavalcade of tandem rickshaws in a long line for mile after mile, and even when night fell, their lanterns formed a continuous stream of light, for they could not bear to tear themselves away. To the former clansmen, my grandfather was still their lord and master. My grandfather finally had to dismount from his carriage, and say: 'You mustn't come with us any further. You must go home now. Let us part here.' It was not until then that they finally stopped following.

Although my father was still a child, the pathos of that night's sad parting of lord and vassals made a deep impression upon him. Sitting in the carriage beside his younger brother Morio, and looking back through tear-filled eyes at the light of those lanterns, he determined in his heart that for the sake of these people of Aizu he must make something of himself so they could be proud of him.

My father did not tell me this himself, but told my cousins, adding, 'You are Matsudairas too. You must never forget the people of Aizu.' My cousins had just lost their father, and their uncle was trying to encourage them.

After returning to our mansion in Tokyo's Koishikawa, my father was sent to the nearby Kuroda Primary School for a year in order to rid him of his Aizu accent. It would never do for him to say *'T'soon gaws dahn in t'West'* at the Gakushūin, the Peers' School, where the sons of the Imperial Family and the nobility went.

From the Gakushūin Middle School, he went on to the First High School, and then to the Tokyo Imperial University (now simply called Tokyo University). In the meantime, in 1892, my grandfather Katamori's stormy life came to an end. Only then, I believe did the feudal era truly end for the people of Aizu.

THE SINGLE PHOTOGRAPH

My father graduated from the Tokyo Imperial University in 1902 and immediately sat for the entrance examination to be a diplomat, which he passed, and his first appointment was to the embassy in London. The reason he wanted to become a diplomat may have been because he was influenced by the international leanings of his deceased father Katamori. But also it may have been due to the persistent image of being a traitor that hung over anyone from Aizu. So much so that satisfying jobs within Japan may well have been limited. At the embassy in London he worked like blazes on furthering the Anglo-Japanese Alliance, which was a very important aspect of Japanese diplomacy. And in those days the staff at the Embassy was not very large so there was no opportunity for him to travel back to Japan to find a bride.

The bride who came as the result of the single photograph was from an exceedingly aristocratic and privileged background. My mother Nobuko was the daughter of Marquis Naohiro Nabeshima, son of Naomasa the last lord of the ducal Nabeshima clan of Saga in the old province of Hizen (now Nagasaki Prefecture). She was one of six girls, the eldest of whom married Marquis Kagatsugu Maeda, lord of the wealthy Kaga clan, whose domain was reputed to produce five million bushels of rice a year. The second daughter married Prince Nashimoto (their daughter Masako became Princess Li); Shigeko, daughter number three, became Viscountess Makino. When it was time to marry off the fourth daughter, my mother Nobuko, Grandmother Eiko, who had apparently wanted one of her girls to marry a diplomat, said: 'Nobuko has a good physique and constitution, and should be able to get along all right abroad.'

My grandmother had been a diplomatic wife herself. Their daughter, my aunt Itsuko, was born when Naohiro was ambassador in Rome, and her name means 'child of an Italian town'. My grandfather Naohiro represented his country with dignity and pride, and my grandmother Eiko devoted herself to being a good diplomatic wife. Dealing with the world at firsthand, she never failed to maintain her Japanese dignity, and I think she wanted her daughter to savour the responsibility and attitude of mind of an ambassador's wife who supports her husband with friendship and encouragement. Unlike today, when one travels nonstop by air, it was an era when travel abroad from Japan was a great undertaking involving weeks and months by sea. Consequently, ordinary private citizens made little contact with people of other countries, so the role of embassies was great, and diplomats were expected to be skilful.

My brother Ichirō told me that the reason most of our ambassadors appointed to leading countries such as Britain, America, France, Germany and Italy were all from the peerage descended from the feudal lords was because the Japanese government had used up all its money on the Sino-Japanese and Russo-Japanese wars, and the Foreign Ministry did not have the funds for the required entertaining. So members of the great *daimyō* families came to the rescue with their own wealth to save the face of Japan.

Eiko Nabeshima's desire to find a diplomat for her daughter found fulfilment in the person of Tsuneo Matsudaira. His university record was brilliant, he had passed the foreign ministry examination with top marks and in addition, he refused to be fazed in the slightest by the gratuitous handicap of being the son and heir of Katamori Matsudaira, which I think impressed my grandmother, as well as the fact that he had renounced his title of Viscount in favour of his younger brother, declaring: 'Since so many gave their lives for my father and for the former Aizu Clan, whose young men of promise are prevented from rising in the world, I feel it would be wrong for me to accept a title.' She admired his having the backbone to choose to live the life of an ordinary citizen. He was just and manly. A person to whom she could entrust her daughter with confidence. No one could possibly be better. My grandfather was of the same opinion, and that is why they set up this proposed marriage across the oceans on the strength of a single photograph.

Not surprisingly, I believe my father at first resisted the idea of marrying the daughter of the lord of the great Nabeshima clan. But it was not feasible for him to find a bride himself, so he finally gave in to the persuasions of an intermediary. His action might sound a trifle imprudent, but I think in spite of his initial diffidence, he suspected that my mother might in fact be just the right one for him.

The House of Nabeshima was indeed very affluent and their main Tokyo residence, a property of 20,000 *tsubo* (about 16 acres) at 1-chōme, Nagata-chō, consisted of a purely Japanese-style manor as well as a purely Western-style house which had been completed in 1892 in time for a visit by Emperor Meiji and the Empress. The subsidiary residence in Shibuya's Shōtōchō was 200 *tsubo* and had a small hill and tea plantation in it. Including the butler and the elderly housekeeper there was said to be a domestic staff of fifty or sixty.

But there was a house rule that the children were not to be pampered, and unless it was raining and blowing hard or snowing, they were not allowed to go to school in a rickshaw and had to walk there with their attendant, and according to my mother their packed lunches were plain and simple.

As I have already mentioned, the bridegroom could not leave London so my mother had to travel across the oceans alone. It was late autumn, 1906, and Nobuko had just left the Peeresses School (later called the Gakushūin Girls' Section) that spring. Nineteen, waited on all her life by maids, with no experience of the world, she was about to set off all by herself on a sea voyage to meet a future husband whom she had never laid eyes on nor spoken to. What a stout-hearted young lady I thought with amazement when I first heard about it. But although I think my mother was brave, my grandparents too were out of the ordinary to have had such confidence in their daughter that they could let her go off like that unaccompanied.

THE FLOWERED BONNET

Journeying alone! And what was more, she had to travel on a French passenger liner. There were no Japanese ships available since they were all on strike after the end of the Russo-Japanese War. And for my mother, travelling to her wedding, it was no simple excursion but an embarkation on a whole new way of life.

Very fortunately, there happened to be on board a gentleman in his seventies from Saga who took it upon himself to look after the daughter of the former feudal lord of his native province. He was the chairman of a liquor company and was on his way to France to purchase wine. If it had not been for him, my mother, who spoke hardly any French or English, for all her stout-heartedness would have felt quite helpless with no-one to sympathize with her seasickness and help her cope with the pity and curious looks of the passengers and crew.

When the forty-day journey was finally over and they landed in Marseilles, she parted with the Chairman, and boarded a train for Paris, where she stayed with a cousin, Count Ichijō, who was Military Attaché at the Japanese Embassy. The Ichijōs gave my mother a great deal of advice of all kinds on things like how to dress and manage one's clothes, and foreign customs and etiquette. In later years my mother told me how thoroughly they had stressed the fact that a diplomat's wife, no matter how low ranking her husband, must be very careful what she does and says.

It was at the Ichijōs' that my father and mother first met one another. My mother asked Count Ichijō to persuade my father to come to Paris to fetch her. Although he was terribly busy, he managed to make time to do so. He was delighted to find that Nobuko Nabeshima was no fancy young lady full of airs and graces, but a nice, healthy girl with a warm personality. As for the bride, my father, who was elegantly slim in those days, struck her as a lively young man concealing plenty of Aizu spirit. Someone she could like and trust.

My father went back to London with Nobuko Nabeshima and their wedding was held at the embassy through the good offices of Ambassador Jūtarō Komura. That day my mother determined to do everything she could to be a good diplomatic wife and help her husband to the utmost. The first thing would be to learn languages, and she made up her mind to start off by becoming fluent in English conversation, for she found she could not even shop with the English she had learnt at school.

What she decided to do was very typical of my mother. She would go to a primary school and make them let her learn together with the children. She would start at the very beginning with basics, just as children do. She got them to let her have a desk at the back of the room, and she learned the same phrases the children did, and sang the same songs, and played the same games and soon mastered the fundamentals, after which she practised intensively and quickly got better and better.

My mother's father had been ambassador to Italy and I think she had learned quite a lot from her parents about what a diplomatic wife should be like, and that together with the advice she had from the Ichijōs in Paris gave her such confidence that I don't believe she was ever timid or awkward at formal occasions. In a photograph I have of the two of them all dressed up, my father, as you would expect, looks dignified and relaxed, and my mother too, while looking modestly artless gives the impression of being a wife who is thoroughly at home in London society. In a becoming afternoon dress and broad-brimmed bonnet, decorated with ribbon flowers, atop her bouffant hair-do, my newly launched mother looks as if she was living the life of a diplomat's wife to perfection.

But even she had a tale of one unforgettable and dreadfully embarrassing incident, which she used to recount to us. It happened just about the time when she had finally become able to go out and about by herself. She set out to do a bit of sightseeing as well as some shopping, and taking an open double-decker bus she was enjoying looking to right and left. When all of a sudden she saw approaching them a carriage in which Ambassador Komura happened to be riding. As the carriage passed beside the bus, she instinctively stood up and made a deep bow towards it. Irrespective of whether or not the ambassador had noticed the gesture made to him from way up there, my mother, satisfied that she had showed him proper respect, sat down and continued to look at the sights. The curiosity of the other passengers, however, was greatly aroused, although they tried not to show it.

Next day she was sent for by the ambassador, and could not imagine why. He said: 'Yesterday, you were on a bus, and it was me that you stood up and bowed to was it not? Well, all you did was make yourself conspicuous. The people around you would not understand why you did it, and find your action strange. They would not realize it was Japanese etiquette. Do not ever do anything like that again.'

In other words, what she should have done was just sit there quietly and think to herself: 'Oh, there goes our ambassador'. My mother said she would never forget her blunder, but I do not think it was terrible at all. I like the story and think it was rather sweet as a first step in the education of a diplomatic wife!

In the process of it all, Ichirō was born, I was born, and eight months later, in April 1910, my father was ordered home and we all went back to Japan, after Ambassador Komura had been relieved by Ambassador Takaaki Katō. Also that year my father's eldest brother Kataharu died, who had suffered such extremes of hardship in Tonami.

Chapter Two

Childhood

◆

THE BEIJING LEGATION

After returning from London we lived in a rented house in Ushigome from which my father went to work at the Foreign Ministry, and Mother worked hard at language lessons so she would not have any trouble no matter where my father was sent.

Promoted to second secretary, my father was posted to China in April 1912, where we as a family took up residence at the Legation in Beijing. It was the beginning of June, and I was only two years and nine months old, so I naturally have no recollection of London, where I was born, or of our brief return to Japan, or my sister Masako's birth in July the year after our arrival in Beijing. Nor was I aware of the epochal event for the Japanese people of the death of Emperor Meiji and the start of the Shōwa era on 30 July 1912. I was oblivious of it all.

I think my earliest memories go back to when I was four and started going to the kindergarten attached to the Japanese Primary School in Beijing. And I can also faintly recollect the face of 'Taka' Takahashi when she was young. I was about four when she came to be our nanny, and later not only we children, but our parents came to depend greatly upon her.

Taka was not her proper name. She was really Mutsu Takahashi. But since Emperor Meiji's name was Mutsuhito, it seemed irreverent to go about addressing her by part of that august name, so they decided to call her Taka. Plain and brusque, she was a typical old maid type, with a stern face, but I think she loved us even more than her own children, for she showed no mercy when she scolded us.

Born into a respectable samurai family of the Aizu clan, Taka studied Chinese classics and Japanese literature as well as etiquette and sewing, and graduated from the Red Cross nurses training school in Fukushima, after which she married into the similarly Aizu samurai Takahashi family who maintained a cottage sericulture industry. They had a son and a daughter. She was called up to serve as a nurse in the Russo-Japanese War. Her husband had been called up earlier, and was killed only five days after she had taken up her post. After the war, Taka worked as a primary school teacher. And then someone she met at the Fukushima chapter of the Patriotic Women's Association was instrumental in getting her the job with the Matsudairas.

As children, we knew nothing of Taka's personal history. It was long after we were grown up that we managed to put it together from her casual piecemeal reminiscences. But from the time we were small, my brother Ichirō and I were brought up on references to things like the fall of Wakamatsu Castle, my grandfather Katamori's hardships and the fief's Tonami exile which she frequently employed to make some point or other whether we understood it or not. As time went by, even though we had not directly experienced the things she spoke of, a subconscious knowledge of them seemed to ooze out of our minds and with age our understanding and feeling of the Aizu spirit seemed to deepen.

Although the birth of my sister Masako was a big event during our two years in Beijing, I have no particular memories of that time, and then my father was suddenly posted to Tianjin as Consul-General, and we all moved there. I learnt recently from my brother that the reason for his sudden posting was because of the unexpected demise of two senior officials, one after the other.

Being a child, my brother did not know the details, but what apparently happened was that Kōkichi Mizuno, the Counsellor at the Beijing legation suddenly died at his post on 23 May 1914, and five days later, Minister Yamaza, who had been at the legation for many years, suddenly fell ill and died too, also at his post. Consequently, our father hurriedly had to act as temporary Minister. The Foreign Ministry then hastily sent a new Minister from Japan, on whose arrival Father was posted to Tianjin as Consul-General.

HEATSTROKE

In Tianjin in those days foreigners – Japanese, British, Germans, etc. – lived and worked in special extraterritorial 'concessions'. There was a Japanese Concession, a British Concession and a German Concession, and so forth, where those countries themselves, and not China, controlled the administration and the policing. For instance, education in the Japanese Concession was controlled by the *monbushō*, the Japanese Ministry of Education, and if a crime was committed, a judge would be sent from Japan to adjudicate. Everything was under the control of the Japanese Government. The Concession even had its own Shintō Shrine.

The Japanese Consul-General's residence, however, where we lived, was in the British Concession, because that was the nicest part of town. But the Japanese School was in the Japanese Concession, and was a primary and secondary school combined. My brother and I thought it strange that we had to go so far to school. We went in a rickshaw they called a *yancho*, and it took quite a while to get there, as we had to go through the French Concession and then pass all the way through the Japanese Concession to its outskirts on the far side.

I was a slowpoke and Taka often had to scold me for dawdling. At breakfast she frequently scolded us both.

'Do hurry up, you two! If you take so long over such a little bit of breakfast, the castle will fall! Eat up quick, and get going.'

I remember her saying that so often. And I dare say she was right.

Another thing I remember was how overawed I was by the rough-and-tumble crowd of boys and girls at the single Japanese school. In the peak of the midsummer heat I was just too timid to push my way past them during break to get a drink of water. I was afraid of being knocked over, or sent flying. No matter how unbearably thirsty I became, I just hung back and went on enduring it, without even enough nerve to confide in my brother.

Finally one day I collapsed with heatstroke and was so badly dehydrated I lost consciousness and was in a coma for three weeks and nearly died.

Fortunately, I made a complete recovery. But that was not the end of it. After it had all blown over, my brother and I were had up on the carpet together by our parents and given a terrific scolding. While I may have deserved being told in no uncertain terms that 'if it hurts, say so; if it itches, say so' I was sorry for my brother. He was scolded severely for not noticing that his little sister was suffering. But after all, he was only a primary school pupil himself, and was in a different class to me, and how could he know I needed water and didn't have the courage to go and get it unless I had told him?

Father ended by saying: 'At any rate, it's clear neither of you is capable of living in a foreign land. That is, unless you learn there is a limit to putting up with things and not speaking up.'

Years later, on the occasion of the third anniversary of my father's death, his friends published a volume of their reminiscences entitled *Memories of Tsuneo Matsudaira*. My father did not care for biographical writings about himself. But I asked to see it, as it was unique and could tell me so much about the father I hardly knew.

In it, I was surprised to find a passage that rang a very nostalgic bell. It described a visit he made to his old fief Aizu in May 1942, where he addressed a group of students. He spoke to them as follows:

'The people of Japan's north-east, particularly Aizu, differ from those of other regions, in that they tend to be more shy and retiring, and have more of the virtue of modesty. It is good to refrain from being too forward. But there can be a limit too. There are times when one should speak one's mind without reserve. I think it is good to do so. If you don't, when you are meeting someone for the first time, they are apt not to appreciate what sort of person you are. Whereas if they do, it is possible that you will become friends and perhaps even be able to help one another. I hope you will keep that in mind, and learn to express your thoughts freely. Tell those who could not be here tonight what Mr Matsudaira said to do!'

There was more, but when I read these words I was reminded of what he had said to us all those years ago when he scolded my brother and me in Tianjin after my heatstroke. Here was his message in full, which he had simplified for us then since we were only children.

Much as my father was strong on patient endurance, he felt that assertiveness, in addition to its negative aspect, had a positive side as well, and should be considered part of the 'Aizu Spirit'. I realized then how this was also reflected in what he taught me when I was marrying into the Imperial Family. The final sentence, with its warmth so typical of him, and which I could almost hear him saying, brought tears to my eyes.

And now let me go back to where we were before my digression. Besides that scolding, I have another memory of Tianjin which I shall never forget. It was at the time of the great Tianjin flood, which the old people used to say recurred every thirty years. It did not affect the British Concession, where we lived, except for the slightly lower ground where the tennis courts were, which were only moderately flooded, making an exciting, first-rate playground as far as we children were concerned.

I think it was my brother's idea, but I aided and abetted him with glee: we set some wooden washtubs afloat and played in them every day. I think the reason nobody stopped us was because Masako, who was a frail baby, was in hospital and our mother was in constant attendance, while Taka and the trainee maids spent a lot of time there too, so none of them had time to notice what we were up to.

Father, being the sort of man he was, had his hands full with involvement in flood countermeasures.

Exactly thirty years later, when my brother was serving as Tianjin branch manager of the Yokohama Specie Bank (now the Bank of Tokyo) he, too, had to help with the flood! He explained to me how it was caused by torrential rain in the upper reaches of the river Hai He that flows through Tianjin. Apparently, when the level of the Hai He rose it breeched its banks around Yangliuchin, which is near Tianjin, and its waters flowed into the valley behind the city, gradually submerging the area outside the castle as well as the adjoining rear section of the Japanese Concession. That time too, the water was deepest in the Japanese Concession, and one had to pole a boat through the worst places. He said the water was so deep in one place that his pole once hit the roof of a submerged bus! It was not nearly so bad in the British Concession, where our Legation was, and in the German Concession, so it was no wonder we children never realized the horror of the flood.

The consul-generals of Japan, Britain, Germany and Italy made a united effort, together with people of other nations, to render assistance, mobilizing their military forces to protect Tianjin as well as bringing supplies, building dykes and undertaking drainage. Japan brought in an engineer corps from the army in Manchuria. Unless such things were done, the flood water would have remained there for years, like lakes, impeding the life of the people, so it could not be ignored.

Thus it was that adult eyes and minds were elsewhere and there was no one to see and reprimand us when we had all that fun for about three whole days in our washtub boats! Otherwise we would surely have been discovered and stood on the mat again together, the two of us, for another monumental scolding. Our parents would have said: 'There are people suffering great distress in this flood. You may be children, but it is utterly unconscionable having fun in it. You should be ashamed of yourselves!'

Those are my main memories of those days: being scolded by my father and by Taka, and the fact that I was such a laggard. Even when Taka came to watch me on school sports days I invariably came in last.

'It's not as if Miss Setsuko was delicate. If only she had a little more drive. She just doesn't seem to have the will to win, or to try to do better than others. I'm always telling her she needs to have a little more competitive spirit.'

It was Taka that I overheard. She was reporting her disappointment to my mother just after we had returned from a Sports Day. But it did not make me say to myself: 'Well then, I'll show them! I won't let them beat me next time.' For I *had* been doing my best, in my own way. Thinking about it now, I'd like to be able to say it was because I was easygoing. But I realize Taka was right.

It might have had something to do with the fact that I was the one who attracted the least attention. My brother, the eldest son, was the important child. My sister, a frail baby whose survival had been in doubt, caused general concern. The youngest, Jirō, born in 1924, was a late child, so naturally he was the darling of us all. Whereas I was healthy and strong, running about with bare feet playing tag in the garden, like my elder brother.

TAKA'S ROOM

The games we played as children, such as washtub boats, blind man's buff, house, beanbags, stilts, swings and jumping rope, all used simple old-fashioned props that were easily available or could be improvised. I'm sure that was better than the things children play with nowadays, like 'Famicom' that is bought for them because they want it for playing computer games. Aside from the question as to which is the most fun, I am sure making playthings out of nothing and inventing games strengthens children's contact with nature, and develops harmonious relations among siblings and deepens friendships. Although I was rather a tomboy, Taka taught me how to juggle with beanbags. Mother being a diplomat's wife was often out doing things with people from the various foreign consulates, but our parents trusted Taka implicitly and left our upbringing to her, which included children's games. Among them my strongest memories are of beanbags, which is what we did most on rainy days, and when it was too cold in winter to play out of doors. It was even more fun when you learned how to sew your own bags, from simple straw bags to complicated hexagonal ones.

'Why Miss Setsuko, what a fine beanbag!'

I remember how happy I used to be whenever Taka complimented me. We used scraps of cloth with as pretty colours and patterns as we could find, and filled them with adzuki beans. If you filled them too full they were roly-poly, and if you didn't put in enough beans they were light and floppy and lacked momentum when you threw them up in the air. By making them yourself you learned how to get them just right.

Taka started me off just throwing one beanbag back and forth with her, like playing catch, as we sat, our legs folded under us on the tatami. Then, following her instructions and using both hands, I had to throw two beanbags up in the air and catch them, over and over again, still sitting down, and I was awfully pleased with myself when I could keep on doing it for one or two minutes. Taka could do it using only her right hand! I think the next step was called 'Breaking down the mountain', and it involved keeping three beanbags going for several minutes without dropping any. And when she did it with four or five beanbags, all I could do was watch Taka with wide-eyed amazement.

In addition to throwing and catching them in endless rotation, there was 'Review', which was also done while sitting on the tatami. One beanbag is thrown up and while it is in the air, any number of others are picked up, or moved about in various specified ways, with the other hand. And while you are doing all this you sing: 'O you one, O you one, dow————n you come!' as you catch the falling beanbag nimbly on the back of your fist, before repeating the sequence over and over.

As I remember, sometimes we sang it as: 'On my hand, On my

hand, Dro——p down!' If the beanbag did not land properly on the back of your fist, you were out, and your opponent took over. Taka hardly ever dropped her beanbag. She always treated me as an equal when we played beanbags, so I don't believe she ever purposely let me win.

There was another game I remember in connection with Taka. The nursery in the Tianjin legation was a sunny Japanese-style room with an *engawa*, an inner narrow veranda-like gallery, and it may have been because we were fascinated by tatami mats, that for a period my brother and sister and I were very fond of drawing floor plans for tatami-floored houses we thought we would like to live in.

My brother initiated the craze by starting a drawing on a sheet of paper, saying: 'My house is going to have the front door here, and here's the drawing room.....' And I, who was sitting nearby, started drawing my own house plan, and I naturally put a room for Taka. My sister being delicate, Taka looked after her constantly, so of course she put a room for Taka in her plan too. We each drew our own plans the way we wanted them, and did not see what the others were putting, except for an occasional glimpse of plain black-bordered tatami mats.

Then Taka arrived, bringing teatime snacks or something, and probably having wondered what had kept us quiet for so long said: 'Oh, do let me see what you've been drawing!'

We lightheartedly handed her our plans, expecting to be praised for so carefully delineating the tatami mats. But Taka just looked at them, comparing them, and abruptly left the room. How odd, we thought, glancing at one another, and went after her. We found her in the corner of a different room with tears streaming down her cheeks. We were speechless. We had never seen Taka cry, and it was a shock. Had we done something bad?

'What's the matter, Taka?'

It was Masako who spoke: the littlest of us all. Taka picked her up and hugged her, while putting one arm around my brother and me and drawing us close.

'It's just that it makes me so terribly happy, to think that the three of you feel that way about Taka!'

She said something to that effect and her face crumpled up and she started crying all over again. She had obviously been touched to the core by the fact that unbeknownst to one another we had each included a clearly labelled 'Taka's Room' in our house plans. But we were too young to understand why Taka was happy, and we were just left wondering why.

She would have scolded us had we asked. She gave the impression of strictness, and one certainly could not say she had a very kind face, but I think she was a woman who, in the recesses of her heart, highly esteemed kindness. That's why we took it for granted that she would always be with us, and why, naturally, we each included a room for her.

Speaking of Taka's kind side, I have an unforgettable memory of her from those Tianjin days. I went through a stage of desperately wanting to arrange someone's hair. I couldn't even try braiding my own because it was bobbed very short. And often Taka used to sit on the veranda while young trainee maids combed her long tresses. So one day I said:

'Taka, would you let *me* touch your hair?'

That was how it began, and she used to let me play with her hair whenever I wanted to. I would say:

'Taka may I do your hair?' and she would reply:

'Please wait a moment' and go off and give her hair a quick wash, and come back, and sitting down with her back to me say:

'Here you are, Miss Setsuko, you can try doing my hair now any way you like.'

I was thrilled and would haltingly start combing her hair and plaiting it. Sometimes in one braid, sometimes in two, and sometimes even arranging it in a chignon. It was all very time-consuming. It was fun for me, but it must have been not only boring for her, but painful, for she had to put up with her hair being pulled and tangled by the comb in my unskilled fingers. But Taka always complied with a good grace whenever I asked, popping off right away for a quick wash and then letting me do whatever I wanted with her hair. I told her she needn't wash it, but she never failed to do so. She would read a classic or something while I played with her hair to my heart's content. Her hair was neither too bulky for me to handle nor too long, but was just right.

Occasionally, Taka was busy and would depute one of the two trainee maids to take her place, but it meant undoing their carefully self-arranged hair-dos, which was a bother for them, and they were never too happy about it. Even though I was a child I could understand how they must feel, so I resigned myself to being Taka's exclusive hairdresser.

I count myself fortunate that my young and formative years, ever since I can remember, were spent in Taka's strict but warm-hearted and broad-minded care.

CHAPTER THREE

GROWING UP

◆

THE PEERESSES' SCHOOL

We returned to Japan in 1918. My father had been appointed Councillor to the Embassy in Washington, and we were all to have gone back together, prior to setting out for the United States. However, plans changed. The Revolution having started in Russia, Siberia was in an unsettled state, and Japan, as one of the Allies in the First World War had declared its intention of sending troops there, and my father was asked by the Foreign Ministry to go alone to Vladivostok as Political Affairs Adviser to the expeditionary army. So the rest of us went back to Japan without him.

After spending some time at another school improving my Japanese manners, I finally passed the entrance examination to the Primary Department of the Peeresses' School, where mother wanted me to go. In the meantime, my father returned from Vladivostok and was put in charge of the European and American Bureau at the Foreign Ministry.

I used to walk to school most days from our home across what were then the wide open Aoyama fields. I remember how lovely they were, especially in spring with wild flowers and butterflies. As summer turned to autumn, we would chase grasshoppers, and oh, how beautiful the fields were in autumn, with silver *susuki*, a kind of pampas-grass. In winter, cold winds blew across the vast expanse, and when the paths were obliterated by snow, one could easily slip and fall unless one carefully traced previous footprints. If I was late, I took the tram.

The first time I rode on the tram to school, and the next two or three times, my nanny, Taka, went with me, but after that I rode on the tram alone, and with the season ticket she had bought me in my purse, I felt quite grown-up and very happy. I had an aluminium lunch box in my bag as well as my school books. My lunch contained nothing fancy, and when I came home from school Taka would look inside the box to make sure I had eaten it all, for I was not allowed to leave anything. She severely scolded me once for leaving one or two grains of rice.

'Do you realize that the Aizu clan members in virtual exile on the snowbound Tonami Peninsula, and their wives and children, had to live on weeds and grass seeds and the tofu lees and leftover rice, usually fed to horses and oxen, which they were given by the local farmers? Even His Lordship had to make do with this animal fodder, and it was filled with maggots, too. So you keep that in your mind, and don't you leave any rice grains!'

Taka made me so deeply aware in my childish mind of how the Aizu clan felt, that after that, I never left anything – and not only in my school lunch.

Taka always referred to my father as His Lordship, although it was his elder brother Katahiro – who had shared the rigours of Tonami with the clan – who first inherited the clan leadership, and when Kataharu died in 1910, my father abdicated the title, that should have come to him, in favour of his younger brother Morio, who was now Lord Matsudaira.

When I was in my early teens, there was a game that was very popular called 'Cormorant's eyes, hawk's eyes'. My elder brother learned it somewhere, and used to be the leader and organized us in playing it, and not only did we children take part, but Mother and Taka and some of the maids too, taking it quite seriously.

My brother, as leader, would place a tray on a table in the large room upstairs. On the tray there would be a set number of objects – say ten things, perhaps, such as a cup and a teapot and things like that. A large cloth would be placed over the tray so the contents could not be seen.

'Ready!' the leader would announce in a solemn voice, and up we would go, one at a time, to be told: 'Now then, carefully observe the objects on the tray and then give a list of them.' Whereupon, he would whip the cloth away, leaving it off for only the space of one breath before covering the tray again. One only had time to glance at the objects before trying to list them. The person who remembered the most objects correctly was the winner. But although one had seen them only the moment before, it was strange how little one could remember. He would start with only three objects, and even then some of us could not remember them all. No matter how hard one tried, staring at the objects with the concentration of cormorants and hawks, it would be almost impossible to recollect what there had been on the tray.

After a while we got the hang of it, and managed to list more of the things. Memory, concentration, and observation improved with practise. As games go, I feel it ranks high. And besides, it was fun. It is not difficult, but you cannot succeed without concentration. I think children ought to play it today, and it would be good for the elderly, too.

THE GREAT KANTO EARTHQUAKE

The summer of 1923, after the usual fortnight with my best friend Masako at the Kabayama's villa in Gotemba, I spent a while as usual in Oiso at the Nabeshima villa with my grandmother, Marchioness Nabeshima, my cousins, my elder brother and younger sister, and Taka, having fun at the seaside. Then, when the summer holidays were almost over and I still had some unfinished homework to do, I returned to Tokyo. The next day, 1 September, was the day of the Great Earthquake. There is no telling what would have happened to me if I had not gone back to Tokyo, since the Oiso house was completely destroyed.

My sister Masako wanted to stay in Oiso until the very end of the holidays and stayed behind with Taka and we had no news of them for almost a fortnight. We were beside ourselves with worry. Communications were not what they are now, and since telephone lines were down, there was nothing one could do.

Fortunately, our relatives turned out to have survived, but many people lost their lives, including classmates of mine, and countless people were injured and lost their homes. The news that gradually filtered through, was heartbreaking. We heard that the elder sister of Princess Kan'in had been killed at her villa in Odawara. We were terribly worried about Masako Kabayama in Gotemba, and I shall never forget the relief we felt when we heard that she was safe.

On the day of the earthquake I was in my room doing my homework. I heard a roar that seemed to be coming from the bowels of the earth and suddenly the room started shaking up and down and sideways. I was thrown out of my chair and rolled about, and remembering being taught to get under a table in an earthquake, I grabbed the legs of my desk and rolled under it. As I did so, the house started to collapse. I wasn't scared so much as in a state of shock, so much so that I could not even cry out for help, but simply waited until somebody came and rescued me and took me outside. I was in such a daze I could scarcely think.

After the second big aftershock, we all took refuge in Prince Nashimoto's palace nearby. My mother's sister Itsuko was married to the Prince. The main building had not even lost a single tile, while the annex had only lost a few. Scary aftershocks continued intermittently, so we spent an uneasy night in a tent set up in a bamboo grove on the grounds. Bamboo groves have always been considered the safest place. Fires could be seen blazing in various directions, which seemed to be spreading. Prince Li – heir to the throne of Korea – and Masako, his Japanese princess, who was my cousin, joined us in our refuge. Aoyama Avenue was said to be a sea of flames, and a great many people whose homes were burned fled to the palace grounds.

Thinking back on it now, I realize it must have been because I was a child, but in spite of all the turmoil, I remember curling up in the tent, sharing a quilt with my cousin Princess Noriko – who was only two years older than I – and falling fast asleep as if I had not a care in the world.

We lived in a sewage pipe for a while afterwards, which was great fun as far as I was concerned. My father was chief of the European and American Affairs Bureau of the Foreign Ministry, and since people from the Ministry and others would doubtless be coming to see him, he felt he could not stay away from the house too long, so, escorted by a secretary from the Prince's household, we went home. Fortunately the house had escaped being burned, but it was uninhabitable. So we copied our neighbours and took shelter in the sewage pipes that workmen had left in the road – living like hermit crabs or snails!

Sewage construction happened to be underway in Tokyo just at that time, and all along the road where we lived, the pipes had been set out ready to be laid down. The pipes were large, and so there was no danger of them sliding into cracks in the ground that might open with further earth tremors, nor would they break apart, since they were made of iron.

Pipes were lying in front of every house, so there were plenty to take shelter in. Lengths of cloth were hung at each end for privacy. Ours had a sheet of paper with 'Matsudaira' written on it hanging at one end, but a man from the Foreign Ministry failed to notice the sign and went to the Nashimoto estate where he expected we would be. When Princess Itsuko Nashimoto heard an equerry say, 'I think they are still in the sewer pipe', she was both alarmed and intrigued, wondering how on earth we would lie down to sleep. That night, escorted by two guards, it seems the princess, together with Princess Noriko, stole out incognito to see how we were faring. After satisfying themselves that all was well, they returned without saying a word to us. When we heard about it afterwards, we agreed that it was just like Princess Itsuko to do a thing like that.

By the time Masako and Taka had returned to Tokyo our house was more or less fit to live in; Taka suggested that I should tour the earthquake damage. What I saw made a deep impression on me which I shall never forget. It was a real eye-opener.

'This kind of disaster must never happen again,' she said, 'but since it has happened, I think it is useful to see with one's own eyes and clearly understand the extent of the calamity and the misery. I will take her myself and accept full responsibility'.

Mother approved of Taka's proposal and agreed, but said my father should under no circumstances be told. Although it was some time since the earthquake, he would be bound to oppose it, saying that the cruel sight of the burnt ruins of what was once a city would be too much for the sensibilities of a fourteen-year-old girl. Besides, he was sure to argue that law and order was not yet properly established.

On the day of the tour, they dressed me in a plain coarse cotton kimono and *tabi* (Japanese foot-mittens) and clogs to protect my feet. The idea was not to wear Western-style clothes or anything conspicuous, but to resemble the ordinary children of the burnt-out area.

Taka and I – just the two of us – slipped quietly out of the house in Aoyama. We went via Kudan and Nihonbashi, finally walking as far as

Ueno. It was hard walking in unfamiliar clothing, and not being used to walking in clogs, I got very tired. It was hard going, and I marvel even now at my perseverance.

Most of the bodies had been cleared away, but there were some left, and I wanted to close my eyes, but instead Taka insisted that I fold my hands and join her in prayer for them. There was no sign of anyone in Nihonbashi, except for a few corpses still floating in the river. Harrowing scenes like that engraved themselves on my young mind. Although I was already familiar with tragic stories of the fall of Wakamatsu Castle, it had all faded into the past and seemed no more than a bad dream, whereas this was naked truth – something I was seeing with my own eyes.

My mother worried terribly, wondering if she had done the right thing to let me go; wondering if the impressions I would receive might not be too much for me; terrified for fear something awful might have happened to us. It was not until we arrived home safely sometime after three o'clock that she was able to stop worrying.

That night, the horrors I had seen did in fact keep me awake until the early hours.

THE AIZU SPIRIT

I think it must have been about a year after the Great Earthquake. I had finished studying, and I do not remember what I wanted there, but on drawing aside the sliding door to the sitting room, there was my father, who had just come home, seated on the matted floor holding a drawn sword under the electric light and looking intently at the blade's *hamon*, or temper-pattern.

'Oh, dear! you do look fierce with that sword!' I blurted out without thinking.

He chided me immediately. 'What a thing for a girl of samurai stock to say! The sight of a sword shouldn't frighten anyone with Aizu blood in their veins!'

I knelt down before him, abashed.

'When Aizu Castle fell, girls younger than you bravely stabbed themselves to death alongside their mothers and their younger brothers and sisters out of loyalty to your grandfather. You must never forget how shamefully treated your grandfather was, and how much the Aizu people suffered.'

I remember clearly to this day that revelation of a side of my father I had never seen before. I had encountered the Aizu spirit that dwelt in the recesses of my father's soul.

The reason my father had abdicated the headship of the family in favour of his younger brother Morio, declining a title for himself, was because he wanted to start from scratch as an ordinary citizen and member of society. He was determined to make a life for himself by his own efforts. He felt that out of respect for the people who had given such loyalty and devotion to his father, Takamori, he had no right to choose the easy path.

And yet, although he told us never to forget the Aizu spirit of our clansmen and their families, he never exhorted his children to strive to get ahead in the world because of it. I think he always just wanted us to be ordinary, good and upright human beings.

But his reprimand that night, as he gazed so steadfastly at the beautiful, gleaming swordblade he held, made me deeply aware of the Aizu blood that coursed through my veins too.

My father had just been appointed to the highly important post of Under-Secretary for Foreign Affairs. It was a time when relations with the United States were becoming difficult. Looking back now, I wonder if he was not gazing at that sword blade hoping its gleam would help to clear his overcast spirit and calm his mind.

Taka never lost an opportunity to talk to my brother and me about the Aizu spirit.

'The reason so many eminent people come from Aizu,' she would say, 'is because of the defiance of the Aizu men who were treated so badly on the Shimokita Peninsula by the Meiji government. They were proud, and their Aizu spirit burned within them. They said, "We'll show them, we will!" It was the same with the women. Look at Miss Sutematsu Yamakawa!'

Sutematsu Yamakawa – later the wife of Field-Marshal Iwao Oyama – went to Vassar College in America in 1871, when she was twelve. She was one of the first Japanese women to study abroad in a group that included Umeko Tsuda, founder of Tsuda College. Miss Yamakawa returned to Japan in 1882, and even after she became Mrs Oyama she was active in social work, in the Red Cross Volunteer Nursing Association and the Women's Patriotic Association. Before Taka came to look after us children, she had taught school and been a nurse, and she had worked in the Women's Patriotic Association, so to her, Sutematsu Yamakawa Oyama was an object of considerable veneration.

My grandfather Katamori, the former Lord of Aizu, spent the last years of his life as High Priest of the Tōshōgū Shrine in Nikko. When he died in Nikko in 1893, he was found to have on his person the two Imperial letters he had once personally received from Emperor Kōmei. According to my brother, the Meiji Government – which consisted almost entirely of Satsuma and Chōshū men – was greatly embarrassed to have Katamori Matsudaira of Aizu in possession of such documents, and while he was alive, repeated attempts were made to retrieve them. But my grandfather was determined that these proofs of Aizu's loyalty to the Imperial House must be preserved at all cost. The Government even offered him a large sum of money for the letters, but Katamori remained adamant. Not knowing when he might be killed by an assassin and the letters stolen, he placed them in a bamboo tube which he wore next to his skin even while bathing.

Ever since then, the Imperial letters have been a treasured heirloom of the Matsudaira family – nay, of the whole Aizu clan – and I believe they will always be a symbol of the Aizu spirit no matter how things may change over the centuries.

SUMMER IN NIKKO

In my days at the Peeresses' School I was neither an honour student nor a particularly exemplary one. I was certainly not a 'swot'; I simply did whatever I had to do to the best of my ability, and I was industrious. The precepts my father gave me were, 'Do what is right and proper' and 'Do the best you can', and I did my best to follow them.

Foreign language study began in the first year of middle school, and one had to choose between English and French. I talked it over with my mother, who said, 'From your father on, we've all gone in for English in this family and no-one has taken up French, so I think it might be a good idea for one of us to learn to speak French.'

My choosing French was as simple as that. Ten of us, including Princess Kan'in, began learning the language from a Japanese teacher. However, I hardly got anywhere before I had to stop, for in less than a year, my father was appointed ambassador to the United States.

How I regretted not having chosen English instead of French! But after marrying into the Imperial Family, I was grateful for even my small knowledge of French, since it was the lingua franca of royalty. That was obviously why the princesses studied it, although at the time, little did I know that I would be needing the knowledge for the same reason.

What concerned me most as I entered First Year Middle was that my best friend, Masako Kabayama, was leaving, on her own volition, to study in America. How enterprising of her, I thought. While I of course admired Sutematsu Yamakawa, the Aizu woman Taka was so proud of who had gone abroad to study at the age of twelve, here was a contemporary of mine doing the same thing! Furthermore, while Sutematsu was part of a group, Masako would travel across the sea alone to go to a residential college in New Jersey. Taka was impressed. 'What a wonderful young lady!' she said. Taka loved Masako's openhearted, lively temperament, and for her part, Masako says, 'Taka always treated me quite impartially, and was so good to me, in spite of my being a child of the enemy!'

Masako's family came from Kagoshima – the former Satsuma fief – and her grandfather had taken part in the attack on Aizu. The Aizu spirit burned with a vengeance in Taka's heart, and she was devoted to the memory of my grandfather, whom she called the Great Lord of Aizu. But while Masako was, indeed, a 'child of the enemy', that fierce Taka made an exception in her case and regarded my friend in a special light. Perhaps it was because they were both forthright people who hated flattery and obsequiousness.

I had always looked forward to our annual fortnight in Gotemba with Masako and her family, but that year we visited the Nabeshima villa in Nikko instead. My grandparents liked to walk, so we used to hike to see the waterfalls and Lake Chūsenji and Yumoto. We never used any form of transport. This time I saw the famous Kegon Falls for the first time.

One day Mother took me and my younger sister Masako to pay our respects at the Imperial villa near Rinnoji Temple. We were graciously received in audience by Empress Teimei. The Imperial villa was not far from the Nabeshima villa, so there was no problem about walking there in our best kimonos. Mine bore our family crest and had medium-length sleeves. Mother had had it made from a bolt of purple silk gauze she had received from the Empress. My sister wore Western dress, as I remember.

I used to have a photograph of the two of us with young Prince Sumi – as Prince Mikasa was then called – in the middle, but unfortunately it was destroyed in the Second World War firebombing. We had been sitting politely, minding our Ps and Qs, when the prince had come over to us and said, 'Let's go out in the garden, and I'll take your picture.'

We went out, and stood in front of a lovely clear stream. Holding his camera, His Highness asked us to move a little this way or that way, and then just as we were expecting him to take our photograph, he handed the camera to a flunky, saying, 'press this', and ran over and got in between my sister and me. So instead of the prince taking our picture, it was he who had his picture taken with us girls! Emperor Taishō watched it all with evident enjoyment from an upstairs window.

I did not meet Prince Chichibu that day, as he was not in Nikko, being away, in the army.

It was not unusual for people to be invited to the Imperial villa or the palace by Her Majesty. When a diplomat was posted abroad as ambassador or minister or some other capacity and their children were old enough, or when the daughter of someone in her service entered high-school, or graduated, Her Majesty would often command her parents to 'bring them too'.

When my mother returned from London, Her Majesty used to summon her often to the palace to help in connection with foreign etiquette and other foreign matters, and when mother returned from Tianjin she was formerly appointed to serve at Court. Consequently, as Masako and I grew older, it became a common occurrence for mother to be commanded to bring us too.

THE DAY I FIRST MET PRINCE CHICHIBU

I never heard any talk at home about who was being considered as a possible bride for Prince Chichibu, but I remember the girls in my class gossiping and speculating about one or two of the young noblewomen who seemed in our inexperienced eyes to have the requisite brains, personality and beauty. It was rumoured that the Empress had visited the Peeresses' School and had spotted a girl she fancied as a bride for her second son.

Empress Teimei – like Empress Shōken, the wife of Emperor Meiji – always attended graduation ceremonies, and often visited classroom sessions, where she would be given a list of the pupils. Girls were not told ahead of time that she was coming and no previous arrangements were made as to what questions would be asked of whom and who would answer. She observed ordinary classes conducted as they normally were. Nor were classes interrupted when Her Majesty entered the room nor obeisances made. We were usually quite unaware of Her Majesty's presence. It did not happen very often. Only about once or twice a year.

It never occurred to us that the purpose of her visits was to find brides. We were simply grateful that she took an interest in us, and it put us on our mettle and made us mind our manners and try harder to be serious in our work so as not to fail.

The first time I was presented to His Imperial Highness Prince Yasuhito Chichibu was in February 1925, when Her Majesty the Empress invited us to the palace shortly before my father was to proceed with his family to the United States as Envoy Extraordinary and Ambassador Plenipotentiary.

My mother, as I remember, wore afternoon dress, and Masako and I went in *furisode* – young girls' gaily-coloured party kimonos with flowing sleeves. The Empress received us warmly, and complimented us on our apparel. 'Nobuko,' she said, 'since you are the Ambassador's wife, you will, I suppose, have to dress and wear your hair in Western style, but I hope Setsuko will not have her hair waved, or anything like that.'

That morning, ordered by my mother, Taka had shaved the down from my face and from the nape of my neck for the very first time. 'It tickles,' I had complained, hunching up my shoulders, and Taka had told me crossly not to make such a fuss. I thought of it as the Empress spoke, and felt very grown up.

My first impression of His Highness the Prince was the sparkle of his glasses and his fine, tall figure.

My mother was bidden to the palace once more by Her Majesty, and took me with her, but on that occasion Prince Chichibu was away on a trip and I did not see him.

But as it happened, I met him again quite by chance in an

unexpected place, at an unexpected time.

We were ready to sail for America and our baggage had all gone off, but a bad storm was predicted and our ship's departure was postponed. Mother suggested that father take us two girls to Nagaoka on the Izu Peninsula to fill in the time before the ship's departure, so off we went. It was the first time we had gone anywhere just by ourselves, with no servants, and we three boarded the train in the highest of spirits. The train was packed, and we had great difficulty finding seats. When we finally did, who should be in the same carriage but Prince Chichibu!

His Highness was in the uniform of an infantry cadet and was accompanied by an aide. My father went up to pay his respects, with my sister and me following behind. The Prince acnowledged our rather stiff bows with a slight nod and asked where we were going. I think my father explained about our ship having been delayed, but I do not remember anything else about the meeting at all. I was so happy to be going on a journey with father that it must have absorbed all my attention. Before getting off the train at Nagaoka, we followed father again in taking leave of the Prince.

What we enjoyed most about those two or three days in Nagaoka was being with father from morning to night. In the peaceful countryside, standing on a bridge over a stream near the hills, using us for an audience, father practised the speech in English that he would give on arriving in Washington.

He rehearsed the speech aloud every day, and each time, when he had finished, he asked us, a little shyly, what we thought of it.

'Well', we would say, trying to sound wise, 'it still sounds a bit flat. Shouldn't you put a little more expression into it?' And taking us quite seriously, he would reply, 'I see,' and, clearing his throat, he would start again from the beginning. I can still hear him now, in my mind, and I cherish the memory.

CHAPTER FOUR

AMERICA

◆

THE REUNION

The danger of the storm being over, we sailed from Yokohama on board the Tōyō Steamship Company's Taiyō Maru on 17 February 1925. I was only fifteen, and at that tender age I found it heartbreakingly sad to leave my elder brother behind all by himself and sail away from my homeland for a far country. It was my first experience of parting and separation.

Taka's daughter Chie was travelling with us. When Taka came to us as our Nanny, her son Ryō was eleven and her daughter Chie was nine. Raised by our grandparents, when they were old enough, they came to Tokyo too, and entered Aoyama Gakuin school. Chie was already twenty-one, and having been at Aoyama Gakuin she could speak English, and was an ideal assistant to Taka.

The Taiyō Maru arrived in San Francisco on time, and from there we spent eight days on a train and reached Washington on 11 March. We were met at the station by Embassy staff and driven to the Japanese Embassy residence.

As we began our life in Washington, the thing that worried me most was the idea of school. Having been in the group at the Peeresses' School who studied French, I knew not a word of English. I had wanted to stay behind in Japan with my brother and graduate. But my mother had considered that it was important for girls in the years to come to learn a foreign language really well and to experience life abroad, so I had left school in mid-term to go to America.

Since the school year there began in September, it had not yet been decided what school we would attend, but whatever school we went to, we would first have to learn to speak some English. That was why I wanted to see my dear friend Masako Kabayama as soon as possible. No sooner had we arrived in San Francisco than I could hardly wait to see her again and was dying to ask her all about her life in America and especially what school was like there.

I was thrilled when I found I could see her during her spring vacation. It was arranged that she should come to Washington for two weeks. But before our longed-for reunion could take place, there were several problems.

Hartridge School in New Jersey, where Masako was a student, was a strict, Catholic boarding school. Masako was the only foreign student there, and she was studying very hard. It was three hours by train from Washington, and it would not have been impossible for her to see Japanese friends, but when he sent her to study abroad, her father, Count Kabayama, had said that while she was a student he did not want her to accept any invitations from Japanese whatsoever. I imagine he felt that if she socialized with Japanese, she would not become really proficient in English. So long as she was a student in America she should cast off her Japanese self and immerse herself in the American way of life and customs.

But he made an exception in our case. However, the school laid down various difficult conditions. First of all, a teacher had to accompany her as far as Washington Station, where my mother would be expected to meet her. It was not sufficient for me to meet her alone. The school would only agree to hand her over to someone they considered responsible. So, although Mother was very busy, she went with me to meet Masako and her escort, who, when she was quite satisfied that Mother was indeed Madame Matsudaira, handed my friend over, on Mother's assurance that she would personally come to the station again on the appointed day to return Masako to the teacher's care. Mother invited the teacher to have tea with us at the Embassy, after which the Embassy car would take her back to the station, but she declined, and went straight back. As we watched her walk away, Masako said: 'I feel like a registered parcel!'

It was the first thing Masako said at our railway station reunion. And she said it in English.

In a mere eight months, Masako could no longer speak Japanese!

She could still read and write it, but the words would not come. She had not forgotten, of course – she just could not summon up the words. I was impressed with the way she had taken such pains to adapt herself and become thoroughly immersed in American life. Her father before her had gone to America to study when he was fourteen, saying it was not for himself, but for Japan. He said that Japan must become internationalized in order to take its place in the world, and so he wanted to learn about the best things in the West and come back and teach his compatriots. Therefore he was very serious about his studies.

Masako may not have been able to summon up her Japanese at first, but no sooner had she arrived at the Embassy residence and relaxed, than, 'Phew! what a relief!' she exclaimed in Japanese, and we all laughed.

Judging by the teacher who brought her to Washington Station, I felt sorry for her being at such a strict school and wondered with some apprehension if that was the kind of school we would be attending. I was dying to start asking Masako all sorts of things about her life in an American school, but I was obliged to contain myself for a while longer. With her Japanese not returning much beyond 'Oh how lovely' and my English completely non-existent, it was rather difficult to communicate.

'Language is like music. If you haven't been hearing it, you get out of practice,' said Masako when she had finally begun to find her Japanese tongue again, and I think she was right. After about three days of uninhibited chatter with my sister and me, she was using Japanese and nothing else.

Hartridge School, where Masako was a student, was unusually strict for an American school. It may have been because it was Catholic, but it was more like an English school. You were not allowed to do this and you were not allowed to do that. There were so many regulations that even talkative Masako had been completely silenced. But one had to admire the way she managed – all by herself as the only foreigner.

Even though she was going to stay at the embassy, the contents of her case had had to be inspected by a teacher. She showed me what she had inside, and I was impressed by the way she had done her packing. She had not been told how to pack, it was done in her own way. She had worked out carefully what she would need and how much for the length of time she would be staying, and how big a suitcase to bring. I could see at a glance how well she had organized her things. On the top she had neatly laid the fan used in the Noh dancing she had studied since she was a child of four.

Masako visited us every vacation, and she never failed to bring her fan, although she did not necessarily dance for us. Ever since she was a primary school girl, Masako had looked stylish and dressed nicely, and on coming to America she had become even more elegant and fashionable, but it occurred to me that underlying her modern exterior she was sustained by the ancient tradition of the Japanese Noh. That, I thought, was probably the backbone that enabled her to hold her own amidst the rigours of an unfamiliar school and dormitory life.

It seems funny to speak of Masako's Japanese becoming more fluent after those three days, but when she had begun to talk freely again in Japanese, she and I stayed up all one night chattering away. 'Oh, aren't these good!' she kept saying, as we helped ourselves to pink shrimp-flavoured *sembei*, seaweed-wrapped Shinagawa Rolls, and the other varieties in the rice cracker assortment known as Edo Arare, talking incessantly. Their saltiness made us thirsty so we drank masses of green tea, and next morning we were so full we couldn't eat another thing.

The other day, Masako – now Mrs Shirasu – was reminiscing about that night and laughingly observed, 'As for what we talked about: one thing just ran into another and didn't make any sense at all!' Watching my friend so thoroughly relaxed and 'letting her hair down' in a way that she could not at boarding school made me feel carefree and happy too.

That fortnight went by in a flash, and before we knew it, Mother was taking Masako back to Washington Station and carefully handing her precious charge over to the teacher, and I had to bear the sadness of parting from Masako – who had become a 'registered parcel' again – until the summer vacation.

As the summer vacation drew near, the decision was made as to what school my sister and I would be attending, which was a relief, but while we looked forward to life at the new school, fears began to assail us regarding the English language.

THE FRIENDS SCHOOL

After a great deal of thought, our parents decided to send me to a private high school on I Street in Washington called The Friends School. My father's predecessor, Ambassador Shidehara's son had been there, and my parents had heard that it was a very good school, so after making various enquiries, they decided to send me there.

The Friends School went from kindergarten to high school, and was co-educational. Classes in the high school were small, with only about twenty pupils. The headmaster was called Dr Thomas Sidwell, and it was a Quaker school, but there was no special religious instruction.

The fact that I could not speak English was indeed a serious trial to me. There I was in an English-speaking country and could not understand a word. For instance, although I could understand what was required for me to do in mathematics, and could write the solution correctly in my notebook, I could not put what I had done into words. How thankful I was that at least the same Arabic numerals were used worldwide!

As for English, we did not of course use language textbooks, but studied novels. Although I knew no English, I was directly faced with English literature, and found myself totally at a loss. Famous novels familiar to everyone there were quite unknown to me. I could hardly write a précis if I could not read the language the novel was written in. The only thing I could do was laboriously look up every word in a dictionary. The dictionary was never out of my hand. Whether I went home, or wherever I went, I was constantly looking up words in the dictionary. It took time. I did not dislike studying, but all that dictionary business was very hard work.

However, in spite of not being able to speak the language, never once did I experience any unpleasantness or feeling of alienation thanks to the deep emphasis placed on international friendship by the headmaster and his wife and its effect on the teachers and pupils, which made them unusually understanding and thoughtful and kind towards foreigners. The only other foreign student at that time besides my sister and me was the daughter of the Chinese Minister, who was in the class below me. We were not treated differently because we were foreigners. All the students were treated with the same warmth, and the teachers showed care and consideration in the way they disciplined us.

Homework was set daily at the Friends School, but it was not taken home. Assignments were generally finished during study periods at school. The idea was that when we got home we could play or do anything we wanted, and spend time with our families. The only students who took school books home were those with special problems, such as those who were badly behind in their studies, or foreigners like us who were not fluent in English. The students were terribly sorry for me when they saw me go out of the school gate loaded down with several books.

Latin was compulsory but I managed to be excused on the grounds that it was more important for me to concentrate on mastering English. Westerners study Latin much as we in Japan study classical Chinese, for the relation of Chinese to Japanese is similar to the relation of Latin to most European languages. Japanese is written in Chinese characters just as English, French, Italian and so forth are written in the Roman alphabet. All my friends were having a hard time with their Latin. Masako Kabayama actually liked Latin. How I admired her talent!

But while I had been excused from coping with Latin, my struggle with English continued unabated. A piano teacher had been appointed for me, but it was decided that the piano was out of the question. I hardly had the time to devote myself to anything like that.

Every other month we had to take a simple test, and twice a year there was a big examination. If one got a grade of over 75 on both these examinations, one could go up one grade, but if one failed, one had to do the course over again.

Whether good or bad, the marks you received were read out in front of the whole class by the teacher without mincing matters in the slightest. In particular, those whose marks were just below the passing grade – 74, for instance – were given a thorough scolding, while the student in question would listen, looking quite unconcerned. Before I got used to this, it made me quite nervous.

When I had got to the stage where I could follow lessons in English, there was a French test in which I got the passing grade of 75. The announcement of my marks was greeted by the whole class with applause and congratulatory cheers. I thought at first that they were teasing me, since no one had applauded girls who had got over 90 marks. I not only wondered why they had applauded, but was somewhat ashamed at what I considered a low mark, having already studied quite a bit of French at the Gakushūin – the Peeresses' School – in Tokyo. But eventually the reason became clear.

I found I was not the only student with 75 marks who was applauded. The students clapped for anyone who got 75, expressing their happiness for that person, who would beam with satsifaction and say 'Thank you' to the teacher. While it was wonderful for anyone to get over 90 marks, it was considered specially good fortune to reach 75, just over the dividing mark of failure. And as for those who got less than 75, they showed no evidence of embarrassment or despondency, and the rest of the students never showed a grain of scorn or contempt.

No one minded in the least whether anyone took three years or five years to graduate. When I discovered what a happy, cheerful atmosphere pervaded friendships and studies at the Friends School, I began to enjoy it thoroughly, and look back with nothing but nostalgia at the happy days I spent there.

Just the other day, when my chief lady-in-waiting, Mrs Shimizu, happened to be looking for something for me, she came to me and said, with a broad smile: 'Your Highness, I think you might like to see this.'

What should it be but a report card and examination paper from Friends School days! Looking at the yellowed pages, I was amazed to see that I had got 85 in English and 99 in Algebra. The 85 in English pleased me much more that the 99 in Algebra, and I was transported momentarily back to those student days.

BRASS BANDS AND CHEWING GUM

My three years at the Friends School comprised the whole of my adolescence. My adolescence began and ended there, so my school memories are all the more precious to me. Those were truly happy, carefree days for me. In spite of my dictionary struggle with English, hard though it was, whenever I think of those days I find myself smiling with pleasure. And sometimes I hear in my mind the sound of an approaching circus band.

Our study hall was on the second floor, facing the road. One afternoon, when we were all quietly doing our 'prep', we began to hear the rousing music of a brass band coming closer and closer.

Everyone became excited, and boys and girls sitting near the window surreptitiously craned their necks to try and see the band. It was advertising a circus. It created a stir in the study hall, making us all want to get up and look, so that we became restless and fidgety and unable to concentrate on our work. Suddenly the teacher said: 'Put down your pencils.'

We all laid our pencils down, quite sure we were going to be scolded. But to my amazement, this is what the teacher said:

'You can have ten minutes. If you want to go down to the street, you may. Or you can watch from the window, if you prefer.'

The band was just passing the school. 'Thank you!' we all shouted, and some ran down the stairs while others leaned out of the window, enjoying themselves to their heart's content. I watched from the window.

After the band had passed by, the satisfied students went back to their seats and resumed their studies with even more quiet diligence than before – and not even ten minutes had elapsed! If the teacher had ignored the students' interest and curiosity and scolded them and made them close the window, they would never have been able to resume their studies with such concentration in the brief space of ten minutes, as they did. I marvelled at the way that teacher handled the situation with such kindness and understanding, and child though I was I could appreciate the wisdom of this kind of educational approach, and I wished it could be adopted in Japan.

There was another incident that impressed me. It concerned a different teacher. This teacher was very strict about students chewing gum during class. One day, after he had come into the classroom, he sat and waited for a very long time without starting the lesson. Students began to wonder what he was waiting for, and started getting restless, but the teacher just ignored this. Then, just when the atmosphere began to change from curiosity to apprehension, he spoke:

'Will the person who is chewing gum please spit it out into that basket, immediately!'

There was no anger in his voice, but the sternness of the command caused one of the male students to spring to his feet manfully and go to the waste-basket by the platform and rid his mouth of the gum. Then to my amazement, he was followed by almost everyone else who, one by one, did the same.

But what astounded me most was that even then the teacher did not begin class. How very odd, I thought, and then the teacher said: 'Someone still has chewing gum in his mouth. Will he please get rid of it?' The teacher quietly waited some more, strolling back and forth between the desks, making no attempt to begin teaching. Not having been chewing gum myself, I could not help feeling impatient about this waste of time. Finally, one last student got up and deposited his gum in the basket, and with a grin, as much as to say, 'Good, now we can begin' the teacher started class as if nothing had happened.

There were only about two others besides myself who had not been chewing gum. The incident taught me a great deal. Firstly, the teacher's warmhearted attitude. Without giving us a vigorous scolding, or lecturing us, he treated us as responsible people and gave us a chance to voluntarily rectify our misconduct. As for the students, I admired their honesty and courage in going up and getting rid of their gum when they might have got away with it by keeping quiet. I liked the agreeable atmosphere of good humour that pervaded the classroom, and the warm, trusting relationship that existed between the teachers and the students. It was something we have never had in Japan, either now or in the past.

I was continually amazed by one thing or another, and in turn, I managed to provide a bit of amazement myself. When I was a child, little girls all learned how to keep several bean bags going in the air. Taka had taught me how to do it, but I did not consider myself particulary adept. One day the cry went up: 'Setsuko's a juggler!'

I had gone to the tennis-club for some afternoon practice. During a recess, I casually threw three tennis balls up into the air and tried the bean-bag routine. It is not considered a particularly high-grade skill in Japan, but my friends made a terrific fuss, and called all the other classmates over and got me to do it again for them to see. They don't play with bean-bags in America, although they have professional jugglers at circuses and vaudeville shows. They could not seem to get over the fact that I could carry off this feat with such ease. They made me do it over and over again, and when I explained that in Japan it is simply a game that all girls play, they couldn't stop marvelling, and came to the conclusion that all Japanese women must be jugglers and that everyone, including women and children in Japan could juggle!

The fact that Westerners are not particularly dexterous may well be because they have never juggled bean bags as children.

Years later, when I visited Washington, an old friend asked, to my surprise: 'Do you still juggle?'

'I haven't tried lately, but I'm quite sure I could.' I replied, remembering with nostalgia the stir I had made.

Speaking of tennis balls, I have a beautiful cup I won at one of the annual school tournaments. I had played a little tennis at the Peeresses' School in Tokyo, where we used a soft ball, but although I joined the tennis club at the Friends School I had no illusions about my abililty. Before I knew it, however, I found myself taking part in a tournament!

The whole school was involved, so I expected it would be quite a gala occasion, but the first round was just like an ordinary day of tennis practice. After letting us warm up for a while, the teacher simply said: 'Now we'll begin the tournament.'

The spectators were no different from the usual onlookers. I was fortunate enough to win that first day and remained in the tournament. I continued to win for the next two or three days and found myself in the semi-finals, which I also won. No-one could have been more surprised than I was to find that I would now be playing in the final! As I stood there in a daze, the girl who was to be my opponent said: 'Well, when and where shall we play?'

I looked completely blank, so she explained that we could play our match on any court we liked, whenever we wanted to.

We decided to play at a club she knew, the following Sunday, and I duly made my way there on the appointed day with a great deal of trepidation. Unlike the previous matches, the very thought that this was the final ladies singles match of the tournament made me feel nervous and tense. I arrived at the appointed place to find no-one there but my opponent – no teacher, not even an umpire. There were no spectators to encourage us and cheer – only the odd passer-by who occasionally stopped and watched. It did not feel like a tennis final at all. We had to act as our own umpire and keep score ourselves.

Perhaps my opponent never got into her stride. Whatever the reason, I won that day too, and so I became the winner. I had won the tournament before I even realized what was happening.

Next day, when we got to the school, the two of us simply reported our score, and that was all. Was it because in America the substance is more esteemed than the form? Or was it to drive home the idea of fair play? Perhaps it was just a Friends School custom that differed from the general form taken by school tennis tournaments. Whatever the reason, for me, it is a happy memory that I have never forgotten.

At the end of term I was presented with a handsome silver cup as the ladies singles champion for that year. Not considering myself a particularly good player, I was rather more embarrassed than thrilled to see my name engraved upon it. But I was truly touched at the way everyone was so happy to see me win it, and never a word of complaint because the trophy was carried off by a foreigner. The announcement of my victory was simple. No fanfare. Just that I had won with such and such a score. I was impressed the the way the school trusted the students enough to award cups based only on the students' own reporting of their scores.

THE LINDBERGH SONG

The memory that stands out most from my Friends School days was seeing Charles A. Lindbergh whose non-stop flight across the Atlantic Ocean made him not only an American hero but a popular world figure. Not only was our school proud of his exploit but it made the school famous, for he had gone through its Primary division.

After flying the 3,630 miles from New York to Paris in thirty-three hours, Lindbergh made a triumphant return in a warship, sailing up the Potomac to Washington on 11 June 1927, where it was said that two hundred and sixty thousand people were waiting to welcome him. The crowd was ecstatic, and young women in particular went wild with frenzy over him.

President Coolidge and the citizens of Washington welcomed the young hero at a ceremony in Potomac Park, where my father was a guest, together with other diplomats. My sister and I went to the park, too, with Taka, where Lindbergh's monoplane, 'The Spirit of St. Louis' was displayed. We were amazed to see how small it was. It was hard to believe that he had actually crossed the Atlantic in it. Lindbergh himself was a tall thin youth of twenty-five, who did not look at all like a hero who had just completed a great, epochmaking feat.

While Lindbergh was born in Detroit, his family had lived in Washington while his father was working at the White House and he had attended the Friends School. After he graduated from university in mechanical engineering, he spent two years doing stunt flying, after which he got a job piloting planes carrying mail. It was during that time that he made his famous solo flight.

He must have been overcome by the unexpected ovation he received. For some time he could not remember what he was supposed to say in reply to the official welcome. He was probably busy thinking, 'Oh, mother, you'd never believe the welcome they're giving me!' Neither he nor his mother could have ever imagined in their wildest dreams the extent of the acclaim. It was not until afterwards that the public learned of the homespun background to the flight. When the story became known, I am quite sure it was their modesty and humility that appealed so tremendously to the public.

Lindbergh may have been staking his life on the venture, but he was quite confident that he could reach Paris non-stop. His mother, however, was naturally very concerned, so he promised his mother faithfully that he would do nothing rash. He assured her that should he be aware of any danger during the flight, he would land on the ocean and radio for help. 'So don't worry,' he told her. As soon as he had allayed her fears, he rushed about, hither and yon, getting people to write him letters of introduction, in spite of being very busy preparing for the flight.

As far as he was concerned, he was just an unknown mail-plane pilot, and he was afraid that if he landed in Paris, where he knew no-one, without proper letters of introduction, he might be looked on suspiciously, and he did not want that to happen. One could not fail to be moved by his sincerity and modesty. It never occurred to him that if he succeeded in his solo non-stop flight across the Atlantic Ocean the whole world would acclaim him as a hero.

His mother, too, had written a letter for him to take, stating that her son was on no suspicious errand and was an honourable mail-carrier pilot, and that she would be grateful for any kindness accorded him. After landing at an aerodrome in Paris, or elsewhere, he intended to take that letter and the others he had obtained to the American Embassy and get them to vouch for his integrity.

Far from arousing suspicion, however, long before the 'Spirit of St. Louis' appeared in the night sky over Paris, the aerodrome was filled with a tremendous crowd of people eager to see this brave, world hero who had accomplished such a daring feat, and his letters of introduction and his mother's affidavit proved totally unnecessary.

Nevertheless, it was hearing about those letters that caused his popularity to soar.

What appeals to me most about America is exemplified in the humility of this mother and her son and the way in which the people took this to their hearts.

Last summer, when I was at our villa in Gotemba, I frantically searched for a gramophone record. I did not think it had been destroyed in Tokyo in the fire bombing, but search as I might, I could not find it.

It was a record of a song in praise of Lindbergh. Many such records came out at that time. I bought one and brought it back with me to Japan. But when I married into the Imperial Family I was told that I should not take anything like that with me. No records of popular music or jazz. But I was sure I had hidden that record somewhere among my things, intending to listen to it secretly to bring back memories of my youth. Someone must have quietly removed it.

I am quite sure the Prince would not have minded at all about things like a record praising Lindbergh. I last listened to it at the Matsudaira house in Shibuya. I wonder what happened to that record with its memories of America and my youthful dreams.

PRINCE CHICHIBU'S VISIT

We spent an unusually quiet Christmas Eve in 1926 on account of the Emperor Taishō's grave illness. His Majesty died the following day. The embassy flag was draped in mournful black, and father received condolences from the representatives of the various nations. We all went into mourning and were filled with thoughts of our grieving homeland far away. My mother wept as she thought of the dear lady she would now have to call the Empress Dowager, and regretted not being there to attend upon Her Majesty. My eyes, too, filled with tears as I thought of how kindly the Empress Dowager had spoken to me, and remembered how affectionately the late Emperor had watched from the upstairs window of the Imperial villa in Nikko as Prince Sumi engaged in a bit of fun with my sister and me in the garden below.

In addition to the sadness, the whole embassy became caught up in a bustle of activity which affected all of us. His Imperial Highness,

Yasuhito, Prince Chichibu was arriving in Washington on the 29th and would be staying overnight at the embassy residence.

The Japanese Foreign Ministry had earlier informed my father that Prince Chichibu, then studying in England, would be returning to Japan via the United States to the bedside of his ailing father, the Emperor, but even so it was rather sudden, and also there was the fact that the Emperor's death had changed the status of the Prince. Whereas he had been the second son of the sovereign, he was now first in the line of succession to the throne, and for the embassy, who would be receiving him, the tension mounted.

It was impossible at that late date to arrange for the Prince to stay elsewhere in view of his higher position, so it was decided that the whole of the second floor, where the best bedroom was, would be made available to the Prince and his attendants, which meant that we, as a family, would have to move to the third floor.

My father went to New York the day before the Prince was due to arrive and was at the wharf to meet him together with three hundred Japanese residents, so mother was left in sole charge and earnestly implored the three of us, over and over again, to be well-behaved.

'We are having a very important guest indeed, so do please try not to cause any trouble.'

Mother knew that whenever there was a lively gathering below, curiosity would get the better of us, and we would peer down from the top of the stairs. It was not surprising on my small brother's part, but since my sister and I were also in the habit of turning out the lights and peeking, I suppose she was worried. 'You definitely are not to do that', she told us, having lined the three of us up together. Thinking about it now, I realize that I was still a child in those days.

The Prince spent one night at the Plaza Hotel in New York and then came on to Washington, where he was welcomed at Central Station by Secretary of State Frank Billings Kellogg.

As the time approached for His Imperial Highness to arrive at the embassy residence, all the staff – my mother, we children and Taka – lined up in the entrance hall, dressed in mourning. Being a high school student I did not possess anything suitable, so a black dress had to be made for me in a hurry. It was the first time I had ever worn a black silk dress, and I still remember the feel of the fabric, and how grown-up I felt.

The car finally drew up, and we all bowed as the Prince got out, and he, in turn, nodded in greeting as my father led him inside, followed by his entourage.

After that, we three children were sent up to the third floor. My sister and I, however, had been entrusted with the duty of serving tea and refreshments to His Highness while he relaxed after having taken a bath, so we remained on tenterhooks. We kept thinking how awful it would be if we dropped a teacup, or spilled some of the *o-shiruko*. My mother had been told that His Highness had a sweet tooth, so she had been busy all morning preparing the sweet *azuki*-bean drink, as well as *sushi*, for she thought these homely Japanese dishes might be a comfort to the bereaved Prince.

Mother sent for us when it was time, and after my sister and I had taken in the tea, *sushi* and *o-shiruko*, I being the eldest, stayed behind to serve them. The Prince seemed to enjoy the hot, thick bean drink, for he asked for a second helping. As I handed it to him, he enquired as to what school I went to, and listened with interest as I told him various things about the Friends School. He wanted to know what I was studying, and what sports I participated in. I remember explaining that although I had at first had difficulty learning English, it was a wonderful school, and I was now enjoying my studies quite a lot.

At the Palace in Tokyo and on the train to Izu I had only been able to bow to the Prince, but this time it was just the two of us, and although I was answering the Prince's questions, I was able for the first time to express my own opinions and ideas. I was in a sort of daze while the conversation was going on, and when I got downstairs I found myself trembling with excitement.

That is why I cannot remember very much about that first conversation with the Prince, but one thing was certain, His Highness seemed quite a different person to me then from the way he had appeared to me before. It may have been something to do with the year-and-a-half he had spent studying in London, but I found him as easy to get along with as any ordinary young man. Apart from the *o-shiruko* and *sushi*, mother saw that His Highness was provided with everything else, so I only had that very brief conversation with the Prince.

On account of the late Emperor's death, no large dinner party was held. Dinner was informal, with some of the Embassy staff and members of the Prince's suite, but we children were not included. Taka brought our food up to the third floor.

Next day, accompanied by my father, the Prince laid a wreath at the Tomb of the Unknown Soldier in Arlington, then after visiting the Lincoln Memorial and George Washington's home, he paid a courtesy call on President Coolidge at the White House. The President seemed touched that the twenty-four-year-old Prince should take the time to call on him on his sad homeward journey, and he put his arms around the Prince's shoulders with genuine compassion, as if he were his own son, and led him into his office for a thirty-minute private chat.

The Prince returned to the embassy residence for a rest, after which he addressed a few words of thanks to the embassy staff and ourselves before setting off homeward via Chicago and San Francisco.

While mother, together with the embassy staff, could not help but feel a certain relief after the inevitable strain of an Imperial visit, all of them, especially my mother, had tears in their eyes at the thought of his father, the late Emperor's sad lying-in-state that awaited our recent guest, imagining what his emotions must be.

The Prince, then a lieutenant in the Infantry, had arrived in London on 7 July 1925, to study in England. He was to enter Oxford University the following year, in October, and until that time was busily learning English as well as indulging in various sports, climbing mountains in Switzerland, going to the cinema, shopping, and generally enjoying himself living the life of an ordinary citizen. He had been hoping to spend at least a year at Oxford, studying modern British History, Politics and Economics, but had only been attending lectures for two months when, after the first term, during the Christmas vacation, he was called home to Japan because of his father's illness.

Nowadays, it would take only a few hours by air, but at that time, the Prince, impatient though he was to be with his critically-ill father, had to cover the six thousand miles from London to Japan by ocean liner and train. The Embassy arranged for the Prince to travel via America as it was the shortest feasible route, and the cable announcing the Emperor's death reached him in mid-Atlantic, only three days after his ship, the '*Majestic*', had sailed from England.

Prince Chichibu finally reached Yokohama on 17 January 1927. He went immediately to the Palace, where he paid his respects to the late

Emperor as he lay in state, and called upon the Empress Dowager. He then called upon the new Emperor and Empress at the Akasaka Detached Palace.

On 20 January, he visited the Palace again, as the representative of Emperor Hirohito, to report his succession to the spirit of the late Emperor, who would henceforth be known, according to custom, by his reign name as Emperor Taishō. It was the Prince's first duty as the next in line to the throne. That day, his aide-de-camp was Lt. Colonel Masaharu Honma – later Commander-in-Chief of the Philippines in the Second World War, who was held responsible for the Bataan Death March and received the death penalty at the war crimes trial in Manila. He was a good, kind, faithful, man. I will write more about him later.

The Prince had left Oxford expecting it to be only a temporary absence while his father, the Emperor, was ill. However, on becoming the first in line to the throne, he had to abandon his cherished dream of returning to the University.

As for me, I knew nothing of all this – indeed, there was no reason why I should know – and I worked hard at my lessons every day. I was beginning to enjoy my studies immensely, although I had no particular ambition to establish myself as a scholar. I found that one did not have to be brilliant, but that just by dilligently amassing bits of knowledge, vistas opened out that one could not see before, and it gave a great sense of fulfilment. After graduating from high school, I secretly thought about going on to study further.

WALTZING WITH DADDY

I saw far more of my father in America than anywhere else, and so my memories of him are closely bound up with my adolescence. I have few memories of him as a child, for although we lived in the same house, the things children do and think are so far removed from the adult world that the lives of one's parents tend to make little impression. Besides, my father was an extremely busy man. After my marriage into the Imperial Family, there was no possiblity for a normal father-daughter relationship. The Imperial Household was not like it is today, and so as far as I can remember, I hardly ever saw anybody much from outside the Imperial circle. It was more or less the same as regards my mother. I probably remember my father more, since it was he who usually scolded me.

My three years in America are precious to me, not only as the years of my adolescence, but as a time spent with my family. My father had a little free time, which he never had in Japan, and was able to spend it with his family. I am only sorry my elder brother was not there too.

Among the scoldings I received from my father, I particularly remember the time my sister and I collapsed with laughter just as a guest had departed. A member of the embassy staff had come to see father on some urgent business just before Sunday lunch and we asked him to join us for the family meal. Something or other had struck us as being funny and my sister and I were in the middle of a fit of the giggles when we were called to come down for lunch. We were at that age when one could start giggling at the drop of a chopstick and we had a hard time trying to control ourselves as we went downstairs to the dining room.

Our guest was someone we knew, but it would never have done to laugh in his presence, so we ate with eyes lowered, avoiding looking at one another in a desperate attempt to prevent our laughter from breaking out anew. Somehow we managed to get through the meal and fortunately, the guest left straight away, but it was all my sister and I could do to control ourselves as we all saw him to the door, and it was hardly closed when we erupted simultaneously in a loud burst of laughter.

My father's anger was like thunder.

'It's frightfully rude to laugh out loud when you've just seen someone off and you're not sure they're out of earshot! You may not be laughing at them, but they'll think you are. It's even inadmissable in a small child, and you're certainly old enough to know better.'

His angry blast extinguished our convulsions at once, and made us realize what a dreadful thing we had done. To this day, I have not the slightest idea what it could have been that struck us as being so hilarious.

Another occasion concerns my father's inordinate sensitivity to smells. He did not smoke, and he even objected to the smell of a packet of cigarettes in the pocket of his secretary sitting next to him in the car.

He was very particular about smells in the house when we were entertaining. We often served *sukiyaki* in Washington – an aroma that tends to linger. Father was very fond of *sukiyaki*, but as soon as the meal was over, he would insist that the windows were opened wide to get rid of the smell, and decreed that this and other similar dishes cooked on the table not be served for at least two days beforehand whenever we were going to have a party, and made quite sure the rooms had been well aired and the curtains shaken out. He maintained it was bad manners to receive guests in any but fresh-smelling rooms, and that unfamiliar cooking odours were apt to be particularly unwelcome to people of another country. I still follow my father's custom from those Washington days and never fail to open the windows after serving one-pot cook-it-yourself meals.

We once were having a Japanese-style dinner party at the Embassy, and everything was ready when father came into the dining room and complained of a funny smell. It was just as the guests were beginning to arrive, and we all sniffed hard to find out what it was, when daddy called out, 'This is it!' and what should it turn out to be but glue that had gone stale in the envelopes containing the pairs of disposable chopsticks! I do not remember what we did about it.

With such a sensitive nose it is not surprising that my father was somewhat finicky about what he ate. The only fruit he would eat was a certain variety of persimmon from Aizu. He had a stern side to him, but called us by affectionate pet-names when he was in a good mood. I was Set-chan and my sister Masako was either Ma-chan or Mak-ko, while our little brother Jirō, whom he adored, was just Ji.

Father was quite plump when we were in Washington, but he loved to waltz, and even when he came home tired after playing golf, he would completely revive in the evening when he heard us playing the gramophone and come and ask us to put on the 'The Blue Danube' or 'The Merry Widow' and ask me or my sister to dance with him. Giggling, we would meekly oblige. He and Mother used to dance a lot together when they were younger, but we were his dancing partners in Washington. He loved Caruso, and often treated us children to a rendition of an aria from *La Traviata*.

At New Year, we always entertained the Japanese staff and their families with traditional New Year food, after which there would be games. In the evening there would be cards and mahjong. Father preferred billiards, of which he was very fond. The Naval Attaché at the time was Isoroku Yamamoto. He was a marvellous dancer, and when he played cards and mahjong, he invariably won. He had a very keen sixth sense, or perhaps it was luck. Whenever we played a game where we drew up sides, everyone wanted to be on his team.

In April 1943, when the war was going badly for us, I heard that Fleet Commander-in-Chief Admiral Yamamoto's plane had crashed and that he was missing. I remember thinking, 'This is the end. Japan's going to lose the war. His special luck has finally run out. We're bound to lose now.' I can say it now. I could not say that to anyone then.

THE FUROSHIKI AND THE HOLE-IN-ONE

Although Daddy had a stern side, he was at heart a doting father and was, surprisingly, more lenient than mother. If there was something we wanted to do, such as an opera we wanted very much to see in New York, we would approach him when he was in a good mood and there was a very good chance that he would take us. There was no use wheedling him if he was tired and irritable after a hard day's work. At times like that, we would do things for him, like massaging his shoulders, or putting on his favourite Caruso record. It was always worth the effort, and the end result as likely as not would be a family visit to the opera, which Daddy enjoyed too.

My sister was the most successful wheedler. She was rather frail, and for quite a few years until the birth of our little brother she had been the baby – and daddy's pet. So when I did not have her help, it was somewhat harder to get my way on my own. I was desperately anxious to go to the Davis Cup match in New York. I had not been allowed to go the year before, and this year I was determined to see it. I was very keen on tennis and the match I wanted to see was an important one between Japan and America. There were some very good players on the Japanese team in those days, such as Hisako Kajikawa and Fumiko Tamura, as well as male tennis stars like Shimizu, Harada and Asabuki. It was the heyday of Japanese tennis.

My father was too busy to take me, and at first he would not hear of my going alone, but after a great deal of coaxing – which I had to do on my own, since my sister was not interested in sports and gave me no support – he finally gave in, to my great joy.

The fact that we happened to be staying in a place not far from New York helped. That summer, instead of going to a resort, as usual, we took a house near New York, since it was convenient for my father's work and there were many Japanese living there. There were tennis courts nearby where I could practise every day, and it was a tremendous thrill being able to attend the Davis Cup matches.

While he was in America, my father used to play golf every week. He even played the day of the Lindbergh Reception after the ceremony in Potomac Park was over – and something awfully funny happened. Mother told us about it, trying hard to control her laughter. Daddy himself never mentioned the incident to us, I suppose because he was not sure whether to be proud of his feat, or the opposite. Apparently, his first drive hit something not far from the hole and bounced out of sight. The three players were carrying their own bags so none of them saw where the ball had gone. After they all searched high and low, it was finally discovered down in the hole itself. Thinking nothing of it, one of them lifted out the ball with the comment, 'So that's where it was hiding!', when a group of students arrived from behind, exclaiming, 'What a magnificent hole in one!'

It had not occurred to my father at all. After all, it was just a fluke. And yet, to all intents and purposes it was indeed a hole in one!

Another amusing episode concerns Taka. She had been with us for so long that it did not bother us the way she dressed while in America. She had her own style. We had accepted the fact long ago that Taka had her own way of doing things, so what she wore in America did not bother us much. At first glance it was difficult to tell whether it was a kimono or a dress. We were also used to her always insisting on taking her daughter Chie with her whenever she went shopping. But one thing irritated me. It was the fact that she made no effort whatsoever to learn English. I considered her refusal to do so downright discourteous to America.

'Taka', I would say, 'since you are lucky enough to be here, I think the least you might do is learn enough English to be able to go shopping by yourself and find your way around.'

'I dislike the English language', she would reply, obstinately.

We frequently quarrelled about it.

Taka was fond of the Japanese classics, and spent any free time she had reading. That was all very well, but she was living in America, so even if she could not read English I felt she should at least *look* at a local newspaper once in a while. I wanted her to get the feel of America, and try to familiarize herself with the country. But Taka was stubborn, and flatly refused to do so. I was stubborn, too, and wanted so much for her to get to know America even just a little.

'Oh, do leave poor Taka alone,' said Masako Kabayama once when she was visiting us during the winter vacation. 'She's a bit eccentric, I know, but it's not that she's just being awkward. It's her nature. She's being true to herself, and I think that's wonderful. And moreover, she gets along perfectly well inside the Embassy.'

Masako's wisdom as an impartial observer gave me much to think about. But a few days later, it was Masako's turn to be embarrassed by Taka. So much so that she actually turned tail and fled. We were all shopping together for Christmas-tree ornaments, when Taka, who was conspicuous enough as it was, deliberately drew out of her bosom a commodious cotton *furoshiki* – traditional dark green, patterned all over with white arabesques – and shaking out the enormous square wrapping cloth she spread it out right there in the middle of the store thronged with shoppers, who started to crowd round with curiosity.

'Oh no!' cried Masako, and rushed out of the store, while my sister and I followed close behind. There was no doubt that the *furoshiki* was an immensely practical way to deal with all the bits and pieces we had bought. Paying no attention to the people around her, Taka wrapped all our Christmas shopping in the cloth square and heaving the bundle onto her shoulders came towards us, leaving Chie to settle up. Taka's courage of her convictions made her completely oblivious to the curious looks she attracted. Hers was not mindless eccentricity. It was bred of education and culture. It was just Taka's way, and as I watched her carrying that large bundle with dignity and self-composure I found myself filled with admiration.

Masako, who had shared this and so many more memories with me, finally completed her studies and returned to Japan. I no longer had her company at holidays to look forward to but I enjoyed my studies more and more and my days were replete with fulfilment.

THE EMISSARY

Washington is a beautiful city, often likened to one great park. In October 1927, just as the trees in Potomac Park and The Mall and those lining the roads that radiate from the Capitol were becoming more and more resplendent in their autumn colours, we heard that Count Kabayama was to visit us at the embassy. He was said to be on urgent, though unspecified business, and had already left Japan when Father received a cable from the Foreign Ministry apprising us of his imminent arrival. I imagined it must be something that had come up suddenly, or Masako would surely have mentioned it in her recent letter to me. But I did not give it as much thought as my parents did, since it was no doubt some government or diplomatic business unlikely to concern me. I eagerly looked forward to his visit, however, since he would bring news of Masako.

Count Kabayama was a Vice Admiral in the Navy and also, as I remember, a director of an iron works as well as being a member of the House of Peers. Countess Kabayama's father – Masako's maternal grandfather – Count Kawamura, one time Secretary of State for the Navy and former Privy Councillor, had, at the instigation of Emperor Meiji, acted as foster father to Emperor Shōwa and his brother Prince Chichibu from soon after their birth until they were three and two respectively. When Count Kawamura died, the two Imperial grandsons moved to a temporary residence in the Aoyama Palace grounds.

Count Kabayama duly arrived, bringing me a gift from Masako. He and my parents were still talking downstairs when I decided to go to bed after having studied until quite late, and I noticed that the downstairs lights were still on when I woke up briefly in the middle of the night. I wondered if the Count's important business had anything to do with some sort of worrisome complications that might have arisen over the recent succession of Emperor Hirohito to the throne. But I did not imagine it was anything I needed to worry about, although I did think it was rather strange that my mother should be taking part the whole time in the conversation. She had never remained before when political discussions were going on.

When I came home from school the following afternoon, they were still at it, and moreover, went on talking until midnight. My parents never said anything to me, but I noticed my father looked sombre, and my mother's face was drawn. It seemed as if it must be something very worrying for it to cast a gloom over the whole house. Even Taka was strangely quiet and her stern features were more sullen than usual and she seemed ill at ease. I came to the conclusion it could not be anything political, and feared that Count Kabayama had brought some awful news connected with our family. My sister Masako, too, seem to sense that something was wrong, but neither of us spoke of it to the other, as there was obviously little we could do, whatever it was. When we came home from school on the third day, we found that Count Kabayama had left. I regretted not having known he was leaving, for I should have liked to have had a letter and gift ready for him to take back to Masako. The tension in the house seemed to have lifted, so I thought the problem must have been resolved, which was a great relief.

But no sooner had he arrived back in Japan than we learned that Count Kabayama was on his way back to Washington. This really must be something very serious, I thought. Nevertheless, neither Masako nor I, nor even Taka, dared ask any questions, for there seemed to be an impenetrable and invisible wall between us and our parents.

Count Kabayama was stony faced when he arrived, and began conferring with my parents straight away, and they talked until late that night. Next day, he sent for me, and spoke to me alone. He told me that this time he had come as the personal emissary of the Empress Dowager to persuade me, Setsuko Matsudaira, to agree to become Her Imperial Highness Princess Yasuhito Chichibu. He had been charged by Her Majesty to obtain without fail the consent of both the parents and the daughter herself.

I was overwhelmed. I was speechless. My head went quite blank, and I sat there stiff and tense, like a stone.

'When I was here before,' said the Count, 'I was given a very definite refusal by your parents, who would not even allow me to ask you myself. On returning to Japan, I explained fully to Her Majesty your parents' reasons for their decision. But Her Majesty is very strong-willed. I am here because she reprimanded me for not having succeeded. Your parents feel that as loyal subjects they can no longer continue to disobey Her Majesty, and so they have given me permission to speak to you myself.'

So 'Uncle' Kabayama – who used to call me by the affectionate diminutive 'Set-chan' when I visited them at their country villa in Gotemba in my primary school days – had been saddled with the painful task, as emissary of the Empress Dowager, of being obliged to prevail over his friends and their daughter against their will!

Count Kabayama gave me the details of my parents' original reply to Her Majesty. My father had said that while he felt greatly honoured, he felt unworthy and that it was his duty as Her Majesty's loyal subject to decline the offer. The gist of my father's reply is a follows:

'The consort of Prince Chichibu, the Heir to the Throne, should be someone of suitable rank and ability. My daughter Setsuko has been brought up as a perfectly ordinary girl and is not capable of filling that position. Furthermore, not only am I, Tsuneo Matsudaira, now a commoner, but in addition, Setsuko's grandfather – for whatever the exigencies of the Imperial army were at the time of the Restoration – was stigmatized as a rebel. It would be inadmissible, therefore, for his granddaughter to become the consort of the heir to the throne. I beg you to consider the Aizu connection.'

My mother too, apparently, had demurred most vehemently, saying, 'Setsuko is just an average, ordinary girl, quite natural and unrestrained, who has never been taught any of the refinements that would prepare her for life at Court.'

My mother having been a lady-in-waiting to the Empress Dowager knew what she was talking about, so when she firmly declared that I was not at all the sort of girl who could suitably discharge the responsibilities of a princess, Count Kabayama had given up trying to pursue the matter any further.

'As you yourself well know,' my mother had reiterated, 'Setsuko has never had any training in manners and etiquette, and is just a plain, ordinary girl with no social graces at all.'

So those discussions I had wondered about that had lasted until the early hours of the morning had been a long verbal battle in which my father and mother had kept on resisting along these lines and Count Kabayama had tried hard to break their arguments down.

When the Count reported his failure to the Empress Dowager, she was greatly displeased and said: 'Well, in that case I shall just have to send somebody else.'

So back he had come, and I heard later that he had made up his mind while on board the ship never to set foot on Japanese soil again unless it be with a positive answer. When my parents heard of his desperate decision, they agonized over it again, and finally said, 'As parents of a girl who is not qualified to become the consort of the heir to the Throne, propriety obliged us to decline the offer, but if Her Majesty's heart is so set upon it, it would surely be discourteous on our part to continue to refuse.'

It was as if my parents had been a breakwater which was suddenly taken away, leaving me about to be engulfed unexpectedly by an immense ocean wave. I had not the slightest idea what to say.

'It is surely incumbent upon me to refuse,' I stammered, 'for I have never been taught how to behave in such a position. Why, it seems quite preposterous that someone like myself should marry into the Imperial Family. There are so many other Japanese girls. . . . Why me? I am not even a member of the nobility, and only managed to get into the Peeresses' School by passing the special examinations. I must certainly refuse.'

I threw at him every reason I could think of to get myself out of the predicament I found myself in. I was not merely unhappy, I was frantic.

'Why me? I'm just not cut out to be a princess, so why me?'

I refused to go to school. I refused to eat. I just stayed in my room and cried my eyes out after leaving the matter in the Count's hands. It could not have been easy for my parents, either, for they stood at the parting of the ways with their daughter.

Guessing how weary the Count must be, Mother offered to have Taka try to persuade me. My nanny having brought me up with such tender care from infancy, Mother thought Taka and I would be able to discuss the matter more easily. But I was torn with anguish at the thought of having to become an Imperial princess so suddenly, with no preparation whatever, after having lived the life of an ordinary girl until the age of eighteen. I did not see how I could manage it. Moreover, it was unprecedented. Count Kabayama had said the Empress Dowager would guide me in everything to do with the Court, and that I need not worry, but it seemed to me that more was at stake than just learning rules – I sensed that the Imperial Family lived in a completely different dimension from ordinary people. Even Taka did not seem to understand this. Or so I thought. But when I confronted her with it, instead of refuting my theory with vigour as she usually did, she said in a choked voice:

'I know exactly how you feel. So does His Lordship; and so does Madam. They are very, very well aware of it indeed. That is why they both look so drawn.'

And she went on, 'The Empress Dowager has sent Count Kabayama here twice. Her Majesty obviously wishes it fervently. So I really think there is nothing you can do but make up your mind to accept.'

Taka also said it would set my parents' minds at rest if I did.

I stopped crying and just sat there, curiously drained of all emotion, and quietly, in my mind – just as if I were turning the pages of a photograph album – I pictured the day at the Imperial villa in Nikko, the time we met Prince Chichibu in the train to Izu, and the time the Prince asked me about my school when he stayed overnight at the embassy.

Why should those images have come into my thoughts just then, when I was in such a desperate frame of mind, driven into a corner as it were and being obliged to say 'yes' just because my parents had already given their agreement?

Looking back now, I think it must have been a desperate attempt to try and imagine what it would be like living in that world that seemed so far apart from my own.

'Taka,' I said, 'if I become a member of the Imperial Family I shan't be able to see much of my sister and my brothers any more, shall I? And it won't be the same any more between mummy and daddy and me, either, will it? It'll be awful.'

There was one more thing on my mind. 'And Taka, it isn't going to affect just me. As relatives of a princess, they won't be at liberty any longer to live as they please, will they?'

Tears suddenly began trickling down Taka's cheeks. When she had dried them, she said, 'No, but they possess the Aizu spirit.'

At the word 'Aizu' I suddenly thought of that night in Aoyama when my father had scolded me for being scared as I watched him gazing so intently at his drawn sword. And as I did so, a strength rose up within me which presently formed itself into the decision to do as the Empress Dowager wished. And I seemed to see the two characters 'Ai-zu' shining through the black, lowering clouds and illuminating the path for me to take.

After thinking it through once more, I said, as I remember, 'I will do as Her Majesty wishes. Please tell Uncle Kabayama and daddy and mummy.' It was Taka who began to cry. I remained quite calm and collected.

I had thought, agonized, and cried myself dry. Now that my mind was made up I would reflect and cogitate no more. Since I had no idea what my future life would be like, I resolved not to be apprehensive, or to fret. I decided to live in the present, to make the most of every day.

That would prepare me best for the future. That was the conclusion I finally arrived at.

But I have to admit I cried the whole night after finally making my decision. I heard years later from my elder brother's wife that Taka had confided to her, 'I am not exaggerating: her bath towel was absolutely soaked with tears, and the poor child's face was swollen with crying.' And Masako – by that time Mrs Shirasu – told me long after that how her father, Count Kabayama, had returned home totally exhausted, saying: 'I was almost at the end of my tether. I didn't get any sleep for three nights, Set-chan was so damned obstinate.'

Looking back over my life, I have come to the conclusion that there are two kinds of grief: one that you can laugh about in retrospect, and another – like that occasioned by the loss of my husband, the late Prince – that grows deeper and harder to bear as the years go by.

1

3 June 1904. Prince Hirohito, aged 3 (left) and Prince Chichibu, 2, at the home of Admiral Count Kawamura who officially fostered them, according to tradition, for their first few years.

2

Emperor Taisho (right) holding Prince Hirohito's hand, with his younger son Prince Chichibu following, in the grounds of Numazu villa

3. 31 May 1911. Three schoolboys. From left to right: Prince Chichibu, Prince Hirohito, Prince Takamatsu.

4. 5 September 1921. Crown Prince Hirohito (left), with the young Prince Mikasa, naval cadet Prince Takamatsu and Army cadet Prince Chichibu in the garden of the Nikko villa.

5. 1925. The three brothers with their mother Empress Teimei: from left to right, Crown Prince Hirohito, Prince Chichibu, Prince Takamatsu

6

9 April 1928. Ambassador Matsudaira and family at the Cherry Blossom Festival in Potomac Park, Washington, D.C.

7

The start of an Alpine ascent c.1925. From left to right: Aritsune Maki, Prince Chichibu, Walter Weston (English missionary and father of Japanese mountaineering), Hachiro Watanabe.

8. 28 September 1928. Princess Chichibu in the ancient 'twelve-layered' *junihitoe* court dress at home before setting off for her wedding.

9. 28 September 1928. Prince and Princess Chichibu dressed for their wedding in ancient court costume.

The Chichibu mansion in Omote-cho (formerly Omote-machi), Tokyo. It was built in 1927 and destroyed in the bombing raid of 17 May 1945.

Rear view of the Chichibu mansion.

22 October 1939, outside the Chichibu mansion. Standing, left to right: Princes Chichibu, Takamatsu and Mikasa. Seated, left to right: Princess Chichibu, the Empress Dowager, Princess Takamatsu.

13

The Prince and Princess taking green tea by the irori, or sunken hearth in Gotemba. (Photo: Francis Haar)

14

1952. Prince and Princess Chichibu watching a demonstration of television at the Yamaha Music Store, Tokyo.

15

August 1948. Prince Chichibu in his study in Gotemba with a silver relief memento of the Matterhorn.

16

November 1951. Prince and Princess Chichibu showing Baron and Baroness Lagerfeld pottery just taken out of the kiln. Left is potter Hajime Kato.

17

February 1962. At the Yoshida residence, Oiso. From left to right: Princess and Prince Takamatsu, Kazuko Aso, Princess Chichibu, Takakichi Aso, Prime Minister Shigeru Yoshida.

18

18 May 1992. Hitachi residence. From left to right: Princesses Chichibu, Takamatsu, Mikasa and Hitachi. (Back row): Princes Mikasa and Hitachi.

19

7 October 2003. Translator/ author Dorothy Britton seated in the Chichibu Memorial Park, Gotemba, with the Chichibu villa in the background.

20

Plan of the Chichibu Memorial Park, Gotemba.

CHAPTER FIVE

UNTIL MY WEDDING DAY

◆

THE MEMORY BOOK

The die was cast, and I had resolved to live each day to the fullest, so I threw myself into my studies. My graduation from the Friends School was but half a year away, in June. I had wanted to go on to university and study science, but there was no hope now of staying on in America for further study after my father's tour of duty was over, so I would have to make the most of the precious time left to me of my student days.

Neither would it be long before I was separated from my family by an immense social chasm, so I wanted each day that was left to be as happy as possible so I could cherish them in my mind. I tried not to let this show, and made a great effort to act as I always had.

But nevertheless, the atmosphere at home was not the same as it had been before. My father and mother spoke less, and even when daddy joined my sister and me when we were listening to records, he was not as animated as he used to be, and I sensed a strange restraint. Even when I persuaded him to dance with me, he seemed ill at ease.

While he presented an imposing figure on the world diplomatic stage, my father was shy and awkward by nature, and try as he might to act as though nothing had changed I could see that he was nervous in my presence, and it made me want to cry. I had heard that fathers become very sad when their daughters leave to be married, so I tried especially hard to be cheerful for his sake, and not to look dispirited.

At the end of 1927, Taka left for Japan, charged by my father to make all the necessary preparations for the wedding. Her daughter

Chie returned with her, leaving the school she was attending. She had similarly interrupted her English Literature studies at Aoyama Gakuin when she came to America with us. They spent New Year's Day, 1928, on the train crossing America, and Taka wrote in her diary, 'My errand seems weightier than the Rocky Mountains.'

Although my betrothal to Prince Chichibu was still unofficial, news of it leaked out and appeared in the American press, which led to it becoming big news in Japan. Facts were garbled, as often happens, and it was made to look as if there had been a romance between the Prince and me. Unkind things were written too, and refutations printed, but I was not told about any of this at the time.

On 13 January 1928, while Taka was still crossing the Pacific, I was officially entered – as his niece – in the family register of my uncle Viscount Morio Matsudaira, for the former Imperial House Act stipulated that princes and princesses of the blood might marry only members of royalty or the nobility.

Then, on 18 January, notice was conveyed to the House of Matsudaira by the Imperial Household Minister as follows:

'Imperial sanction is hereby granted for the matrimonial alliance of His Imperial Highness Prince Yasuhito to Setsuko, niece of Viscount Morio Matsudaira, Senior Grade of the Fourth Court Rank, Third Order of Merit Fifth Class.'

An official announcement was made simultaneously by the Imperial Household.

Having no royalty or nobility of their own, the Americans are greatly attracted by it, and the fact that the Japanese Ambassador's daughter, a student at one of their schools, was about to become a princess caused a furore among the media. Thankfully, my mother took care of the numerous newspapers and magazine people who came wanting interviews. Japanese reporters were particularly tiresome.

Everyone congratulated me at school but were very considerate and allowed me to go about my studies in peace like an ordinary student, just as before.

Taka and her daughter arrived in Yokohama at dawn on 21 January and were besieged by the press in spite of the early hour.

'Look here, I'm not the one who's getting married', Taka is said to have declared indignantly. When I heard about it I could not help laughing. It was so like her. But judging by later press cuttings, she obviously learned how to deal with them splendidly. Always prefacing her comments by an assurance that she was being quite impartial, in spite of having brought me up, she was so profuse in praise about my character and personality and even my scholastic ability that reading it now makes me blush. She was, however, realistic and objective about my daily life and categorically refuted the myth of a romance between the Prince and me.

Until our return home in the middle of June 1928, Taka worked tirelessly on the preparations for my wedding, with both public and private help and the advice of my uncle and aunt and others such as Itsuko, Princess Nashimoto, my Nabeshima grandparents, and Count Kabayama.

Princess Nashimoto, who was my mother's elder sister, and my cousin, her daughter Masako, Princess Li, were able to give many a tip from their experience, which helped my aunt and Taka considerably. Taka also had to make arrangements for our mansion in Tokyo's Shibuya ward to be renovated in time for our return, as well as dealing with media harassment. The extent of Taka's anxiety and concern is evident in the entry in her diary in which she tells of how she kept a dagger tucked into her *obi* at all times, and whenever anything happened, she placed her hand upon it for reassurance.

However, the entry for 26 April reads, 'Today's evening paper joyfully announced Lady Setsuko's arrival date and the date set for the official exchange of betrothal gifts. It included happy comments from many well-meaning citizens. As I think of her ship as it sets sail with fair spring winds, I am grateful. . . .'

Taka was obviously relieved to read that I had millions of people on my side.

Meanwhile, I had many things to think about as my 18 May graduation approached. After graduation was over, I was to leave Washington for Japan on 1 June. I might never see my teachers and friends again, and wanting something to remember them by I went around asking each of them to write something in my memory book.

But their reaction was curious. In spite of having been such good friends, no-one seemed to want to do so. A few grinned sheepishly and merely signed their names. I was very disappointed. A few days before graduation, however, there was to be a talk of some sort and we all gathered in the assembly hall, where after it was announced that my sister and I would be leaving for Japan, to our surprise we each received a gift. And what should mine turn out to be but a magnificent, large, handsomely-bound, specially-produced memory book!

Not only did it contain signatures, but there was a photograph of the headmaster and his wife and all the teachers, as well as group photographs and close-ups of the students, and all sorts of nostalgic snapshots. And to cap it all, my teachers and schoolmates had written messages of warmth and friendship, wishing me happiness in my future life as a princess – messages brimming over with encouragement and inspiration.

I was overwhelmed. I hardly knew what to say. 'Thank you so much. I shall treasure this all my life.' That was about all I could manage.

But alas, the memory book is no more. It was reduced to ashes in the fire bombing during the war, together with the palace we lived in. Only my graduation certificate, in its thin leather case, survived. Although it had been in a safe, it was badly shrivelled by the heat – but it proves that I am a graduate of the Friends School.

On the night of 18 May 1928, when the graduation took place, little did anyone imagine there would be a horrible war. There were fourteen of us graduating – seven boys and seven girls – and we sat in a row on the stage in the assembly hall, the boys in tuxedos and the girls in white formals carrying bouquets of crimson roses. After congratulating us and bidding us farewell, the headmaster presented us each in turn, with a final benediction, our parchment certificate tied with a maroon and gray ribbon – the school colours.

On the platform that day, the Rising Sun was displayed in my honour beside the Stars and Stripes, which the headmaster presented to me in his warm thoughtfulness. I still remember how deeply touched I was.

As they carried away their graduation certificates – their passports to the future – I wondered what hopes and dreams my classmates carried with them as they spread their wings and flew away out into the world. As for me, as I set off on the path of my destiny, I vowed to myself that I would follow it faithfully and do my very best.

RIGHT AND PROPER

The days following my graduation were busy with preparations to leave Washington for good, for in addition to having obtained leave of absence on account of my wedding, my father had been designated ambassador to Great Britain. The post of ambassador to the Court of St James is considered the diplomatic pinnacle, but my father did not seem happy about it at all.

Taka told me that it had been for two reasons that he had persisted so long in opposing the Empress Dowager's wish for me to marry her son. The fact that he considered me quite unsuitable had been the prime consideration, but in addition to that, he did not want advancement in his career by virtue of his daughter being a member of the Imperial Family.

'He is that sort of man,' she said. 'When they wanted to make His Lordship a member of the present nobility, the reason he renounced the headship of the family and the title in favour of Master Morio was because he felt, as a member of the former Aizu clan, that it would be unfair to those clan members whose own chances of advancement had been ruined.'

My father had climbed the rungs of the diplomatic ladder by his own efforts alone, as an ordinary person, with no influential backing, so having reached the position of ambassador extraordinary and plenipotentiary in Washington, it would seem only natural that his next appointment would be to the prestigious London post, so it saddened me to think that he should have misgivings. My heart ached to think that becoming an Imperial in-law might have the effect of changing the personality of my dear father – so strict but so magnanimous, and with such an endearing childlike quality.

One day not long before we left Washington, my father called me to him, saying he would like to have a nice quiet chat with me since it might be hard to find time to do so once we were back in Japan.

'I want you to know', he said, ' how happy I am that you have turned out to be the kind of girl I had always hoped you would be. I wanted you to grow up just an ordinary girl who was good and upright – someone who could be counted on to do what is right and proper in any situation. You will need that more than ever now. You must not just make do and pretend, hoping it will look right. You must know your place, and always be aware of your position. A student, for example, acts like a student, and does whatever is required in that capacity. Since fate has decreed this for you, put your heart and soul into doing the very best you can.'

Daddy pointed out that suddenly entering Court life like this out of the blue, there were bound to be many things I would not know how to do, so it would require great dilligence on my part. He warned me against pretence and muddling through, for I would not be able to keep it up. If I tried my very best with wholehearted sincerity and then failed, there would be nothing to be ashamed of. It would be quite different from failure for lack of effort.

'And as I'm sure you already know,' he added, 'if you do not think of effort as a trial and tribulation but try to gain satisfaction from it, and even joy, you will be able to continue that effort all your life. Above all, put sincerity first.'

My father spoke with deliberate calm, holding in check the multitude of thoughts crowding his heart. As for me, his manner of speech gave me a wrench. My sister had told me that on the day of the official announcement of my betrothal, daddy had said to her and our brother: 'We mustn't think of Setsuko any more as one of us. We must think of her as having been entrusted to our care by His Imperial Highness,' so I realized that his use of the formal rather than the familiar 'you' in speaking to me now had been his way of distancing father from daughter. But his smile, and the warmth that I could feel told me my father had not changed. I loved him so much and wanted to throw my arms about his neck as I used to do as a child, but I also realized that now that I had made the decision to marry into the Imperial Family I would have to move away step by step from those I loved.

It was not long, however, before our tête-à-tête took a lighter turn.

'Here you are, beginning to speak English fluently, but you've got an American accent. I suppose now you'd better try and learn the King's English!' said my father, laughing. 'It's just as well you studied that bit of French in Japan.'

It was our last serious talk together.

On 1 June, I said goodbye to Washington and my adolescence. We were given a big send-off as we boarded the train for San Francisco to embark on the *Shunyo Maru* for Japan, where the beginning of a new life awaited me.

I realize now how thoughtful it was the way my parents planned that sea voyage. They knew those two weeks would be my last carefree days so they saw to it that I thoroughly enjoyed myself, without thinking about the future. Nothing was said about my forthcoming life at court, for I am sure my father felt that to do so would only be counterproductive and plague me with anxieties and doubts.

I treasure a snapshot I have of my father lying in a deck-chair looking amused as he reads something on a small bit of paper. I had sat down beside him after a strenuous game of deck golf or quoits, and the two of us look relaxed and happy. My parents left me quite free to play to my heart's content. I mostly played deck games alone, except for table tennis, for which I had found a congenial companion.

I would have liked that happy voyage to go on forever, but the two weeks were over in a flash. On the other hand, it was nice to be coming home again after having been away for three years, and nostalgic thoughts crowded my mind as we dropped anchor off Yokohama early in the morning on 22 June.

In spite of it being June, there had been a storm the previous night, and the air was chilly. I put on a white coat over my blue dress, and completing the ensemble with a white hat, I went up on deck, where I could see a launch speeding toward us. Among the people at the bow I saw the smiling faces of my uncle and Count Kabayama. Soon, they were on board, accompanied by the Vice-Minister of the Imperial Household and other dignitaries, all of whom had come specially to greet me – who only yesterday had been playing on deck with complete abandonment! It brought home to me with a start that I was now on the way to belonging to another world.

A champagne toast was drunk in the lounge, and when the *Shunyo Maru* finally tied up at Pier No. 4, I was in for another surprise. I looked down from the deck to find the pier crowded with people. Surely they could not be there on my account, I thought, but the masses of schoolgirls standing in the rain, cheering and waving little rising sun flags were, in fact, to my great amazement, all there to welcome me. I waved back.

I followed my father down the gangway, led by the captain, in a blaze of newspaper flashbulbs and banks of newsreel cameras, to vociferous cheers of *'Banzai!'* I walked through it all in a daze, smiling and waving my handkerchief, to a room that had been prepared for us, where welcome speeches were made, and where I was reunited with Taka. Security was so strict that my brother Ichirō was unable to get in. Apparently the guards had refused to believe that he was Ambassador Matsudaira's eldest son.

We travelled to Tokyo in a special train, where another tremendous welcome awaited me. Among the crowd of well-wishers at the station I was particularly moved to find members of the former Aizu Clan as well as five hundred girls, lined up in rows, representing all the girls schools in Tokyo.

I got in an automobile, my arms filled with bunches of flowers, and as we proceeded to our new house in the Shōto district of Shibuya Ward in a motorcade of ten cars, I knew there could be no turning back. I had already started out on the irrevocable path to a royal life. And no matter how difficult or strange it might be, I would not flinch. I vowed to do as my father had said and strive with all my heart to do my very best.

I have to admit that in spite of all my earlier determination and vows, at times I had been petrified and full of misgivings. But the fact that I had now seen for myself how delighted the people of Aizu were, and so many ordinary citizens too, and how they all wished me happiness, was a great source of strength to me.

LEARNING TO BE A PRINCESS

The very day I returned home I received a message from the Empress Dowager to say I must be tired from the journey and would probably need to rest the following day, but that she would like me and my mother to come to her palace the day after that.

It was three years since Her Majesty had received us in audience. She graciously offered to teach me everything about court observances and etiquette, and asked me to come to her palace every day. Since there was no course of royal bridal instruction, with special teachers, as there is now, it was indeed reassuring for a completely unqualified ignoramus like me to know that I would be instructed personally by the Empress Dowager herself.

I had heard that the Empress Dowager, when she became the wife of the then Crown Prince, had herself received a rigorous training from those ladies-in-waiting who had served at court for a long time. The first thing I learned was how to walk. A good posture is essential for a princess. Long silk dresses, either low-necked or high-necked – referred to as *robes décolletées* and *robes montantes* – were worn at court functions, and it was considered indecorous to let one's shoes show when walking. One had to move gracefully, with elegance. And one had to learn how to put on ancient ceremonial robes and how to deport oneself in them. And when required to stand in attendance, one had to remain absolutely motionless for no matter how long.

My aunt Itsuko, Princess Nashimoto, did not marry her Prince until three years after their betrothal, since he was with his regiment in Hiroshima during that time. My cousin Masako, Princess Li – who was royal from birth – had a two-year wait. In my case I had barely three months. I could hardly be expected to learn everything in so short a time. I visited Her Majesty for instruction as frequently as possible and tried to remember everything she said, but it was all very difficult, and many were the times I shed tears in private.

Furthermore, only two months after our marriage, I would be required, as the consort of the Heir Presumptive, to attend upon the new Emperor and Empress at their enthronement in Kyoto.

Aunt Itsuko helped me a great deal, and said not to worry about the ceremonies – that I was sure to be instructed in the details at the time. She gave me much encouragement, urging me to relax and take things as they came. The words of cheerful, serene Aunt Itsuko always made my fears melt away like snow in springtime.

Writing poetry is a required accomplishment at the Imperial court, so I was given lessons in composing the traditional thirty-one syllable *waka* by Dr Taneaki Chiba, who had edited Emperor Meiji's poems for publication. I had calligraphy lessons from Dr Masaomi Ban.

On 12 July my parents, my uncle and aunt and I were invited to dinner by the Empress Dowager. Others invited were the Lord Keeper of the Privy Seal, the Minister and Vice-Minister for the Imperial Household, and other dignitaries. At this dinner I met Prince Chichibu for the first time since returning to Japan. A week later, on the 20th, His Imperial Highness hosted a dinner, to which I was invited, together with my parents, my elder brother, my sister, and my aunt and uncle. He invited my parents and me to dinner again on 29 August, and on 8 September, shortly after, we Matsudairas reciprocated with a dinner for the Prince.

I had now met His Highness four times before the ceremonial

exchange of betrothal gifts took place on 14 September. For this occasion, my parents and I went to Uncle Morio's house, since I was now officially a member of his family. There, my uncle and aunt and I received the Prince's envoy. For this ceremony I wore a low-necked formal dress of snow-white silk and a necklace the Empress Dowager had given me.

The gold braid on the equerry's full-dress uniform sparkled as he relayed a message from His Imperial Highness, Yasuhito, Prince Chichibu, and a subordinate official gave orders for the betrothal gifts to be brought in. They consisted of an *uchiki* (a loose-fitting lined court robe of ancient design), a *hitoe* (an unlined summer court robe), a cedar-wood fan, sheets of special paper, a box containing a fresh sea-bream and a barrel of *sake*, each presented on a plain wood stand.

When the envoy had left, our old retainers, who had come up to Tokyo the week before specially for this event, rejoiced together, with tears in their eyes.

Next day, the fifteenth, at ten in the morning, there was a ceremonial trying-on of the ancient-style court costume, called *junihitoe* (twelve unlined robes), that I was to wear at the wedding. The number of layers had fortunately been somewhat modified.

First, I had my hair done in the traditional way, stiffened with thick camellia oil and puffed well out at the sides into a sort of heart shape, with the rest tied in a pony tail and hanging down at the back, greatly lengthened by the addition of a switch. The hairdresser began by combing the solid, lard-like pomade through my hair with a fine-tooth comb, which, as I remember, was very painful – much more so than with an ordinary old-fashioned Japanese hair-do – and needed great skill on the part of the hairdresser.

Even more skill was required on the part of the dresser. My dresser, seventy-year-old Seichoku Aoyama, had been with the Empress Dowager since her marriage. First, over a royal purple *kosode* (a short-sleeved under-kimono of soft silk), I put on a royal purple court *naga-bakama* (a full pleated divided skirt). It was so long that it seemed to be made for a giant, my feet coming where the giant's knees would be, and the rest trailing a long way behind. How would I ever walk in this without tripping! Next came the *hitoe*, a linen robe – unlined because it was summer – also in royal purple, followed by the *itsutsuginu*, or 'five robes', of deep royal crimson silk damask. Once they were five separate garments, but now just one, simulating five, with folds of shaded colours at the neck, the openings of the sleeves, and the edges of the skirt. Over all this went a lustrous purple linen *uchiginu* with wide sleeves, a pale blue double-woven outer robe (*uwagi*) lined with yellow silk, and finally a *karaginu*, or 'Chinese jacket' of blue brocade. A trailing, pleated fan-shaped train was attached at the back from my waist. Combs, hair ornaments, a cedar-wood fan and a brocade paper-case completed my outfit.

I learned of the importance of neatly lining up the collars of the first three robes, and that it was essential that the hems of the garments as they trailed out to either side from the sash, being longer than one's height also be neatly aligned. The dresser and assistants arranged the robes while I merely stood there like a mannequin. Although the garments were 'summer weight', some were lined, making the costume heavy, and the many layers made it hard to move my arms. I wondered how I would get through the ceremony. I quailed at the thought of the 'winter weight' set I would be wearing for the ceremonies connected with the November enthronement.

My mother was obviously relieved that her sister, Princess Itsuko, was on hand to advise and guide me. As the wedding day drew near, she relayed to me a message from my aunt that I should drink very little tea and other liquids from the day before the ceremony.

I noticed that Mother spoke to me employing verbal forms used when addressing a superior. She had started doing this the day of the Exchange of Betrothal Gifts. Although I knew that our old mother-daughter relationship was bound to undergo this change, I could not help but feel sad. 'You must not think of Setsuko as a Matsudaira any more', she had told my sister and brothers. 'And you must change your way of speaking to her.'

THE LAST FEW DAYS

Before the betrothal ceremony, on 26 July 1928, I toured our old family fief of Aizu – now Fukushima Prefecture – for four days with my aunt and uncle, my parents, my elder brother, my sister, and Taka. I went to report my forthcoming marriage at the graves of my ancestors and to bid farewell to our former clansmen, who shed tears of joy, exclaiming that the honour of Aizu had been restored.

I had only been once before to Aizu, and that was to the spa at

Yanaizu on the Tadami River, and it was my parents who had been wined and dined and made a fuss of then. This time it was I who was the VIP – already royal in their eyes. 'Princess Setsuko comes to Aizu' proclaimed a local newspaper headline.

I was getting used to being addressed as Princess, but I found crowd ovations unnerving. It was not until I listened to the solemn declaration made by my uncle Morio at Hanitsu Shrine – dedicated to the memory of Lord Hoshino, founder of our clan – that I fully understood the import of what was expected of me:

'I hereby inform the spirits of my ancestors' he intoned, 'that Morio Matsudaira's niece and Tsuneo Matsudaira's daughter Setsuko is to be married to His Imperial Highness Prince Chichibu. I hereby vow that she will endeavour to bcome a paragon of Japanese womanhood.'

As we visited various parts of the province, I was given a tremendous welcome by four hundred thousand former vassals. The knowledge that the people of Aizu were so overjoyed about my marrying into the Imperial Family made me determine anew to strive my utmost, no matter how difficult it might be, to live up to the Empress Dowager's expectations.

On 17 September, the spelling of my name was changed, because the Empress Dowager's name, though pronounced Sadako, was written with the same first Chinese character as mine – namely that meaning 'season'. From several alternative characters suggested by the Empress Dowager's chief chamberlain, Mr Irie, Her Majesty chose the character for 'se' as in Ise, the site of the Great Shinto Shrine, and the character for 'tsu' (also pronounced 'zu') as in my ancestral Aizu.

On the twentieth, my trousseau was sent from our house to Prince Chichibu's palace in Akasaka. There were various chests, and chests of drawers – some lacquered black, others plain wood – as well as personal effects, clothes and other paraphernalia. The same day, accompanied by my mother, I called upon the Emperor and Empress, the Empress Dowager, and all the princes and princesses to pay my final respects as Setsuko Matsudaira.

The following days were full, with farewell parties being given for me almost every day by former schoolmates, friends, teachers and associates, which fortunately left me little time to brood on my forthcoming marriage. One whole room in our house was filled with wedding presents, including gifts from the President of the United

States and the Secretary of State.

The lingering summer heat was finally over by 26 September, and there was a slight drizzle when the Ceremony of the Announcement took place at Uncle Morio's house, at which Prince Chichibu formally made known to the Matsudaira family the date set for the marriage. From early that morning the principal members of the former Aizu clan began converging on the house, and in due course the Prince's envoy arrived. My uncle, in his rear-admiral's dress uniform, my father in tails, and my mother and aunt in formal kimono, waited in a row in the upstairs drawing-room, while I stood in my appointed place in a pink frock. As soon as he had been led in by the butler, the envoy – the Prince's private secretary – solemnly announced, 'I hereby inform Setsuko Matsudaira that the marriage ceremony will take place on 28 September in the third year of Shōwa', to which my uncle replied, on my behalf, 'With humble duty, she will be pleased to comply.' It was all over in half an hour.

'What a moment of emotion,' wrote Taka in her diary. 'A half year's agonizing gone like ice in the spring sun.'

That evening, we gave a dinner at home for me to say farewell to my close friends as well as those who had served the family for many years. Taka's diary describes it better than I could.

'We, too, were invited,' she wrote, 'the butler, the houseboys, the maids, and I, on the same equal footing as the distinguished guests. "There's to be no formality," His Lordship told us warmly. There was a feel of autumn in the air as we sat down to dinner a little after six. You could not blame those members of the Aizu clan for their joy after years of grieving over the fall of the Castle. I, who had never danced in my life, was so overcome with emotion that I found myself joining in the folkdance with tears in my eyes, although I did not know the steps. How Lady Setsuko must have smiled to herself when she saw me. To think this was Lady Setsuko's last night in this house! To think this was her farewell to those of us gathered there. During a pause in the dancing, she stood up, looking like a flower, and thanked us all in a clear voice, and the guests started dancing again around her like a garland of flowers.'

'She had gifts for us all. Mine was a wristwatch she had bought in Washington. She handed it to me saying, "You've been so good to me for seventeen years. Take care of yourself, won't you." Then she said,

"I've got something else for you," and went to her room and brought me a little box with three drawers, which she said I was not to open until afterwards. It reminded me of the fairytale and the treasure casket the princess gave the young fisherman, Urashima Taro, when he left the Dragon Palace under the sea. Tears welled up in my eyes, as I wondered what was inside. "You've been crying ever since this morning," she chided me, but I could see something glistening in her bright eyes too. "Just today," I replied. "Please allow me to cry a little, just today."'

Late that night – the last night I would sleep in my old home – I expressed to my mother and father, in just a few words, my heartfelt gratitude for all they had done for me, and the way they had brought me up these past twenty years. It was my way of saying goodbye. As for daddy, all he said was, 'I can only repeat what I've always said you must do: put your heart and soul into doing your very best.'

Mother said, 'I am praying for your happiness. Be sure and take good care of your health.'

Their eyes overflowed with love and affection and the myriad thoughts that filled their minds. We did not give way to tears.

> *May integrity*
> *Be my strength, as like a ship*
> *On the stormy sea,*
> *I ride out the wild billows*
> *Of this world's deceit and lies.*

My father liked this *waka* and used to inscribe it in his graceful calligraphy. I remembered the poem, and it gave me courage as I thought of the bumpy road ahead that I must do my utmost to negotiate well.

CHAPTER SIX

IMPERIAL BRIDE

◆

THE TWELVE-LAYERED ROBE

On 27 September, the day before my wedding, I ate my last lunch as a member of the Matsudaira family, and after going with my mother to the Empress Dowager's palace to pay our respects, we set off from home, bound for my uncle Morio's house, at about four in the afternoon – my parents, brothers and sister, Taka and I. A crowd of neighbours were gathered outside the gate to see me off, including children from the nearby primary school waving little Rising Sun flags.

As soon as we arrived, Taka helped me change into kimono for a farewell family dinner to which our domestic staff had also been invited. Not wanting it to be a sad occasion, Aunt Tomoko said cheerfully, 'Setsuko, you may not have much opportunity to eat tomorrow, so you must eat as much as you can tonight and get plenty of nourishment.' Everyone laughed. Aunt Tomoko was the widow of my uncle Katamori, the late Lord Matsudaira, and was the oldest there. Although I was under a certain amount of strain, knowing it was my last family dinner, it was a jolly and enjoyable evening.

Mother, Taka and I spent the night at Uncle Morio's. As soon as the others had gone, I had my bath after which the imperial hairdresser washed my hair and completed its preliminary pomading. The moon, which was almost full, had just risen, and I entered my bedroom to find it flooded with brightness. I opened the window. If only Mother and I could enjoy the view for a few last intimate moments together, I thought. But it was not to be. Reminding me that I must make a very early start the following morning, she insisted that I go straight to bed. I had to rise just after two – long before daybreak. I breakfasted between the various stages of being made up, having my hair done, and being dressed in the so-called 'twelve-layered robe'. The great weight of the combined garments seemed to me to symbolize the weight of the duties I was taking upon myself in becoming a member of the Imperial Family.

I left the house at 8.15 – exactly the same time, as I learned later, that His Highness, Yasuhito, had left his palace. The whole Matsudaira family were gathered under the *porte cochère* of my uncle's mansion, where a maroon state carriage drawn by two horses awaited me. A lady-in-waiting, Mrs Yamaza, dressed in white, took my hand and helped me into the carriage, neatly arranging the trailing trouser-legs of my divided skirt, and sat opposite me. I must have been nervous and apprehensive as we started off, for I scarcely took heed of the servants and Taka, who stood dabbing their eyes with handkerchiefs.

My uncle's residence stood in a rather hilly area and apparently there had been some question as to whether the carriage could safely negotiate the slopes, but the journey went off without hitch and lady-in-waiting Yamaza was a most considerate companion. The roads were lined with people, and I can still see them in my mind's eye, waving their little Rising Sun flags.

When we arrived at the entrance to the *kashiko-dokoro* – the sanctuary inside the Palace grounds – the lady-in-waiting helped me out of the carriage, and I bowed low to the waiting Prince, who bowed in return.

In a dressing room, the traditional three-pronged gold coronet-like ornament was placed in my hair, and in my hands was placed the ceremonial cedar-wood fan symbolizing feminine modesty.

At precisely nine o'clock, to the strains of the *shichiriki* and *shō* – the flutes and mouth-organs of the thousand-year-old court orchestra – the Chief Ritualist in traditional robes made an offering to the gods and intoned a prayer. Then, led by another ritualist, His Highness proceeded along the gallery, holding a sceptre, followed by me, and we entered the outer chamber of the sanctuary. Although nowadays much of these ceremonies is televised, cameras are still not allowed inside the sanctuary, and since my recollection of the actual marriage service has become dim, I shall quote from an account by one of the ritualists.

'His Highness sat on the right facing the altar, and Her Highness on the left. First, His Highness bowed to both sanctums (Her Highness doing likewise) and then reported earnestly and in a clear voice: "At this auspicious time on this auspicious day, we conduct this ceremony of marriage before Thee. We solemnly vow that henceforth and forevermore we shall live together in mutual love and fellowship that shall not change for one thousand, nay, ten thousand generations." Then a ritualist set a small wooden stand with an earthenware cup on it before each of Their Highnesses and Chief Ritualist Kujō took the vessel of sacred *sake* and poured it for them. At exactly eight minutes past nine, the loud boom of a cannon rent the silence of the autumn air above the Palace, followed by another and another as the twenty-one gun salute continued and Their Highnesses quietly left the palace looking as beautiful and elegant as figures in the Hina Festival. What a splendid and congenial pair they made!'

Guests had been invited to observe the procession to and from the Sanctuary. They included all members of the nobility, the Minister for the Imperial Household, and other high government officials. My uncle Morio and my aunt, as well as my parents, were special guests. I wondered what they thought when they heard the gun salute and watched me leave the Sanctuary as a princess.

Yasuhito, Prince Chichibu, born in June 1902, was twenty-six, and I had just turned nineteen.

'PINETREES TWAIN'

A state coach was drawn up outside the Sanctuary, and I followed the Prince into it and sat by his side. Led by a cavalcade bearing the Imperial standard, we crossed Nijū Bridge and left the Palace grounds, where we were joined by a mounted guard of honour in white-plumed helmets, carrying standards, and proceeded in ceremonial order to the Prince's residence in Akasaka. Both sides of the road were thronged with people holding little Rising Sun flags, and I could hear their cheers of *'Banzai! Banzai!'* as I sat rigidly facing straight ahead, trying not to lose my balance as the carriage swayed.

In those days, people had to bow respectfully when royalty passed by, and were not allowed to look at them. It was not like it is now when people can freely look at us and wave their flags, and we can wave back and smile.

When we arrived at the *porte cochère* of the Prince's residence, the guard of honour lined up as the Prince's private secretary, Mr Maeda, opened the door of our carriage and the lady-in-waiting took my hand and helped me out. I stood with my head bowed as the Prince alighted, and stood beside him to bow our respects to his four aunts, who had arrived ahead of us – Nobuko, Princess Asaka; Toshiko, Princess Higashikuni; Fusako, Princess Kitashirakawa; and Masako, Princess Takeda; – the daughters of Emperor Meiji. I remember being very nervous, as these were the elder princesses whose guidance I would be seeking, and whose admonitions I would have to heed.

The ceremony of the 'three-times-three' exchange of nuptial *sake* cups was performed anew, after which we sat down to a banquet – I still in my 'twelve-layered' robe and the Prince in his ancient court costume. A friend who was a young lady-in-waiting at the time tells me how graceful I looked as I poured the *sake* for His Highness, but I felt far from graceful, and I imagine it was the beauty of the ancient Heian Period garb that fascinated her. Neither she nor I can remember who poured the *sake* for me. It was probably Lady-in-Waiting Yamaza. Neither can I remember what exactly we were served at the ceremonial banquet – only how varied and colourful the many dishes were.

After the meal, we had our photographs taken and then, in what was to be my upstairs living quarters, Lady-in-Waiting Yamaza and a maid had hurriedly to help me out of the many robes, wash the stiffening out of my hair, and dress and coif me anew for the ceremonial audience with the Emperor and Empress.

Removing the hair grease was a dreadful ordeal. My hair first had to be wiped with benzine and then given a good scrubbing, and even though they bound a cloth tightly around my eyes, the fabric inevitably became wet, and the soap, mixed with fumes from the benzine, got into my eyes. They stung excruciatingly, but worse than that, I was temporarily blinded. It was frightening. I wondered if my sight would ever return. The relief was enormous as the pain and the blackness gradually receded.

With feverish haste, my hair was arranged anew, and I was dressed in the formal European court gown provided for me by the Empress Dowager. It had a long train, which I would carry over my left arm. When worn at the New Year's Day ceremony it would be held by two young boys of the nobility. The sash of the Order of the Sacred Crown, First Class, worn by consorts of Imperial princes, was fixed across my bosom diagonally down from the right shoulder, and the heavy diamond-encrusted badge was fastened nearby. A sparkling diamond tiara and gold brocaded pumps completed the outfit.

The Prince changed, too, into the ceremonial dress uniform of an infantry lieutenant, and held his plumed hat while we had our photographs taken. Meanwhile, the Prince's secretary kept coming in, at ten minute intervals, to inform us of the arrival of wedding gifts – a sword, a clock and a magnificent sea-bream – symbol of good fortune – from the Emperor, a brooch from the Empress and another bream from the Empress Dowager.

We then took our places once more in the state coach to ride back to the Imperial Palace. The crowds lining the road were still there, and greeted us with undiminished fervour. This time I felt a little more relaxed, and in my heart I kept saying, 'Thank you, everybody!'

We crossed the moat again by the graceful bridge called 'Nijū-bashi' and alighting at the Western Chamber, we made our way into the Phoenix Room, I dragging my heavy train. This was an important ceremonial occasion in which we formally announced our marriage to Their Majesties.

As soon as the Emperor and Empress had taken their places on the dais, the Grand Chamberlain led us to our places below, and after the Prince had expressed his gratitude to the Emperor, His Majesty conveyed his felicitations to us in ancient court language, and so did the Empress. Then, the Prince and I sat down in the seats that had been provided for us, and a chamberlain and a lady-in-waiting brought us each a tray with *sake* and food and poured *sake* for Their Majesties. It was a special thick, black *sake* called *kunen-shu*, or 'nine-year *sake*', made by boiling black soybeans, *sake* and *mirin* (sweet *sake*). Before Their Majesties had partaken thereof, the chamberlain first handed the Emperor's cup to the Prince, then the lady-in-waiting handed the Empress's cup to me, and we partook. After that we took up our chopsticks and made as if to begin eating, but did not in fact do so, since it was only a symbolic gesture. This ended the ceremony, and the Prince and I rose and bowed deeply as Their Majesties departed.

We continued in our carriage to the Eastern Palace in Aoyama to pay our respects to the Empress Dowager, who received us warmly, and gazing with great affection, first at the Prince and then at me by his side who was now his wife, she spoke the ancient words of felicitation, but the message she conveyed with her eyes as she spoke was a fervent hope that we would be happy together in love and comradeship. And she composed the following poem:

> So many people
>   Wish you great happiness,
>   With all their heart.
>   Let their joy not be in vain,
>   O pinetrees twain!

The autumn dusk was falling by the time we arrived back at our residence. The lamp at the gate was already lit, and glows faintly still in my memory, like a daytime moon.

There was no relaxing yet, however. I had to be helped out of my court gown and into a formal black kimono patterned with cranes and ocean waves woven with gold and silver threads.

Since the day before, I had been dressed by others, just as if I were a doll or mannequin. It seemed appropriate then, as the garments were all so unfamiliar, but now it was different. I bent down quite naturally, without thinking, to fasten the clasps of my *tabi*, the white silk foot mittens one wears with kimono.

'No, no!' cried my elderly lady-in-waiting emphatically, 'You must let me do that.' I was taken aback. Was I to remain a mannequin forever, I wondered in dismay. My sister had been a delicate child and Taka had spent more time looking after her than me, so from the time I was quite small I had learned to do everything for myself. The idea of allowing someone else to fasten my footwear seemed preposterous.

But I had no time for thoughts such as this. Whilst my costume was busily being changed, a messenger came to say that Prince Sumi had arrived to see us. The sweet playful youth I had last seen at the Nikko Imperial Villa was already a pupil at a military preparatory school. I went downstairs to find that Prince Chichibu had also just come down – now dressed in a formal black crested kimono jacket and *hakama* trousers – and together we received the congratulations of his young brother, who cut an imposing figure in his uniform.

The night was brilliant with the light of the full moon. Led by bands, groups of marchers had been coming by since early evening – local residents of Akasaka, five thousand boy scouts, groups five thousand strong made up of each of the other Tokyo wards – and finally five thousand people carrying paper lanterns. Representatives from each group had come in through the side gate and were lined up opposite the *porte-cochère*. They probably only intended to express their felicitations to a footman or secretary and retire, but when the Prince heard they were there, he jumped up, motioning me to follow, and hurried outside – in his indoor slippers! I did not take the time to change into outdoor footwear either. In fact it all happened so quickly there was no time, anyway, for anyone to have got them out.

The Prince, with spontaneous ease, thanked the representatives most warmly, while I bowed beside him. In those days, to be spoken to personally by a member of the Imperial Family was so unbelievable and awe-inspiring that the representatives were rendered speechless with emotion. Some time after we had returned inside and the people had gone, we heard thunderous shouts of '*banzai!*' coming in waves from the crowds. Perhaps those representatives had passed the word to those outside of their unexpected encounter.

That night, I was told, people from far and wide had gathered in Hibiya Park, thrilled to see a newsreel of the wedding, although it merely consisted of a few minutes of the procession, sandwiched among sports items. What a far cry from television coverage today!

The hum of voices from the lantern parade had receded into the distance like the sound of far-off surf when the Ceremony of the Rice Cakes – symbolizing the conjugal tie – took place in our bedroom, conducted by Lady-in-Waiting Yamaza and Private Secretary Maeda. Inside a box made of beautiful, heavy handmade paper, were two earthenware bowls, each piled high with twenty tiny white rice cakes the size of *go* counters – twenty because that was my age. After the Prince and I made symbolic gestures as if to eat the rice cakes, the box was left in the room, and after three days it was buried in the garden in a spot deemed propitious.

The fateful day in which I took my first steps as a princess, 28 September 1928, finally drew to its close. It had been a long day, with one new experience following another in quick succession. 'You must be terribly tired. It'll all take a lot of getting used to, I know. But don't worry – I'll always be there for you to lean on.'

The Prince's voice was warm and caring, but I was too stiff and awkward even to raise my face to his.

'I know so little. I wish to learn from you, my lord.'

I think I said something like that, and I faintly remember making a deep bow.

THE CHRYSANTHEMUM AND I

As soon as I awoke on my first morning as a princess, Lady-in-Waiting Yamaza, who was on duty in the next room, came in, with a respectful bow, to help me wash and dress. I greeted her with special warmth, for not only was I grateful for her devoted help the day before, but I had discovered who she was. By one of those curious coincidences, Shizuka Yamaza turned out to be the widow of Enjiro Yamaza – *chargé d'affaires* at the Japanese Embassy in London when I was born – who had been asked by my father to select a name for me. I did not learn of this connection until just before the wedding, when I had little time to think about it. There could be no familiarity between us, of course, for court protocol dictated that Mrs Yamaza and I must treat each other as mistress and servant, but as she waited upon me I sensed a touching solicitude, and although we could not express it in words, we both were aware of a deep understanding between us.

As I explained earlier, the *chargé d'affaires* in London, my father's boss, had suggested two names: Setsu (season) or Kiku (chrysanthemum), since I was born on the ninth day of the ninth month – the Chrysanthemum Festival of ancient observance. My father chose Setsu, and my mother then took the chrysanthemum for my emblem. (It used to be the custom for members of royalty and the aristocracy in Japan to have their own sign, or emblem, with which to mark their clothes and other possessions.) When my mother, the daughter of Marquis Nabeshima, chose this flower as her daughter's mark, little did she know that her child would one day ascend the precincts of the Chrysanthemum Throne. It was strange how fate was to bind us – the Yamazas, the Chrysanthemum and I.

The Prince's emblem was a young pine.

The first visit we made together on the day after our marriage was to the Emperor and Empress to express our thanks. The Empress spoke to me most kindly, which was very heartening. After that we called upon the Empress Dowager, who seemed particularly delighted to see us and said we must come often, urging me to come in kimono.

Nowadays it is permitted to wear kimono openly at court, but before the war the official dress was Western-style. Kimono could only be worn, after dark, at private family gatherings, and one had to enter the palace by a side door, passing through the gardens. I therefore had very few kimonos in my dowry, but I used to try and wear a different one each time we called upon Her Majesty.

Having only sons, I believe she enjoyed seeing me in my colourful kimonos, and I think the Prince did too. Many was the time she would not let us go until after eleven.

The second week after the wedding our household was kept busy with celebratory dinners, teas and audiences, as well as state visits to the Ise Shrine and the Imperial mausolea. In addition, my personal effects and clothes had to be carefully organized and sorted out. The people of Aizu shed tears of joy when they learned that the court had given permission for me to use the Matsudaira hollyhock crest on my things, and that on the day of the marriage I had with me the fine family heirloom sword by Kunitoshi Rai, in its brocade bag.

I was not allowed to help sort and put away any of my belongings, except for making a few suggestions. Merely touching a bird ornament in the garden to adjust its position brought a cry of, 'I will do that Ma'am!' I should have known better by then, having been prevented even from fastening my own *tabi*, but on my first evening visit to the Empress Dowager in kimono I thoughtlessly started to turn my footwear around at the entrance after slipping them off, but was hurriedly prevented from doing so. I would have preferred to carry out this point of Japanese etiquette myself, for I knew how I liked to place them for easy slipping into on departure. Moreover, I was amazed to note that services to do with the lower part of the body and those to do with the upper part were rendered by different attendants. Oh dear, I thought, and wondered what other surprises were in store for me. How I wished Taka were there. I thought of the little box with three drawers that I had given her the night of the farewell dinner, telling her not to open it until later, and pictured her laughing and perhaps shedding a few tears at what was inside. I cannot remember exactly what they were, but they were the things I treasured as a child. I was leaving my childhood in her safekeeping as I set out to do my best as a princess, and I am quite sure she understood.

My aunt, Princess Itsuko, had said, 'Patience and perseverance are the most important attributes. If you have these, you will soon learn to be a princess.' I realized I would have to forget the ways I was used to, and learn to do things the court way as fast as I could. It would indeed require patience and perseverance.

October was soon upon us and a string of formal functions began on the fourth. On the third, the Prince went alone to Yokohama to welcome back his brother Midshipman Nobuhito Prince Takamatsu who was returning from a cruise that had prevented him attending our wedding.

On the fourth, there was a banquet at the Akasaka Palace attended by the Imperial Family, ambassadors and ministers from twenty-five countries, and their wives, Grand Master of Ceremonies Hirokuni Ito, Lord Keeper of the Privy Seal Count Makino, and various Foreign Ministry officials including my father, the ambassador designate to Great Britain. It was my first experience of such an international gathering.

On the fifth, we received the congratulations of three hundred members of the various embassies and the Imperial Household staff at a reception at the Akasaka Palace.

On the sixth, we hosted a purely family banquet at which the Prince's maternal family was represented by Prince Kujō and mine by Viscount Matsudaira – my uncle Morio. His daughters – my cousins – were invited too, and were entertained with lively conversation by Prince Takamatsu, sun-tanned from his recent overseas voyage.

One day I gave a party for the ladies-in-waiting, and on another day we held a reception at the Akasaka Palace for over two hundred people who included our former teachers, close friends and classmates, as well as the Prince's sports associates.

And then on the eleventh, there was a banquet at the Akasaka Palace for the Imperial Family and senior members of each princely house, as well as the Prime Minister and top brass. Finally, on the twelfth, there was a luncheon for almost two hundred military and government personnel, among which the Prince was especially happy to honour Colonel Nagata, the commanding officer of the Third Infantry Regiment, of which the Prince was an officer.

There had been a reception that same day for over six hundred of the men of the regiment – so many there was hardly enough room for them all in the Akasaka Palace. I was deeply impressed at the way the Prince meticulously observed respect for the senior officers with no sign of the fact that he was heir to the throne, and by the easy camaraderie he showed to his fellow officers. It was a side of him that I had not seen before.

All the official receptions and banquets were now over, leaving me quite depleted both mentally and physically, so new and unfamiliar had everything been to me, but the days that followed were still full of engagements.

On the thirteenth we attended an international swimming meet in honour of our marriage at Tokyo's only fifty metre pool, which was in Tamagawa. The contestants were all swimmers who had taken part in the Amsterdam Olympics, and afterwards the Prince chatted with many of them, including America's Johnny Weismuller of Tarzan fame.

The following evening we dined at the home of Mr Devison, the British Consul, to meet the visiting wife of retired Major-General Laurence Drummond. The Drummonds had provided a home away from home for the Prince throughout his year of study in Britain, so the reunion was a nostalgic one for him. The Prince had a special affection for Britain, and had been Patron of the Japan-British Society since that January. He wanted the Empress Dowager to meet Mrs Drummond, so we arranged a tea in our garden the following day to which we also invited the British Ambassador, Sir John Tilley, and Lady Tilley.

Not only was I a very new member of the Imperial Family, but I was a totally inexperienced hostess, and having to entertain foreigners made me very nervous indeed. But the Empress Dowager, the Ambassador and his wife and Mrs Drummond were so congenial that I felt a great sense of relief.

Needless to say, I could never have coped with all these unfamiliar duties that had been thrust upon my shoulders had it not been for the support and help of the staff. But above all, it was the moral support given me by the Prince that kept me going from day to day. He was my source of spiritual strength with his encouragement and his caring consideration. Three days after our wedding, when there was still so much to learn and I seemed to be confounded whichever way I turned, the Prince was obviously concerned for me in my predicament and did his best to reassure me.

'I know how it must be,' he said, with sympathy and understanding. 'There's far more than I could teach you. It's best if you just take things as they come. Don't worry! You'll absorb it all naturally, bit by bit.'

From that day on, I knew I could rely on the Prince to be my tower of strength, and that everything would be all right if I did as he said. I also knew that I would do anything in the world for him, and that nothing would be too hard.

All the Tokyo ceremonies in connection with our marriage were now over. It only remained to pay our respects at the Grand Shrine at Ise and the Imperial tombs. We set off on a special train westbound for the area around Kyoto and Nara – the ancient capitals of Japan – and within the month had made our obeisances at Ise, at the mausoleum of Emperor Jimmu – the first Japanese emperor – which stands at the foot of Mount Unebi, and at the tombs of the Prince's grandfather, Emperor Meiji, and his father, Emperor Taishō.

CHAPTER SEVEN

THE SILVER BOX

◆

A BROTHERLY CHAT

Even though the functions connected with our marriage were over, there was no time to start living the life of normal newly-weds for preparations had to be made to depart for the Enthronement on 6 November in Kyoto where we would attend on Their Majesties. I would have to lead all the other princesses during the ancient ceremonies, and I was sure I would find myself completely at sea. I would just have to do the best I could. I did my utmost to learn what I had to do. I am sure the Empress Dowager and the Prince were as worried as I was about my performance. I was instructed in the rules of etiquette by the ritualists, but would I remember what do do when the time actually came to do it?

On the sixth of November we left Tokyo as part of the imperial suite, spending the night at the Tokugawa mansion in Nagoya. The following day, we continued the journey to Kyoto, where we spent the night at the Sumitomo mansion in Shishigatani. On the tenth, the first two enthronement ceremonies took place – one before the Imperial Sanctuary (the *kashiko-dokoro*, which had been brought with us from Tokyo) and the other in the *shishinden*, or State Ceremonial Hall. The following day there were ancient ceremonial shrine dances, and on the fourteenth, the *daijōsai* – the Emperor's mystical rite of all-night communion with his ancestors, which goes back to time immemorial.

Banquets were held on the sixteenth and seventeenth, and after that we accompanied Their Majesties to the Grand Shrine at Ise and the Imperial Tombs.

With the Emperor and Empress and their Court all dressed in the ancient style, the age-old enthronement ceremonies must have seemed like a beautiful antique screen or scroll come to life. I remember, however, the enormous weight of my 'twelve-layered' robe – winter-weight, as opposed to the summer-weight robe I wore at my wedding. I heard later that it probably weighed between fifteen and sixteen kilograms!

I also remember the care we princesses had to exercise in regard to the Parisian gowns – both high neck and *decolletée* – worn at the state banquets and some of the ceremonies, to ensure that the colours we chose did not clash with that worn by the Empress or predominate over it. If Her Majesty was not present, it was the colour of my gown which took precedence, since I was the bride of the Heir Presumptive, and the ladies-in-waiting of the various princesses would enquire of mine as to what I intended to wear.

The same rule applied, whatever the occasion. I could not see the point of this at first, and wondered what was wrong with variety in dress, but that was the way it was and one had to abide by palace custom. For example, if we wore a fur, it would not only have to be the same kind as the others, but worn with the head of the animal facing exactly the same way. I simply could not understand why one could not wear one's stole any way one wished, and the sight of us all wearing identical silver-fox furs in an identical manner used to strike me as most odd.

I think it was the day before the Enthronement Ceremony that I came upon Prince Chichibu and the Emperor having a happy *tête-à-tête* in a dimly-lit room of the Palace in Kyoto. The brothers had not had the opportunity for a chat for some time, and they were talking and laughing in a relaxed, informal way about something that interested them both, although I do not recall what it was.

In those days, in accordance with the Meiji Constitution, the Emperor, since his succession, had become a divine sovereign up in the clouds. And so, as I watched these two, between whom there now existed such a clear line of demarcation talking together for a little while just like any ordinary brothers, I realized anew the awesome character of the realm into which I had married. I still remember the qualms that assailed me at that moment.

We accompanied Their Majesties back to Tokyo on the twenty-seventh and attended the *mikagura* shrine dances before the Palace

Sanctuary on the following day. That evening, we hosted a dinner for the American Ambassador and Mrs McVeigh. I had not met them before, but after having lived and studied in their country for three years, they seemed like old and dear friends.

The days that followed were filled with official engagements – some for the Prince alone, some for us both. We attended a dinner at the British Embassy, and there were lunches and dinners at the palace for the foreign diplomatic corps, and I discovered how busy members of the Imperial Family were, with their schedules crammed with diplomatic engagements and public service duties.

On 20 December, my parents invited us to dinner. It was not only my first visit home since my marriage, but a farewell to my parents, who were to leave in a week's time for London, where my father had been appointed Ambassador. Outwardly, we were making a royal visit to the house of a loyal subject, so we were naturally attended by equerries and ladies-in-waiting, with a police escort, and my family were formally lined up at the entrance to receive us.

I felt strange and uncomfortable being received as royalty by my own kith and kin, and thought how curious it was that I had stood myself in a similar line at the door of the Japanese Embassy in Washington when the Prince had arrived there the year before.

The Prince chatted to everyone with friendly ease, and when my father showed him over the house, he nonchalantly sat on the railing of the upstairs veranda and gazed into the garden, giving my mother palpitations for fear the railing might give way. He wanted to see everything, including my room, which was still just as I had left it.

I was wearing kimono, and formerly Taka would have taken a lively interest in how I looked in it, but now she kept her eyes lowered the whole time and hardly said a word, which was like her, but still made me sad.

The Prince enjoyed talking to my father regarding his prospective London appointment and about his own time of study in England. My parents did their best to make it an enjoyable evening, and the Prince seemed to relish the family atmosphere, which was a pleasant change from the usual formal banquet.

Four days later the Prince entered the military staff college. He had been ordered to do so by Imperial command. He had already been tutored in military history, strategy and tactics by Lieutenant-Colonel

Honma, his aide, who had once been an instructor at the college, and who had been appointed aide-de-camp to the Prince just after the late Emperor's death. The colonel had spent three years in England studying military affairs and so the Prince found him most companionable.

On 26 December, my father left for England with his family to take up his appointment as Ambassador, again leaving behind my elder brother Ichirō, now a student at Mito High School, and taking with them Taka and her son Ryō.

A YOUNG PINE AND A STAR

So unused was I to my new life that at times I felt like a bird that had lost its way and flown into the wrong place, and I would be filled with despair at my incompetence.

'Don't let it worry you if you make a mistake', the Prince would say. 'Nobody can get used to a new life right away. You'll learn it all gradually.'

But I could hardly bother him with every little thing, so what used to provide me with constant comfort was the *bonbonnière* given to me by the Empress Dowager.

At the Japanese Court it is the custom to give small silver confection boxes – known by the French word *bonbonnière* – as mementos to mark special occasions. Much thought is given to their design, with the occasion in mind, so that each one is unique. The boxes contain those tiny old-fashioned sugar-drops that used to be known as comfits. It is a custom peculiar to the Japanese Court and aristocracy, and is reminiscent of the Fabergé easter-eggs once exchanged by Russian royalty.

The Empress Dowager gave me the *bonbonnière* at the dinner she gave for me upon my return from the United States. The Minister for the Imperial Household had been invited, and other dignitaries, and after the banquet, Her Majesty called the Prince and me over to her and handed the gifts to each of us personally. She had designed the silver memento herself. It was a miniature *tsuzumi*, the ancient Japanese hand drum shaped like an hourglass. Fine rose-coloured silk cord had been used for the tension-adjusting drum-rope, and the body of the drum was embossed with a pattern of tiny young pines and stars. The young pines were the Prince's symbol, the rose-coloured cord was for England, where he had studied, and the stars were for the Stars and Stripes of America where I had been to school. Her Majesty's hope that our union would bring England, America and Japan closer together was beautifully expressed in her touchingly thought-out gift.

Looking at this ancient musical instrument reproduced in miniature I cannot help feeling how modern it seems today. The rose-coloured cord has been replaced, but the silver is as bright as ever and I keep this treasured memento in a glass case in my drawing-room. I often pick it up and marvel anew at Her Majesty's extraordinary originality and aesthetic sense. Sadly, the one I personally received was destroyed in the bombing during the Second World War. This is the one she gave the Prince, and it survived because it had been put away in the fireproof storehouse.

As is evident from the wish she embodied in her design for the *bonbonnière*, the Empress Dowager was deeply interested and concerned about Japan's future as a world power and her relations with other countries. Her Majesty's outlook was truly international and she took a keen interest in learning about conditions abroad and foreign culture. She was particularly interested in the life of British and other royalty. She had never been abroad, and it was an age without television, and not many sources of information, but nevertheless she was well-informed in a large variety of fields. I realize now more than ever what a remarkable person Her Majesty, the Empress Dowager, was.

Her knowledge included the latest French fashions, and it was she who designed all the formal wear for us princesses, even choosing the materials. She may have enjoyed doing this because she had no daughters of her own. She also may have enjoyed the freedom that was hers as Empress Dowager – denied her while Empress – of being able to invite whom she liked when she liked, for she often invited the Prince and me over for an informal chat.

So the Prince and I decided to invite Her Majesty to our residence one evening for a real English dinner. The dining table and chairs and dishes had all been brought back from England by the Prince, and all the dishes we served that night were typically English. She was delighted. So we repeated the invitation several times, including the Prince's two brothers, Prince Takamatsu and Prince Sumi, and these family gatherings were greatly enjoyed by all. When we went out to dinner there was always a great to do with police security, but between houses in the same compound, as ours were, one could slip backwards and forwards without any fuss at all. We often invited the Empress Dowager for a typical English tea as well, which she enjoyed tremendously.

I meant to write about the comfort and encouragement I used to derive from the Empress Dowager's *bonbonnière* whenever I felt sad and dejected, but happy memories have come tumbling out one after the other instead. Many were the times when I in my youth and inexperience committed the most dreadful blunders. I blush even now when I think of some of them. The first one was when we returned to Tokyo after the enthronement ceremonies and visited the Tama Imperial Mausoleum with Their Majesties. I should have ascertained carefully beforehand when and how many times I was expected to bow, but the Prince had assured me that all I needed to do was to copy him, which I did – only to hear someone's discreet chiding voice behind me, 'Since Your Highness is on the distaff side, you should have turned once more, stopped, and bowed. Remember to do so next time.'

I was cut to the quick. Moreover, I had no idea what was meant by 'the distaff side'. Later, back in my own room I remember how downcast and dejected I felt. And then, suddenly, the rose-pink cord on the drum-shaped confection box caught my eye, and shed a warm glow in my heart. It seemed to say, 'You've learned something today. Be thankful for that.' At times like that I would pick up the little *bonbonnière* and hold it in my hand, and it never failed to bring calmness and peace.

My second *faux pas* occurred four days later when I attended the Grand Military Review on the Yoyogi Parade Ground in which the Prince took part as Commander, Sixth Company, Third Infantry Regiment. This time it was the coat I wore. I had a rather nice leather coat I had brought back from America, where they were all the rage. Now they are fashionable in Japan too, but nobody wore leather coats here then, and eyebrows were raised in considerable disapproval. Being midwinter, and expecting the parade ground to be cold and windy, I, in my ignorance, had thought it was just the thing to wear. Realizing that I knew no better, I was let off quite easily, although in private I think I was considered quite hopeless. I tremble to think what the consequences would have been had I worn that coat wilfully in full knowledge of the facts.

The dear little silver drum was to comfort me again on another occasion. While the Prince was attending the military staff college, he used to walk there every day accompanied by his aide, Colonel Honma, returning some time between half past four and a little after five. Long before we could hear the sound of their footsteps on the gravel path, I would join the staff lined up at the front entrance to greet them. If the Prince was not giving an audience to some ambassador, or if there was no dinner party that evening, or some palace ceremony, he would have a cup of tea and *anpan*, soft breadrolls filled with bean jam. The Prince had a sweet tooth, and was particularly fond of them, and usually ate more than one, after which he naturally was not very hungry at dinnertime. He knew that, but just could not resist them.

I, however, have never been very fond of sweet things, nor do I think that adzuki-bean jam goes well with bread, so I never had any. Looking back now, I wish I had joined him occasionally and had one. How stupid I was!

Since I never touched the bean-jam rolls, the servants finally took to serving me little sandwiches, which, in my *naïveté*, I ate with relish.

And that, too, was apparently a dreadful thing to have done. I was severely reprimanded for being selfish and allowing myself to be served with something I enjoyed for tea instead of keeping His Highness company. They were right, of course. There was no excuse for my behaviour. This time I realized how thoughtless and insensitive I had been, and I dissolved into tears.

In Washington, although we often had an English-style four-o'clock family tea together, I was still considered a child and excluded from adult entertaining. Then I was suddenly thrust into court life without having even had any experience of ordinary Japanese social life. I think that was why I kept making so many mistakes.

It would have helped, perhaps, if I could have consulted my parents from time to time, but they were in far-away England. The telephone was not yet fully developed, and letters took forty days each way. Besides, I had been casually warned not to write too much of a private nature.

These were some of the many hurdles I have had to cross.

STAFF COLLEGE HOMEWORK

On 1 January 1929, I attended my first New Year's Day ceremony at the Palace. All the members of the Imperial Family were lined up in ceremonial dress in the corridor leading to the Grand Audience Chamber. Each of the princesses were provided with two train bearers – boys dressed as pages who had been selected from among the pupils of the Peers' School and meticulously rehearsed.

We proceeded to the Phoenix Room, where the members of the Imperial Family offered felicitations to Their Majesties. Then we followed Their Majesties to the Main Hall, where we stood in attendance at their side while dignitaries, as their names were called by the Grand Master of Ceremonies, came up in turn and offered felicitations to Their Majesties. After that, we proceeded on through three reception rooms receiving greetings from the people standing in rows therein. This continued until four o'clock, when we attended upon Their Majesties' departure. A similar ceremony took place the following day.

As for the New Year rituals at our own residence, our servants and ladies-in-waiting had all been previously trained in various other princely households so although I was a new Imperial bride I had nothing to worry about and could leave things to them. Incidentally, Senior Lady-in-Waiting Sagawa, who had been trained in Prince Takeda's household, was from Aizu. Looking back now, I realize how much both she and Lady-in-Waiting Yamaza must have done to shield me in my ignorance.

That year, it is recorded that 850 people came to our palace to offer New Year felicitations. We did not, of course, receive them all. Most of them simply wrote their names in the book. Relatives, intimate friends, and special persons, however, were invited inside and received by the Prince and me. I remember the Prince greeting at the entrance a large number of soldiers who had once served under him in the Third Infantry Regiment and had come to offer their New Year felicitations to us both.

New Year evenings were usually free, and we often played poem-card games. The Palace version – called the 'Noh card game' – was much more sedate than the usual 'Hundred Poems by a Hundred Poets', and simpler, provided one could read the difficult calligraphy peculiar to Noh chants and knew the plays in the Noh repertory. It was a good way to widen one's knowledge of the Noh, but many members of the Imperial family, such as young Prince Sumi, much preferred the more generally popular version of the game based on poems from the famous thirteenth century *A Hundred Poems by a Hundred Poets* anthology of thirty-one syllable *tanka* – also known as *waka*.

It is a much livelier game. There are two decks of cards, one set bearing the first three lines of the poems and the other the final couplets. While one player, designated 'reader', intones each triplet in turn from his shuffled deck, the rest of the players compete in picking up the relevant couplet from the cards of the second deck, which have been shuffled and placed face upwards at random.

Their Majesties and the Empress Dowager invariably played Noh cards, and many's the time I was invited to her palace to partner the latter, but it was always 'A Hundred Poets' at our Residence. We used to invite Prince Takamatsu and Prince Sumi (later called Prince Mikasa) over for a game, and I would head a women's team of ladies-in-waiting, while the three princes would be joined by Chamberlain Watanabe. The rest of the male staff used to try and avoid playing poem cards, making all sorts of excuses, but Watanabe invariably got roped in.

The Prince was very good at Noh Cards, but not having played Hundred Poets until my arrival, his team always lost. He was a keen competitor, and tried hard to memorize the poems, but being more experienced at the game I usually won. It was the only game in which I was able to beat him.

After taking part in the first military review of the year on 8 January 1929, the Prince began a busy schedule which combined studies at the staff college with his official duties as a member of the Imperial Family.

He attended the staff college for three years, during which time hardly a night went by without copious homework that had to be done. When there were no evening functions to attend, he would come home from the college, have a leisurely tea, read the newspaper and seem so relaxed that I would think to myself, how lovely, he has no homework to do today. Then, after a leisurely dinner and another perusal of the newspapers, just when I was quite sure he had the evening free, he would settle down to his homework at about half past seven – and he would not finish until one or two in the morning, and sometimes even later than that.

Once in a while, some professor would come to the Residence after dinner to give the Prince a lecture, which usually lasted until eleven. And then there were the many diplomatic and other dinner parties we attended, when we did not get home until eleven-thirty. The Prince would begin his homework very late on those occasions, and always urged me to go on to bed, but somehow I could not bring myself to do so. Instead, I used to wait up for him in the middle room as it was called. This was the room between my sitting-room and the Prince's.

I realize now that it would have been sensible to snooze, but being young, it never occurred to me. Or I could have studied too. I could have read books, and practised the poetry and calligraphy required of a princess. But I was tired and sleepy after those parties and did not feel like studying. Although I was aware that the Prince was probably just as tired as I was, I simply whiled away the hours playing games I could play by myself, like Corinthian, a simple form of pinball popular then. Sometimes a member of the staff who happened to be on duty would keep me company. I tried to think of ways I could help my husband – but there was little I could do other than sharpen his pencils.

The Prince would ring for a cup of green tea after he had worked for about two hours, and I would think, ah, I'll be able to go to bed now. But no, he would drink his tea and begin work again. Sometimes he would come into the middle room and ask me to order the tea. Then I would really think, with relief, that his work was over, but I would be wrong again. He had just been taking a breather.

It went on like this night after night, followed by an early departure for the college the following morning. He never even slept late on Sundays, but would be up by 8.30 a.m. Some nights he worked all night and did not get any sleep at all.

Shigesada Hayashi, a classmate of the Prince's at the college, writes as follows in a biography of the Prince he compiled twenty years after the Prince's death.

> The difficult assignments we took home would often take us until one or two in the morning to complete, so when we read in the paper next morning that HIH Prince and Princess Chichibu had attended a dinner at the America-Japan Society or something like that, good heavens! we thought, and used to ask him what time he managed to finish his homework. He would often reply that he had not slept at all that night.

One cold snowy Saturday afternoon after classes were over, as I accompanied His Highness as far as the main road, I said 'Tomorrow's Sunday so we can take it easy for a change!' and he said he couldn't as he'd got to see some ambassador or other. I felt terribly sorry for him.

I once remonstrated with him and said I thought he was working far too hard.

'There are lots of my classmates', he replied, 'who have to do the same work in cramped quarters with an infant bawling its head off. Here am I working in quiet, palatial surroundings, so I've little to complain of.'

The quiet. I remember those nights of the Prince's Staff College days as if it were yesterday. I remember the silence – made all the deeper by the occasional hoot of an owl or the cry of some other night bird in the great deodars and oak trees of the spacious garden.

After completing his courses at the staff college, the Prince continued his studies of poetry and calligraphy. As for me, with no basic training in these arts I was a mere beginner. Taneaki Chiba had given me a brief pre-marriage course in the composition of *waka*, but now I submitted my original poetic efforts to Koji Torino for correction. It embarrasses me now to remember how poor my early efforts were! All I tried to do then, as I remember, was to express my feelings, and I did not worry too much about the form.

I had hoped to have piano lessons too, having never studied properly with a teacher. I could read music a little, and often after lunch the ladies-in-waiting would gather around the piano and we would sing some of the popular war and regimental songs. 'Blossoms at dawn' was a new favourite, and the words had been written by the Prince's aide-de-camp, Lieutenant-Colonel Honma.

As a matter of fact, the Prince had a hand in Colonel Honma's composition of the poem. Just about the time I arrived back from America, the Prince was taking part in a military exercise at the base of Mount Fuji and he had not allowed his aide to accompany him. This was because he wanted to be on the same footing as his fellow officers with no privileges accorded to him as an imperial prince. Colonel Honma, therefore, having accompanied the Prince as far as the barracks at Takigahara, was obliged to wait there for twelve days with nothing to do and whiled away his boredom by composing an entry for a nationwide competition for the words to a new war song.

The announcement that Honma's entry had won came just after our wedding, and the Prince was overjoyed. The music, composed at the military band school in Toyama was very catchy, and the song was a great hit.

Colonel Honma had become the Prince's aide-de-camp at the instigation of the Empress Dowager, who expressed the hope that he would stay with the Prince in that capacity for a long time. The Prince had the fullest confidence in Colonel Honma's sincerity and faithfulness. The Colonel taught me and the ladies-in-waiting how to play bridge, and often played tennis with us, too. When he went away to London as Military Attaché in June 1930, I regretted that I had not had him help me improve my English, as well. Few Japanese had as good a grasp of the language as he did. When the Prince and I attended King George VI's coronation in London in 1937, Colonel Honma was one of our suite, and towards the end of the Pacific War, just before his ill-fated departure for the Philippines, he made several visits to us to see the Prince, who was then ailing.

HIKING IN THE SUMMER HOLIDAYS

Not long ago, a former member of our staff came to visit me, and we had a great laugh together over the roller-skating the Prince and I used to indulge in at midnight.

'Your Highnesses used to do it,' he said, 'just when we all thought you were asleep. It must have been a wonderful relaxation for His Highness to have that bit of exercise roller-skating in the upstairs corridors for a little while before turning in after studying all those hours. I remember how startled those of us downstairs were the first time. We thought it was thunder.'

Reminded of it sixty years later, I did not know at first whether to be embarrassed or to laugh! The former staff member went on to remind me how the Prince and I used to skate on our pond when it froze over in winter, and ski on the gentle slopes of the landscaped garden.

The Prince loved sports of all kinds, both to participate in and to watch. We had a tennis court, and we played together whenever the Prince could find the time, which was not very often. He also had a squash court built in the house with the help of someone from the British Embassy. It enabled him to take short amounts of exercise and work up a healthy sweat even on rainy days. Squash rackets is played a lot in Japan now, but it was the Prince who first introduced the game to this country. He felt it was ideally suited to Japan.

Mountaineering was the Prince's favourite sport. He climbed the Matterhorn in the Swiss Alps while a student in England, and there is hardly a peak in Japan which he did not scale, from the Japanese Alps to the Chichibu Range from which he derived his title. Mountains gave him spiritual freedom and peace of mind, and he liked the discipline.

He took me with him once on a hike during one of his vacations from the military staff college. Takeji Asō came along as our guide. I knew the Prince wanted to introduce me to the joy of mountain climbing, but to me it was far from a 'hike'. We started from Nikko and made our way over the Konsei Pass to Ikaho, where we spent the night. From there we climbed Mount Haruna, and then drove by car to Karuizawa. Next day, we walked all the way from Kanbayashi to Hoppo, and the day after that we climbed Mount Iwasuge, 2,295 metres above sea level.

As far as I was concerned it was a forced march. Although I had been a tomboy as a child, I had never walked in the hills. Moreover, I was not dressed properly for mountaineering. It was the hottest time of the year and the paths were dizzyingly steep. I only managed to finish the course by taking frequent rests. I began to wonder if being walked off one's feet was another of the requirements of a princess.

But the Prince had not been trying to make it an endurance test for me. It was only later I realized that not having any sisters, he had no idea what an ordeal it would be for me. I still remember how considerate he was on the way down. When we came upon a slope of slippery red earth, Mr Asō passed me his mountaineering stick and the Prince took hold of my other arm and together they helped me safely down.

Looking back, I think of that trip as our real honeymoon. Admittedly it was rough. There were no lights where we spent the night in Hoppo. But it was a trip I shall never forget as long as I live.

The Prince was a professional-class skier, having been coached by Kunio Igaya. And he used to scull in Hayama, where we had a summer villa. The Prince tried very hard to teach me to row but I was no good at it at all. It was such a shame, as he was so eager to have me experience the exhiliration of gliding through the sparkling blue ripples the way he did. The Prince loved taking part in all sports except boxing. Rugby was one of the sports he enjoyed watching most. But more about that later.

Just before I married Prince Chichibu, the Imperial Family Social Club had been formed, of which he had been one of the founders. Meetings were held once a month in a different princely house each time, and a speaker invited to lecture on some timely topic, after which there would be a pleasant get-together. There were so many aunts and cousins that sometimes there would just be games – the poem card game if it were New Year – and dancing. The Prince was always the life and soul of the party.

We had film shows, too, since we were not able to go to the public cinema. The Empress Dowager often came to these. I remember how much we all enjoyed *'Morrocco'*, *'The Merry Widow'* and *'Tom Sawyer'*.

Besides taking a lively interest in so many things, I think the Empress Dowager missed not having had any daughters of her own. The spring following my marriage, she expressed a desire to see my Doll's Festival display, and came to see it every year.

CHAPTER EIGHT

OUR DAILY LIFE

◆

A VISIT TO THE CHICHIBU MOUNTAINS

On 4 February 1930, Prince Chichibu's younger brother Nobuhito, Prince Takamatsu, married Lady Kikuko Tokugawa. The Empress Dowager was, of course, delighted, and as for me, I was overjoyed to gain a royal sister-in-law, and she proved to be a great source of strength to me. Prince and Princess Takamatsu were always so helpful and kind to both of us over the years.

Prince Chichibu graduated from the military staff college on 28 November 1931. People may imagine that Imperial princes attending the college are invariably helped by their aides-de-camp in their studies and in the field exercises, but Prince Chichibu exploded that myth once and for all. Not only his aides – Colonel Honma, and later Colonel Okada – could attest to that fact, but every single one of his classmates.

At the graduation ceremony, the officer with the highest marks receives a sword from the Emperor. The Prince's marks were not announced, but when he entered the college, as a member of the 43rd Graduation Class, his academic record at first was disappointing. However, his marks rose higher and higher each year through his own dedicated efforts – all privilege and leniency having been strictly forsworn – so that he, too, received a sword from his brother, the Emperor.

On graduation, the Prince was appointed Company Commander of the Third Infantry Regiment so his days continued to be full with his combined military and Imperial duties. It was just three months after the Manchurian Incident, and after an expeditionary First Division, which included sixty men from the Third Infantry Regiment, had made their obeisances in front of the Imperial Palace, the Prince saw them off at Tokyo Station. He had taken a fatherly interest in each of the men under him, and their families, so I know his heart ached to see them go.

I went to the Palace Plaza, too, in a private capacity, to see these brave men who were about to cross the sea for sovereign and country, and I hoped fervently that war would not spread in Manchuria.

On 8 April 1932, the Empress Dowager expressed a wish to see how ordinary soldiers lived, and made a tour of inspection to the barracks of the Third Infantry Regiment, in which I accompanied her. This kindly lady wanted the soldiers to know of her warm concern for them.

On 15 May, we returned home from attending a student field-and-track meet to find our residence bristling with policemen, guards and members of the Kempeitai. It seemed that there had been an attack on the homes of the Prime Minister and several other cabinet ministers. We were greatly alarmed, and the Prince left immediately for the Palaces of the Emperor and the Empress Dowager.

Following this dastardly affair, which became known as the 'Five-one-five Incident' from the date it took place, the Prince participated in a succession of marches and exercises, and owing to the serious and precarious national and international situation, he had little time now for sports, and on 1 September he was posted to the Second Operational Division, General Staff Headquarters.

Once again, as in his staff college days, the Prince would come home in the evenings and shut himself in his study until all hours – very often all night long. As for me, I could not help but worry about his health as I whiled away the time working on my poetry and calligraphy and doing embroidery.

The work he brought home from Headquarters concerned important operational plans which he would ponder thoroughly, going over them again and again. It was all highly secret, and so he had to do any mimeographing and hectographing himself.

On 15 August 1933, however, we made a six-day trip to the Chichibu Three Peaks and spent five nights at the summit Guest House. On the second day, after worshipping at Mitsumine Jinja, the celebrated Three Peaks Shrine, we had intended to walk through the forest to the observation platform, but the fog was so heavy that both the Prince's hat and my parasol were soon wringing wet. Visibility was nil, so we returned to the Guest House and decided to make it a day of rest. But not for the Prince. As was invariably the case, he had brought along work to do. When he turned on a lamp at dusk, however, he was plagued by insects of every description.

The Prince had visited the Three Peaks Shrine soon after he was first made Prince of Chichibu in November 1922, and again when he was about to set off for England to study in 1925. This time it was because he wanted me to see 'his' mountain and to introduce me to the people of the district.

The mountain scenery was indeed beautiful, and the tall cryptomerias, with their tops hidden in the mists reminded me of Japanese paintings. The fourth day of our trip dawned fine and sunny, and we walked up to the observation point and then, after breakfast, we climbed Mount Myōhō. The mountain, whose contours stood out boldly that day against the clear autumn sky, had several sections that were very difficult to climb. Iron ladders had been affixed in some places, and in others, the wet rock faces were so slippery that one had to find footholds on old imbedded tree roots. Finally, there was an iron chain for hauling oneself up. My simple frock, ordinary walking shoes and staff did not help much as I frantically tried to keep up with my companions. The Prince, an experienced alpinist and rock-climber, had no trouble at all with the ladders and would be out of sight in no time, only to reappear from some hidden path to encourage me.

'Just hold on tight and you can do it. There's nothing to worry about!'

We reached the summit at last. Chichibu is famous for its fog and so there was no view, but we heard a beautiful burst of song from a bush-warbler somewhere down below the sea of mists, and on the way down, we flushed out the occasional pheasant and butcher-bird. It was like being in an enchanted kingdom, far from the everyday world.

The next day we set off for Swallow Rock on Mount Shiraiwa's Jizō Pass. We could see craggy Mount Myōhō on our left as we climbed through fields of alpine flora. It was a far gentler environment than that of the previous day. We sat down for a while among the wildflowers, and I particularly remember how lovely the columbines were.

We left Mount Mitsumine – Chichibu's Three Peaks – the following day, on the twentieth, and were given a warm send-off by the local people. Back in Tokyo, the Prince became caught up again in his busy schedule of military and Imperial duties, with hardly a moment to spare. Every Wednesday evening Professor Hiraizumi of Tokyo University came to lecture him on 'Japanese Political History' and I always joined in these sessions.

On 23 December 1933, an event long hoped-for by the nation came to pass – the birth of Crown Prince Akihito. The whole country celebrated this happy event with flag parades and lantern processions, and joy was universal. His birth was like a bright light that shed hope on a dark and foreboding period in Japan, when the future seemed so uncertain – a time of crop failures, economic panic and undernourished children.

THE TEMPORARY IMPERIAL RESIDENCE, HIROSAKI

On 2 June 1934, not long after Pu Yi, the last Emperor of China, had been made Emperor of Manchukuo, the Prince, as the representative of his brother, the Emperor of Japan, made a trip to Changchun, the capital of Manchukuo, to carry a personal letter from His Majesty and to present Pu Yi with a decoration.

The following April, the Prince and I were at Yokohama to meet Emperor Pu Yi when he officially visited Japan, and we accompanied him to all the various functions, including tea with the Empress Dowager.

Then in August, the Prince was posted to the castle town of Hirosaki in Aomori Prefecture. Promoted to the rank of Major, he had been appointed Commander of the Thirty-first Infantry Regiment which had its headquarters in the extreme north of Honshū, Japan's main island. We left Tokyo together on 9 August 1935, by train.

The Prince had volunteered for a posting in the cold north-east, since no member of the Imperial Family had ever been posted there before except for a brief sojourn by Prince Fushimi. My husband had actually asked for Hokkaido, but being only accessible by sea, Hokkaido was deemed impracticable in the event of an emergency which might call him back to Tokyo.

I believe the reason he wanted to go to such a cold region stemmed from his Third Regiment days, when most of the new recruits he trained came from poor homes in the 'East End' of Tokyo. Feeling responsible for these men, he would ask them about their living conditions, and when he discovered how wretched these usually were, he was appalled to think of how many people there were living in conditions so different from his own. I think that is why he wanted to experience for himself the harsh conditions of the cold north-east.

In actual fact, however, it turned out to be the most relaxed posting he could have chosen. There were no Imperial duties, so while he was quite busy with military duties he did not have to cope with the other and could enjoy to the full the pleasures of life in the country. If only he had been able to complete his two-year tour there, instead of having to cut it short after only a year-and-a-half, I think his health would have greatly benefited.

We lived in a house in Konya, outside Hirosaki, belonging to a Mr Kikuchi. While we were there it was known as the Temporary Imperial Residence. It was surrounded by rice fields, and we could watch all the aspects of rice culture as well as feasting our eyes on the lovely green of the young rice, waving in the breeze and stretching off into the distance beyond our windows. Although we had only just arrived, we were soon hoping for a bumper crop along with the farmers, our neighbours. The Prince photographed the whole rice cycle from planting to harvest with his sixteen-millimetre movie camera, to show to the Empress Dowager. The Iwaki River flowed nearby, and its gentle murmur was most soothing. Hirosaki Castle, the seat of the feudal lords of the Tsugaru domain, was not far away, and from our upstairs windows we could see Mt Iwaki and Mt Hakkoda where we often took walks.

The Prince's private secretary and my ladies-in-waiting had come with us from Tokyo, but we had local cooks and maids, so there was plenty of direct contact with the people of the region – nice, relaxed people we found soothing to live amongst.

Winter comes early to Japan's snow country. Each day, after the Prince had left for Headquarters, I used to sit with my feet in the *kotatsu* – a table-topped quilt-covered framework over a charcoal brazier – and spend the time painting, or practising poetry. We also learned the local folksongs with their complicated melodies and refrains. I can still hear some of those lilting Tsugaru songs in my mind. Snowed in for days on end there was plenty of time to spare.

It also snowed in Tokyo, of course. Two years before we moved to Hirosaki, we once had five or six inches of snow in our garden and the Prince gave me my first skiing lessons on the garden slopes. But while the snow I was used to drifted down silently, the snow up north seemed to beat down mercilessly, with great thuds, quickly blotting out the landscape. Next morning, you would find snow had even forced its way in through the shutters.

Until quite recently, I used to receive quilted jackets from an elderly Hirosaki friend. They were in traditional Hirosaki *kogin* work – dark-blue homespun linen with geometric patterns stitched in amongst the weave in heavy white yarn. During the snowbound months the women used to make work clothes like this for themselves and their daughters' trousseaux – garments to last a lifetime. They were so beautiful we found it hard to believe they were only worn for work, but that was indeed their purpose – clothes to keep you warm while doing heavy work like sawing snow when the weather was coldest.

Snow shovelled off the roofs several times a winter to keep the weight down would pile up on the ground and become rock hard, eventually having to be sawed into blocks and carried away. On an appointed day at winter's end, each household was expected to clear the snow in front of their house. What a cheering sight it was to see the children playing ball on roads whose earthen surfaces had reappeared: one knew then that spring had come. The Prince no longer had to ski to brigade headquarters. After 'snow-sawing' he could make the four-kilometre trip by car.

On 24 December, when we had been at Hirosaki four-and-a-half months, the Prince was given a fortnight's holiday and we both went down to Tokyo to attend my brother Ichirō's wedding. After paying our respects at the Palace we called upon the Empress Dowager, who was delighted to hear all about our life in the Tsugaru region. She had been concerned about our going to such a cold place, and had enjoined us to be careful about our health, so she was especially relieved to see the Prince looking so well. She expressed pleasure to see that it had apparently agreed with me, too.

Besides visiting the Mausoleum at Tama, we managed to attend a meeting of the Imperial Family Social Club. It was nice seeing everyone again, and there was much to talk about. My father's tour of duty as Ambassador in London had ended in August, and he was back in Japan, so my parents were able to be at my brother's wedding on the twenty-seventh.

We took the night train back to Hirosaki before New Year's week was up, arriving in a blizzard, so that the Prince could be back in time for the first review of the year on 8 January. Busy days of military duties followed. But on Sundays, we went skiing in the foothills of Mount Sasamori. Though still a learner, I was beginning to enjoy the sport and practised dilligently, longing to be good enough to accompany the Prince to more advanced slopes. I do not think we ever had more time to ourselves than in those Hirosaki days.

The coldest time of the year in Hirosaki began about the middle of January, with blizzards almost every day, making driving impossible so that the Prince had to ski to work most of the time. But it was in good health and high spirits that he participated in night skiing exercises, reviewed the Thirty-second Infantry Regiment (Yamagata Corps), and took part in a cold-weather endurance march involving a two-night bivouac. I went too when he inspected the Ski Corps in Owani. We stayed overnight there, and for me the opportunity to meet more local people was a joy.

And then there was one morning I shall never forget. It must have been two or three days after we returned to Hirosaki from Owani. There had been a blizzard the day before, and the morning sun was dazzling as it sparkled on the snow. It was the day of the 'Two-two-six Incident' in Tokyo, so-called because it took place on the twenty-sixth day of the second month – February 1936.

There had been a telephone call from Prince Takamatsu early in the morning, and I sensed something was wrong. 'Nothing to worry about,' my husband replied when I asked him about it, and left for duty as usual. Radio news was censored in those days, and long-distance telephone calls took hours to put through. Various rumours reached us around noon, but the staff and I only had a vague idea about what had happened. We were on tenterhooks all day.

The Prince left for Tokyo late that night. A second telephone call had come through from his brother in the afternoon, asking him to come, and his private secretary had gone to regimental headquarters to relay the message. Some junior officers leading a large number of soldiers had taken control of central Tokyo and assassinated several cabinet ministers. The Emperor was determined to quell the insurrection, and Prince Takamatsu decided his brothers should assist him in doing so. My husband already knew from the morning telephone call of His Majesty's anger and had been planning to go to Tokyo as soon as possible.

The Prince's anger, too, knew no bounds. He could not condone the act of the rebel officers in using national military forces to try to further their own ideas, killing and injuring a large number of people in the process. The Emperor welcomed him warmly and together with the Empress, entertained him to dinner that night.

The Prince telephoned me once but did not give me any details. Again, all he said was not to worry. Eventually I read in the newspaper about the insurrection and that it had been successfully put down. I was greatly relieved, but the Prince was away such a long time I could not help feeling uneasy.

He returned on 9 March and left immediately for regimental headquarters. When he came home that night he told me he had seen my parents and they were well. I was extremely touched by his thoughtfulness. He also told me something I did not know. When the new Hirota cabinet had been formed after the 'Two-two-six' Incident, I had read in the newspaper that my father had been appointed Imperial Household Minister, but I was unaware that he had declined at first and that his refusal had been overruled.

By the end of March, the Prince had managed to clear up the backlog of work that had accumulated while he was in Tokyo, and every Sunday we went to Mount Sasamori to ski.

Spring comes late to the snow country and the cherry blossom season is not until the middle of May. The blossoms surrounding the old manor house and the vermillion-lacquered bridge over the moat are breathtakingly beautiful. We often joined the crowds that flocked to see them. Sometimes we went to see them at night, and when the petals began to fall, the pale pink 'blizzards' as they swirled down into the moat were also very beautiful.

In June, we picked edible bracken shoots on Mount Iwaki, and in August there was the five-day Neputa festival for which Hirosaki is famous. Now Aomori Prefecture has turned the festival into a large-scale show, with big, elaborate floats, but in those days, the displays were small affairs – handmade paper models of every description, with candles inside, which would be carried about the town from house to house from dusk until midnight to the sound of fifes and drums. They also used to bring them around to our Temporary Imperial Residence. Then on 7 August, the last day of the festival, the models were set adrift on the Iwaki River to the accompaniment of a special song. It was all quite fairylike as the models drifted along, their inner candles flickering. There was an indescribable sadness about it, too, as one savoured the emotions peculiar to the region.

In addition to these peaceful pursuits, the Prince worked hard at his military duties, conducting overnight bivouacs and protracted military exercises, as well as umpiring war games. Once he even had to stand for hours on the summit of Mount Iwaki in the middle of the night in the rain. The result of their training was plainly evident in the special exercises in Hokkaido in October, where the Hirosaki Thirty-first Regiment won first place and high commendation, which pleased the Prince immensely.

Very soon after that, we received word from the Imperial Household that we were to proceed to England, and so, on 7 November, I accompanied the Prince to the Palace to wait on His Majesty's command.

ATTENDING THE CORONATION

Britain's King George V had died and was succeeded by the Prince of Wales, who became King Edward VIII, and was to be crowned in May, 1937. We were to attend the coronation as representatives of the Emperor and Empress. To enable us to prepare for the trip, it was decided that the Prince should be transferred to First Division, Army Staff Headquarters in Tokyo on 1 December.

In the meantime, as a result of what became known as the love affair or the century, the new king abdicated on 11 December, and his brother the Duke of York succeeded to the throne as King George VI. The Coronation, however, proceeded according to schedule.

When we left Hirosaki on 7 December, we left part of our hearts there. Although we had not been able to stay for the full two years, it was our first experience of living in the country, and we loved the warmth and simple kindness of the people.

We sailed for England on 18 March 1937, on the *Heian Maru*, with a suite of eleven including the Grand Master of Ceremonies, Chief Lady-in-Waiting Yamaza and two others. After crossing Canada by train, we embarked on the luxury liner *Queen Mary* from New York. To be in America again nine years after I had been at school there filled me with nostalgia, and most moving of all, we were met by the Japanese aeroplane *Divine Wind* which had flown to New York to greet us after its ninety-two-hour flight from Tokyo to London. When he heard they were coming, the Prince had worried that they would not be able to see where we were on the deck and devised the following plan. He had the ladies-in-waiting sew a red circle – cut from some scarlet damask I happened to have with me – onto a white sheet, and when the *Divine Wind* appeared in the sky we spread it out for them to see. It was a great success. Pilot Iinuma and his engineer, Tsukakoshi, in their tiny low-wing monoplane, circled the part of the ship where we stood, over and over again. I thought of Lindbergh's *Spirit of Saint Louis* as the Prince and I waved to them.

We arrived at Southampton the evening of 12 March and were greeted by Japanese Ambassador Shigeru Yoshida, after which we were conducted on board the battleship *Queen Elizabeth* by Admiral of the Fleet Sir Dudley Pound for dinner and to stay overnight.

Next day, we went by special train to London, where the Duke of Gloucester met us at the Hyde Park Hotel. It was eleven years since the Prince and the Duke had met, and they greeted one another like old friends. As for me, since I had left London only eight months after my birth there, everything should have seemed quite new, but curiously, everything seemed strangely familiar.

Our days, before and after the Coronation on 12 May, were filled with all sorts of engagements, both private and official, and what with the Prince renewing his acquaintance with people he had known while at Oxford University, every minute seemed to be taken up, and there was little time left for rest and relaxation.

The very first person the Prince wanted to see was Major General Laurence Drummond (Ret'd.), at whose home he had lived while studying in England, and who had looked after him so kindly. The General was greatly moved to see the Prince again after eleven years and to receive the gift he had brought from his mother, the Empress Dowager.

After we had moved from the Princess Hotel in Hove to the more central Hyde Park Hotel in London, I accompanied the Prince to see some of his favourite rugby, and we also went for walks in the area around Kenley House on Kingston Hill where he had lived with the Drummonds.

On 11 May, the Prince made a nostalgic visit to Oxford, his *alma mater*, to receive an honorary degree from the University together with Paul, Prince Regent of Yugoslavia. I treasure the photograph taken then of the Prince in his academic gown. He looks so young, so healthy and so handsome. It is so apparent in that photograph how that was the time in his life that he was the most fulfilled, both spiritually and physically.

Rather than giving my own faltering impressions of the Coronation, I shall quote from the Prince's 'Memories of England'.

> Sixty-three countries were represented among the guests at Westminster Abbey for the Coronation. The ceremony itself was both solemn and magnificent. There was no-one who was not intensely moved, after the two hour rites were over – three hours in King George V's day – when, to the strains of the national anthem, the king left the hall with quiet dignity.
>
> The climax of the ceremony was the moment of crowning. The Archbishop of Canterbury says, 'May God crown thee with honour and righteousness' as he places the crown on the sovereign's head, at which moment all the members of royalty and the nobility put on their coronets. There is a shout of 'God save the King!' and a salute is fired at the Tower of London. The royal and noble ladies put on coronets too, together with the Queen Consort. Up until then, the king has been sitting in King Edward's Chair below the altar, but now he sits on the throne for the first time and the Archbishop of Canterbury says: 'From now on, in the name of God and the power and majesty thou hast been given as king and emperor, may thou maintain it with all thy power.'
>
> The Archbishop of Canterbury, followed by the other bishops, then kneel before the king and swear their allegiance, followed by his two younger brothers and representatives of all the peerage.

There was just one thing that bothered the Prince about the ceremony. It was the fact that only the nobility seemed to have been invited to witness this once-in-a-lifetime ceremony for a beloved monarch, and that no representatives of the people took part. But he came to the conclusion that with their deep regard for tradition, the people were satisfied that it should be that way. There was no sign of class dissatisfaction or jealousy, and the people lining the route were at one in their hearts with the people in the Abbey.

As representatives of Their Majesties the Emperor and Empress of

Japan, the Prince and and I were happy to find that we were always given precedence over the representatives of the other nations. There was no advance notice of the order of precedence, but when the day came, we discovered that our carriage headed the cavalcade of guests, as did our seat in Westminster Abbey and at all the other functions afterwards. At the state banquet at Buckingham Palace the Prince led the Queen in to dinner and sat on her right, while I went in on the arm of the King's younger brother, the Duke of Gloucester, and sat on the left of the King. The Japanese Imperial Family was treated with especial respect by the British Royal Family. Whatever the reason, the extraordinary friendliness expressed to us by the British Royal Family was quite remarkable.

When the Prince was studying in England, King George V and Queen Mary invited him often to an informal family lunch, and the king gave him a pair of diamond cuff-links. He also learned to know the Prince of Wales quite well, too, and as it happened, he had the same rooms at Oxford that the Prince of Wales had used.

When Prince and Princess Takamatsu visited England after their marriage, and were having a private lunch at Buckingham Palace, to Princess Takamatsu's initial bewilderment, the very young Princess Elizabeth asked her, 'How is Ichirō?' She was enquiring, it seems, after my elder brother, and I was delighted to hear from the Takamatsus on their return to Japan how popular my family had been with the British Royal Family when my father was Ambassador in London.

When we attended the Coronation, it was in the interim period before the Manchurian Incident had escalated into the Sino-Japanese War, and world feeling towards Japan was not especially cordial, and the fact that Japan had signed an accord with Germany must have affected British feelings. That the Royal Family should have treated us so warmly at such a time touched us deeply.

After the Coronation was over, the Prince still kept to an energetic schedule, even going on to a ball at Buckingham Palace after a dinner hosted by Foreign Secretary Anthony Eden. I accompanied him to the ball given by the Duchess of Sutherland, which was attended by the King and Queen and Queen Mary, the Queen Mother, and I enjoyed it very much. The Prince was a good dancer, easy to follow. His English manners were impeccable, and he was very much at ease and popular with everyone.

On the nineteenth, we presented a letter and a decoration from the Emperor to the King at Buckingham Palace. The following day we watched a naval review at Portsmouth from on board the battleship HMS *Queen Elizabeth*, and visited the Japanese cruiser *Ashigara*, which was taking part. But whenever there was any time in between official duties, we would take the opportunity to enjoy the freedom we could never have at home. The Prince rode horseback in Hyde Park, and I joined him in going to the opera, the cinema and shopping. There were no police escorts, and we felt like caged birds that had been set free.

Once, when the Prince was in a shop buying a gramophone, the assistant handed us a record with no label on it, saying, 'what about this as well?' We were mystified. It turned out to be a recording of King Edward VIII's abdication speech! To think that those unforgettably moving words with which the monarch of the great British Empire had given up his throne for love – that speech which was the culmination of the drama of the century, each single word of which resounded with pathos – to think that it had become a commercial commodity! We were shocked.

Ever since arriving in London we had taken such care to avoid the subject of the abdication. And here was this record blatantly on sale in a shop! After his initial amazement, however, the Prince was pleasantly amused at this new side of the British character which he had not seen before. In fact, he bought the record as a memento of his friend, and brought it back to Japan, where he listened to it several times.

In spite of the lovely June weather, I caught a cold, which kept me in for several days, and no sooner had I begun to recover than the Prince came down with one, so we had to miss the King's Birthday celebrations. Then no sooner was he well enough to take a walk than I became ill again, this time with pneumonia, requiring the services of two nurses.

But from then on until 8 July the Prince insisted on carrying out his full schedule of engagements without a single day's respite, in spite of not having fully recovered from his cold, since there was no-one to take his place. As for me I was distraught at not being able to help him at all.

It had been His Majesty the Emperor's wish that we travel to Europe after Britain, but cables had to be hurriedly sent to the Kings of

Norway and Sweden sending our regrets and cancelling our visits there.

On 7 July, the Marco Polo Bridge incident in Beijing took place, followed by a cease-fire agreement on the eleventh. But although the situation seemed to be under control, we were, in fact, already bogged down in a Sino-Japanese war.

Thankfully, I was finally well enough to get up, and prepare to travel to Switzerland on the fourteenth, where I was able to recuperate until the end of the month at a hotel in Grindelwald. Here, at an altitude of 1038 metres, the invigorating air and the views of the sparkling snow-capped alpine peaks not only restored our health but brought back happy memories to the Prince of the ascents he made of the Jungfrau and Wannehorn while on vacation in 1926.

We made the most of this carefree time devoid of official engagements. There were glaciers merely a short stroll away, and many were the picnics we enjoyed in the sunshine, among the gaily-coloured wild alpine flowers, soothed by the tinkle of cowbells. One glacier had been hollowed out and contained an ice rink, where we skated – an unforgettable memory. I remember how amazed we were by the iciness of a stream that flowed all the way down from the glacier to the village. Each day I felt better, and the Prince even felt up to visiting the League of Nations and the International Labour Organization in Geneva, as well as a clock factory.

After our fortnight's recuperation, we finally set off for the rest of our European tour. We arrived at the Hague on 2 August, attending a luncheon hosted by the Queen of the Netherlands on the third. We were invited to dinner that night with Princess Juliana and Prince Bernhardt, but my cold flared up again and I had to take to my bed, so the Prince went alone. But alas, he too took to his sick bed on returning.

It was obvious that to continue the tour would be not only a worry to Their Majesties the Emperor and Empress and the Empress Dowager, but to a great many other people involved as well. It was decided, therefore, to cancel the rest of the European tour and return to Japan as soon as our health would permit after some further recuperation in Grindelwald, which we finally left, reluctantly, about the middle of September. I went to London to await the Prince, who first paid a visit to Germany.

It was the Army's idea that he should go there, as the German-Japanese Anti-Comintern Pact had just been formed, and they felt it would boost relations with their new ally to have a Japanese prince pay them an official visit. The Prince attended a lunch given by Hitler at Nuremberg Castle, at which the Fuhrer launched a vitriolic verbal attack on Stalin, saying how much he hated him, in reply to which, the Prince retorted: 'Is it not wrong to express such prejudice against the Head of State of another country?' The Prince's candour disconcerted Hitler considerably, the Japanese ambassador, Kintomo Mushanokōji, gleefully noted.

Two or three days after the Prince joined me back in London we embarked at Southampton bound for home via Canada, arriving in Yokohama on 15 October. We had been away for seven months.

The Prince was clearly tired from the trip, but the political situation being what it was, he reported to the General Headquarters on the eighteenth to assume duty in Section Two of the Operational Planning Department.

CHAPTER NINE

UP TO THE OUTBREAK OF WAR

◆

PAPIER MÂCHÉ STRING

The Prince could not seem to get rid of the cough he had had ever since London, and even though his attending physician said he should rest for at least a month, the Sino-Japanese War had begun and he felt he could not take any leave. Numerous X-rays were taken, but we were told later that the condition of his lungs had been difficult to observe because of thickened scar tissue on the pleura resulting from an early illness.

Soon after returning home, I had gone down to our villa in Hayama for a change of air to rid myself of the lingering traces of my bout with pneumonia in London. To my relief, the Prince finally was able to join me for a spell at the beginning of December, although I doubt he had any peace of mind because of the hard-line policy towards England being advocated by the Army in the controversy between the military, politicians and diplomats of how to bring the Sino-Japanese War to a conclusion before it escalated. The Prince was the Honorary Patron of the Japan-British Society, and through his knowledge of both England and America he was convinced that to break off friendly relations with those countries would only lead to Japan's ruin. Also, at this critical time, it pained him that the Army and the Navy did not see eye to eye.

News of the fall of Nanking reached us in Hayama.

The Prince returned to Tokyo before the New Year, but although I had fully recovered my health by about the middle of January, I stayed on in Hayama for another reason. The attending physician and I both thought that if I were in Hayama, the Prince would at least come down there for the week-ends, which would help towards the recovery of his health. Just as I expected, he did indeed join me every Sunday, and Saturdays when possible. I do not know how much of a help it was. There is no doubt that it gave him much-needed rest and recreation, but at a time when the root of his illness should have been thoroughly eradicated, I am now filled with remorse at my insufficient knowledge about his illness and the way I just kept harping on about Hayama.

During this time the peace negotiations being negotiated by Germany between Japan and China were broken off and the Government broke off relations with Chang Kai-Shek and the war with China became a prolonged conflict.

That year, 1938, in March, the Prince was appointed Lieutenant-Colonel in the Infantry, and promoted to Colonel in August the following year. The pressure of work at the General Headquarters became extremely hectic. A long tour of duty in Manchuria was followed by analyses of each battle after continuously exhausting all-night observation of the battles standing on the bridge of the cruiser *Yura*. Most people would try and spare themselves as much as possible, but not the Prince. He was so dedicated, so conscientious. Truly a man of undiluted integrity. Being like that, he had always driven himself hard, even before entering the military staff college, and now in spite of continued ill health, so that ultimately he succumbed to a disease he was unable to overcome.

And I kept on believing only that all the Prince needed was sufficient rest. In July 1938 we went up to Hakone to stay at Baron Fujita's mountain villa in Kowakidani. Again, I remained there all through August so the Prince could join me whenever he had a few days leave. He seemed so well on these occasions – except for his nagging cough.

Back at General Headquarters in Tokyo, when he was not on manoeuvres, he was never home until after dark, even in summer when days were long. The building was old, and Colonel Kumao Imoto wrote of the unhealthy conditions of the sunless Operations room in which the Prince worked:

'His Highness, just like the other members of the staff, always worked until late in the dimly-lit inner room, sitting straight upright maintaining correct military posture. He did everything himself, never delegating any of his duties to men under him. He was not very good at making those pieces of papier mâché string you had to use in those days to hold one's papers together at the corners, and sometimes his were a bit clumsy. Once, without thinking, I offered to help him make his. With due respect, thinking back to those days, it seems to me that the unhealthy environment in which we worked was partly responsible for undermining His Highness's health.'

Such work conditions were undoubtedly bad for the Prince's health, but the real cause lay in the strain he constantly subjected himself to in those working years as he strove to carry out both his Imperial duties and his military duties with a high degree of excellence, even when he himself was aware that his physical strength was far from up to it. That desire stemmed from the humility he felt regarding his upbringing as a member of the Imperial Family which was so vastly different from that of the poor army recruits. That is why, even when he let his men rest for an hour while on manoeuvre, he would not even allow himself to sit down. And during a cross river 'attack' at night in mid-winter, if someone had to lead the men into the cold muddy water, it was always he who would assume the rigorous task himself.

Now as I re-read Colonel Imoto's words, I picture the Prince at the War Office struggling with the unfamiliar task of rolling his own papier maché string to fasten the pages of his reports, and it blends in my mind's eye with the memory of one of those same hands ceremonially taking the hand of the Queen at Buckingham Palace.

THE ANTI-TUBERCULOSIS ASSOCIATION

The Prince and I spent a weekend together at our Hayama villa at the end of January 1939. But soon after that he left Japan in connection with the attack on Canton. He lived aboard a warship for some time, and after returning to Japan he was so busy with official duties and observing manoeuvres that he was not able to take time off in Hayama again for quite a while. I stayed on at the seaside until April, still obsessed with the conviction that I could thereby induce him to join me whenever possible.

One day in May, Hidetada Hirose, the Welfare Minister, called on me to ask if I would agree to become President of a proposed new organization to be called the Anti-Tuberculosis Association. He told me that my name had been suggested by Her Majesty the Empress, whose desire it was that I take on the job. Of course I said yes.

Earlier, the Empress had summoned the Prime Minister, Kiichirō Hiranuma, to the Palace on 28 April, where she had expressed satisfaction that something was being done for the prevention and cure of tuberculosis and handed him a personal contribution of five hundred thousand yen.

When we were at Hirosaki I had heard from the Prince of the large number of men in the army suffering from tuberculosis. Many of the soldiers there came from impoverished farming villages in Iwate Prefecture. Already suffering from malnutrition, the rigours of their training caused many to develop the disease.

Not only soldiers in Hirosaki but people all over Japan were succumbing to tuberculosis in increasing numbers every year as a result of malnutrition. Although the government was anxious to do something about this, counter-measures were inadequate, what with the military budget so stretched by the escalating war.

I knew nothing about the disease, but began to study material I obtained from the Association, wondering what there was that I could do to help in its prevention.

I read that in 1936 a total of 145,160 people had died – one tenth of those with the disease. It meant that of the entire population, one in fifty had contracted tuberculosis. What is more, these figures were three years old. One could assume that both the numbers who had died and the numbers who had contracted the disease – mostly young people in their teens and twenties – were now even greater. In Tokyo alone, the possibility of students and school children showing a positive reaction to a tuberculin test falling ill as a result of their environment was more than fifty percent. It was horrifying. It was no longer a question of whether I could be of any help. I was stirred into action. I simply *had* to do something.

Further study revealed that in Europe and America such strides had been made in the prevention and cure of tuberculosis that the numbers of both cases and deaths had been halved. While in Japan, facilities for the prevention and treatment of the disease were very poor. If things went on like that, cases would just go on increasing.

The means for the prevention of tuberculosis had, in fact, been in existence here since 1919. X-ray examination and tuberculin testing was available, but so much of the national budget had been allocated to defence that this important counter-measure had not been adequately taken, and had been left to the private sector to deal with. The Japan Anti-Tuberculosis Association had been founded by the internationally known doctor Shibusaburō Kitazato, and included groups such as The White Cross Society, organized on Christian principles by a group of doctors, and Kazuo Tanabe's 'Nature Cure Society'. Depending precariously on donations alone, they did their best to try and stem the ferocious onslaught of the disease. On one hand there were the scientists carrying on their research, and on the other these private citizens fighting alone against great odds, until finally the government got around to doing something at last. The Department of Health within the Ministry of Home Affairs had managed to secure 100,000 yen to organize prevention measures, and just as it was on the point of being made a separate Welfare Ministry to grapple with tuberculosis, Her Majesty the Empress made her gift of 500,000 yen. This provided a great impetus, and the Cabinet immediately held a meeting and granted the Anti-Tuberculosis Association a state subsidy. The formal inauguration took place on 22 May 1939.

On the 30th, the Prince and I were received in audience by Their Imperial Majesties, and when I assured the Empress that I would do my very utmost to repay her trust in me, she must have felt my lack of confidence, for she smiled most kindly and, nodding, replied, 'I know you will do your best.' I was twenty-nine. I may have been the President in name, but I felt then that the true Head of the Anti-Tuberculosis Association was Her Majesty.

What with two weeks in Manchukuo and north China in June, followed by a spell at the front in central China in November, once again the Prince was too busy to take any time off. The day after his return from central China he resumed work straight away at the Staff General Headquarters in addition to his Imperial duties.

The ceremony inaugurating me as President of the Anti-Tuberculosis Association was held at the Tokyo Kaikan on 20 September. I sat on a dais before a gold screen, flanked by dignitaries, and read a message from Her Majesty the Empress. It was indeed a brilliant ceremony, and I was deeply moved to think that a movement started by the people, with faltering steps, should finally have attained this high government recognition. The eradication of tuberculosis was now no longer just a dream!

After I had read Her Majesty's message, there were speeches by the Chairman, Prime Minister Nobuyuki Abe, and my father, who was the Imperial Household Minister.

That December, the Prince and I attended a dinner at my father's official residence. The Prince was relaxed and seemed to enjoy himself, and I was immensely happy to be able to spend an evening with my parents, something I had not been able to do for some time. The only sadness was that 'Taka' Takahashi was not there. Taka had died that March from a stroke, on the eve of her fifty-eighth birthday.

THE PRINCE FALLS ILL

1940 was said to be the 2,600th year of the Imperial reign, and the Prince was appointed President of the commemmorative celebrations to be held in November. But in mid-June, he was obliged to take to his bed with a cold. Then, before he had completely recovered, he had to visit the Shrine at Ise to report on his appointment, as well as performing other duties, returning to Tokyo on the 20th and reporting to Their Majesties on the following day. That night he developed a fever. It proved to be the start of a long illness.

It was thought at the time to be bronchitis, and on 29 July he was considered well enough to be allowed up to attend at court for two days, and on 1 August we went up to the Fujita villa in Hakone for a change of air. The Prince was free of any temperature for two or three days, and enjoyed walks around the estate, but presently, his temperature rose and remained high. For the first time, the palace physicians diagnosed it as pulmonary tuberculosis. They informed the Prince, and ordered a complete course of medical treatment. It is impossible to put into words the emotional shock it was to me. And I could not possibly allow any of this to show. 'Pull yourself together' I kept telling myself. Although I tried to look calm, I was overcome by remorse and the feeling that I had somehow let the Prince down.

Among the material I had read on being appointed President of the Anti-Tuberculosis Association was an article headed 'The Importance of Early Detection'. At the time I had had a sort of uneasy feeling about the Prince's cough, since the symptoms sounded similar. But on his regular medical examinations they never discovered any lesions, so I decided my fears were groundless and faintheartedly said nothing, preferring to look on the bright side.

But it was no use chiding myself. I realized the most important thing I could do now was concentrate on helping the Prince have the best treatment to make him well.

The medical staff was headed by the Emperor's chief physician, Dr Hatta and the Army's Dr Nakamura, as well as Dr Endō, director of the Manchurian Railway's South Manchuria Sanatorium, well-versed in the treatment of TB, who was brought to Japan to head the team. Nurse Fumi Kawabe was brought in from the Red Cross Hospital.

The first thing prescribed by Dr Nakamura and Dr Endō was rest, both physical and mental. The Prince was made to realize that he must give up his overcrowded schedule and resign himef to a prolonged period of medical treatment. He handed over his duties as President of the 2,600th Anniversary Ceremonies to his brother Prince Takamatsu, and moved down to Hayama from Hakone to begin his life of treatment in earnest, realizing he had no alternative.

He became a model patient, characteristically conscientious and thorough in this as in everything else. During the twelve years of his struggle with the disease, never once did he entertain any lack of confidence in his phyisicians, trusting them completely. Even when his condition took some new turn, he would simply listen to the doctor's explanation and reply, 'I see', never asking for more details, and never questioning the treatment. Should the doctor suggest an operation, he would always agree. If no progress seems to be made over a long period, some think of changing doctors or hospitals, but the Prince never once wavered, always faithfully following doctor's orders. He was consistent in this to the very end. Indeed, pitifully so, I have sometimes thought.

In my studies I had read that there were two methods of treatment for TB. Neither of them were cures, since at that time the disease was considered incurable, but depended on whether the lesion had become a cicatrice or calcified, whether the bacillus had spread through the bronchi and veins. The aim was to prevent it from breaking through the membranes and spreading.

One method was called the 'general whole-body treatment' and consisted of keeping the patient quiet in a clean atmosphere and building up his strength with proper nutrition. The other method, called 'specialized treatment', involved any of the following: chemotherapy, atrophia or 'direct treatment'. As for chemotherapy, streptomycin had not yet been discovered, and there was no effective drug, while atrophia involved pneumothorax or thoracoplasty to close the focus of the lesion in order to stop the activity of the bacilli. The 'direct treatment' involved completely taking out the vomica, which is the source of progress of the tuberculosis, and the lesion which will become aggravated sooner or later, but at that time Japan lacked the expertise, the facilities and the equipment to do this.

The method chosen by the Prince's doctors was the generalized treatment. He was only thirty-eight when stricken by the disease, and if only streptomycin had been discovered, he would most certainly have recovered.

A ROOM WITH A VIEW OF MOUNT FUJI

At the beginning of summer, after six months of convalescence at the seaside, in Hayama, the Prince became feverish again, and it was thought that perhaps the less humid air of the mountains would be better for him. The foothills of the Japan Alps, where there was a sanatorium, was considered, but would be too far from Tokyo for the doctors to commute by train. Gotemba was finally chosen. Although the air was not particularly dry, it was clean, and the winters were cold but the summers cool, and there was a fine view of Mount Fuji and Mount Ashitaka. It also met the important criterion of being within a day's commuting distance of Tokyo.

We heard that Count Kabayama wished to sell his villa there. I had spent every summer there as a child and knew it well. It was large, had two storeys, and we would be able to put up visitors. It faced south, and was just what we needed in every way.

Except for one thing. I had a feeling that the Prince would be bedridden for some time, and thought how wonderful for him it would be to be able to see Mount Fuji from his bed. And I remembered, alas, that at the Kabayama's one had to go outside in order to view the mountain. So we finally settled on a villa belonging to Junnosuke Inouye, and moved there from Hayama on 16 September 1941. Being wartime, petrol was unavailable, and cars had to run on charcoal. One was apt to have numerous breakdowns, but we managed the trip comfortably, without incident.

All eighteen of us, including secretaries, nurses, maids and kitchen staff, settled in at what came to be called the Prince Chichibu Imperial

Villa, Gotemba. The house was situated in a forest on the left of the road from Gotemba to Hakone, and the trees were beginning to change colour. The air was chilly but redolent of mountain freshness, and I sensed the Prince's satisfaction.

The house was a wooden bungalow with a thatched roof, and in addition to a spacious Western-style living-room, there were several Japanese-style rooms with tatami matting, and before we moved in an annex was built, joined to the main house by a corridor, with a large, comfortable combined bed-sitting-room and study for the Prince.

Almost all the rooms had a view of Fuji, the Prince could gaze at the mountain from morning till night, enjoying its varied aspects even as he lay in bed.

The mountain air agreed with the Prince, and he seemed so happy in the mountain villa that his temperature finally returned to normal, and by October, he was well enough to go down the veranda steps and walk a little in the garden.

On 18 October came the announcement that Hideki Tōjō had formed a new cabinet and would also be acting as Minister of Defence. I am quite sure the Prince did not feel the policy being advocated by the Army was good for the country, and now that he was relieved of his duties at General Headquarters he accepted his retirement with resignation and without regret.

On the 22nd, the Prince's younger brother, Takahito Mikasa, married the lovely Yuriko, second daughter of Viscount Masanori Takagi, and I attended the ceremony alone. I had known him since he was a boy, when he had been known as Prince Sumi. He was now an officer in the Army and led a busy life, often visiting the front line. We were all very happy for him and wished them a long and happy life together.

On the 27th, my father, in his capacity as Imperial Household Minister, came with my mother to call on the Prince, who received my father in the study while my mother came to my room so I could ask her about the family. There was so much we wanted to say to one another, but we did not know where to begin. In the end we just talked about Mount Fuji and the birds that came to the garden.

The Minister was relieved to find the Prince looking so well, and after I had shown my parents around the house, they left.

The days that followed were without incident, and most days the

Prince sat outdoors in the autumn sunshine from about 9 o'clock until noon. He weighed 154 pounds, and life seemed peaceful and quiet.

November brought with it severe winter weather. Mount Fuji grew whiter each day, with snow. I prayed that the Prince's first winter here would have no adverse effects upon his condition.

At about that time, Prince and Princess Takamatsu paid us their first visit, which we had looked forward to eagerly.

'What on earth have you done to your hands?' said the sharp-eyed Princess Kikuko on noticing my chilblains. I had never had them before in my life. Like a scolded child I hurriedly hid my hands behind my back.

'You can't help it here,' I explained. 'The wind is so cold. It's not that I've been doing a lot of washing, or anything!'

They went back to Tokyo after spending the night, but came back again at the end of the month, for another overnight visit, when the two men enjoyed a nice long talk together. Prince Takamatsu was a staff officer on the General Staff, and in a position to know details of the national policy and told Prince Chichibu that war with Britain and America was already inevitable.

The Princess and I were discussing the same thing in another room, feeling that the outlook was gloomy indeed. America and England had deep connections for both myself and the Prince, symbolized in the pattern on the little silver comfit-boxes the Empress Dowager had given us. I was so afraid the news would upset the Prince and worsen his condition.

On 6 December, the newly married Mikasas visited us. It was the first time the Prince had met the bride, and he dressed in his formal *hakama* for the occasion. The following day being Sunday, the young couple spent the night, and after they had gone, the Prince was in a particularly happy mood, full of affectionate reminiscences about his mischievous youngest brother.

Both my husband and Prince Takamatsu were born while Emperor Taishō was still Crown Prince, and being grandchildren of the reigning sovereign, Emperor Meiji, were known as Their Highnesses the Imperial Grandsons, while Prince Mikasa had been born when his father was Emperor, and therefore was a Prince in his own right straight away. His elder brothers used to tease him, saying they were of different birth! It was clear the Prince felt that his little brother, now grown up and married, had become a fine young man with a promising future before him.

The next day after the Mikasas returned to Tokyo – 8 December – Japan declared war on Britain and the United States. That day, a detachment of twelve men from the Sixth Eastern Corps was posted to mount guard at our villa, and we were immediately put on air-raid alert. When he was told the news, the Prince said nothing and only nodded.

It was a war that ignored the nation's resources. Moreover, the Prince had so many good British friends, from the Royal Family down, not to mention teachers. For some while after the start of the war, the Prince hardly spoke at all. He refused to even mention anything to do with the war. When not resting, all he did was sit silently in his study, only gazing for hours at Mount Fuji.

CHAPTER TEN

IMPERIAL VILLA, GOTEMBA

◆

FUJI'S FOUR SEASONS

In the old days, it was generally accepted in Japan that women did not discuss politics. They were not supposed to comment or make judgements, and had to refrain from expressing opinions. I trusted the Prince, and believed that all would be well if I only did as he wished. But since the Prince became an invalid, I tried not to trouble him any more than necessary, and therefore had to make decisions and organize some things on my own.

War with America and Britain had just begun. Not only were US Ambassador Joseph Grew and British Ambassador Sir Robert Craigie envoys of countries we had personal connections with, but they and their wives were very good friends of ours. They were about to be repatriated, and we hated to end our friendship in this way. There was no question of being able to meet them and bid them a proper farewell.

It occurred to me that I could ask Shunichi Kase – who had served under my father, and was now head of the North American section of the American Affairs Bureau of the Foreign Ministry – to see the Grews and the Craigies on our behalf. Together with messages, I entrusted to Mr Kase a jewel-box for Mrs Grew to commemorate our long friendship, and for Lady Craigie some mutton I had managed to obtain in Gotemba and other foodstuffs, since they would be interned for some time yet.

When Mr Kase arrived at the American Embassy, the Grews greeted him in their best clothes, and accepted my message and the jewel-box with tears in their eyes. They were apparently so overcome with emotion it was some time before they could speak. 'We are deeply grateful for such kind treatment by the Imperial Family', said the Ambassador, finally. The Craigies, too, I heard, were delighted, and I believe Sir Robert said to Mr Kase: 'I did not know the details of the negotiations between Japan and America. If only I had known, I could have acted as an intermediary.' As for me, it was a great relief to have been able, thanks to Mr Kase, to let the two Ambassadors and their wives know of the Prince's and my feelings.

About the end of January 1942, it was decided to build a new annex for the Prince that would be light and airy and get plenty of sunshine, for unless he was forced to rest owing to a slight temperature, he passed the time reading in his study. It was not really a proper building, but more like a makeshift prefab, hurriedly put up with used timber, and had only a plywood *tokonoma* alcove. The main feature was the fact that the whole south side consisted of sliding glass doors, but even the six foot long screen in the bedroom painted by Joyō Nozawa of Hirosaki did little to make the place – with its naked wiring – look less like a warehouse. The Prince felt badly about having new living quarters built for himself in wartime, but I wanted him to get better, and was determined to see that he had the best conditions towards this end.

The Prince moved into his new quarters on 5 April. At this time, besides reading, he used to enjoy working out problems in *shōgi* – Japanese chess. He used to say that working out *shōgi* problems was not only fun, and a solace, but helped him to keep up his powers of reasoning and made the time pass more quickly.

The Prince was also very fond of *rakugo*, the traditional art of comic storytelling. While convalescing in Gotemba, he frequently listened to it on the radio. This somehow became known, and the leading exponents of the art volunteered to take turns visiting us to entertain the Prince, who used to laugh so hard his glasses kept misting over. Each time he took them off to wipe them, he would turn around to see if I and the staff were laughing too.

When we were trying to find a house in Gotemba I had been insistent that the Prince have a room with a view of Fuji so that he could see the mountain even while lying in bed. He never told me at the time in order to spare my feelings, but it turned out that climbing it once had been quite enough of the mountain for him, and he never wanted to climb it again. But the fact was, that gazing at the mountain from Gotemba, he said he began to see many aspects of Fuji he had never dreamed existed: the way it changed according to the season, and even in the space of a single day, the way its colour and cloud-shapes changed moment by moment. It was a mountain you could never tire of observing. Indeed, he told me, there was something awesome and unapproachable about the way it soared, quietly aloof.

Of all the aspects of Mount Fuji – Fuji in early autumn, Fuji in winter, Fuji in spring – I think the Prince's favourite Fuji was its still snow-capped spring countenance.

The Takamatsus and Mikasas came frequently to visit their elder brother, always staying overnight, and brought news of the outside world to the Prince, who did not listen to the radio or read the papers since he knew how far removed from the truth their reports were. Even when they referred to the Battle of Midway that June – the battle that led to Japan's defeat – the people were not told the true state of affairs. Prince Takamatsu, who was on the General Staff, felt it was essential for Japan to bring the war to a conclusion as soon as posible. Prince Takamatsu, in whom the Prince had every confidence, wrote frequent letters to his brother, as well as telephoning, and made many visits to Gotemba, keeping the Prince well informed regarding the progress of the war. And Prince Mikasa, who visited frequently with the Princess, kept him *au fait* with what the army officers were saying and thinking.

Although the Prince – a reluctant invalid at the foot of Mount Fuji – was forced to be merely an onlooker, he never ceased being anxious about Japan's future, and like the Emperor, was sick at heart.

About the midldle of August, a dear friend came to see us – Lieutenant General Masaharu Honma, who although only fifty-five had been retired from his post as Commander-in-Chief, The Philippines, and sent back to Japan to be put on reserve.

'To think I am actually here visiting Your Highnesses!', said the General, his face lowered to hide his tears and his body shaking with emotion.

Having been the Prince's aide-de-camp, and knowing the Prince so well, he must have known how wretched this secluded life must be for the Prince. And the Prince knowing the circumstances of General Honma's being placed on reserve, could feel for him, too. There was no need for words between them on this memorable reunion. The General had a good grasp of world affairs, and we had heard that the personnel reshuffle was connected with his great anxiety to avoid the fighting on the mainland of Japan, which he knew would inevitably cause tremendous loss of life.

When General Honma was at the Philippine front, the Prince had sent him a fan with a painting of Fuji by the great Taikan Yokoyama. 'Indeed, my cup runneth over', said the General. 'Fancy being able to gaze like this at the beauty of the mountain, in the presence of Your Highnesses'. That day, Fuji soared majestically, in all its summer clarity, above the trailing clouds below.

General Honma came several times to visit the Prince, who enjoyed their conversations together so much. But, alas, the further possibility of that pleasure was to end with the end of the war. General Honma entered Sugamo Prison as a war criminal for having been C. in C. in the Philippines, and was taken to Manila in December 1945, where, charged with being responsible for the Bataan Death March, his life was ended on an execution ground, and he just faded away from this world like dew.

We, who knew so well what a gentle warrior he was, could do nothing to help him. Nothing but bow our heads, silently, toward Mount Fuji, and say a prayer.

We shed tears anew when we learned that in General Honma's diary, an entry in February 1946, addressed to his children, had included the words, 'Your father bows every morning towards the Imperial Palace, and prays for the recovery of Prince Chichibu.' And still, whenever I think of General Honma – and all the others who died as a result of the war – I am filled with grief, even today.

At the end of September 1942, Her Majesty the Empress Dowager, who was staying at the Numazu Imperial Villa down on the coast not far away, honoured us with a visit for the first time since the Prince had fallen ill. The Prince had been without a fever for some time, had just had a haircut, and did not look at all emaciated. He was able to greet his mother outside the front entrance looking fit and well in his formal *haori-hakama*.

Because of the contagious nature of the Prince's illness, it had not been possible for the Emperor and Empress to visit him, and the Empress Dowager had also been prevented from visiting him for the same reason. The mother and son had so much to say to one another that it was as if a flood-gate had been opened, and the obvious joy of their meeting brought tears to my eyes. When it was time for her to leave, I was almost embarrassed by the profuseness with which Her Majesty thanked me for nursing and caring for her son.

That day, Fuji looked truly a Sacred Mountain – soaring in splendid majesty and elegance.

For some time afterwards, the Prince was without fever, and was able to walk as far as the summer-house. There, at the spot in the grounds with the best overall view of Fuji stands a statue of the Prince as mountaineer. It is by Fumio Asakura, who was Japan's leading sculptor, and was a wedding present from the Emperor. The Prince often lingered there, with his hand resting on the statue. I used to think it was not so much nostalgia for his mountaineering days, but nostalgia for his elder brother the Emperor that was probably in his mind – mixed with sadness for his inability to be of use to the sovereign, and grief that they could no longer meet.

Although it was not possible for Their Majesties to visit us themselves, they often sent their chief physician up to Gotemba from the Numazu Villa on their behalf with comforting messages.

Alas, the feverless period did not last long. From the middle of October, the Prince was running a temperature of 37 degrees centigrade.

ARTIFICIAL PNEUMOTHORAX

From about April 1943, blackouts and firefighting drills had begun – in which I, too, participated – which brought home to us the gravity of the situation.

Although the Prince was running a temperature, I was required to deputize for the Empress on a tour involving three days in Shizuoka Prefecture and three days in Kanagawa Prefecture. Each of the Imperial Princesses were being sent by Her Majesty to visit all the naval hospitals to cheer up the patients. Because of the Prince's illness, I was sent to prefectures nearby, but even then I worried about him and always telephoned as soon as I had reached my lodgings. Previously, the Prince's condition had invariably worsened whenever I was away, but this time it fortunately did not. It was for their country, but oh, how it pained me to see all those sick and wounded servicemen!

On 5 June, there was a state funeral for Admiral Isoroku Yamamoto.

The only happy occasion that year that I can recall was the wedding of the Emperor and Empress's eldest daughter Princess Shigeko to Prince Morihiro Higashikuni on 13 October, which I attended. Being wartime, everything was done very simply, but nevertheless the bride looked young and beautiful. It was a nice change to be able to describe to the Prince, on my return, the details of such a joyful occasion and the great happiness of Their Majesties.

The Prince's health seemed to reflect the hopelessness of the military situation, and was worsening. There were no more walks, just complete bed rest. The poems he wrote then are dispirited with the hopelessness of ever being up and about.

> *To be well again,*
> *And to serve my Emperor!*
> *Was my pledge in vain?*
> *For I see no hope ahead*
> *Of ever rising from my bed.*

I could not bring myself to read those poems until after the war, when he was better. He himself wrote about that period:

> When I woke at night, all was quiet, and I could not even hear Setsuko breathing in the next room. There was no sound even from the nurses' room on the other side of the hall. I would suddenly have to cough, and I knew someone would come running if I did, and not wanting to give anyone trouble, I used to bury my head in the quilts and try my utmost to stifle the sound of my coughing.

He was always thinking of others, and trying so hard not to cause anyone any trouble, trying not to disturb our sleep, always maintaining a stiff upper lip so as not to worry us by betraying his despair. If only he had let me share some of that despair!

From 2 January 1944, Dr Denji Terao took over from Army Doctor Junichi Nakamura as a member of the Prince's medical team. Dr Terao was the Health Advisory Chief of the Anti-Tuberculosis Association, as well as being the man who developed the Terao Pneumothorax in 1934. As I explained earlier, when the lung is contracted, the point of entry of the disease is closed off, the discharge of bacilli stopped, and recovery begins. Pneumothorax treatment consists of removing the air from the pleural cavity so that it naturally contracts. It was decided to add this treatment to the general regimen of fresh air, rest and nourishment he was already following.

Dr Terao describes his first impression of the Gotemba Villa as follows:

> The sick room was a Japanese-style room of eight mats, separated from the corridor partly by a plywood wall, and partly by papered sliding doors behind which was His Highness's bed.... The bed faced the veranda on the south side, and on His Highness's right was a *tokonoma*, the sides of which were also plywood. I was astounded at the simplicity. The veranda was of ordinary cypress and only three feet wide. The Princess sat on a blanket spread on the wooden floor. I was amazed at what a plain and humble sick room it was.

Dr Terao always seemed surprised that I never sat on a cushion, but I had my reasons. In one of his poems, the Prince had written,

> *The sound of my cough*
> *Changes, and I know that I*
> *Must be getting worse.*
> *How my heart sinks...*

Being unable to take his pain upon me and suffer in his stead, I felt the least I could do was to inflict some discomfort upon myself in sympathy with his condition.

The Prince was no longer able to walk to his study, but spent all day in bed. In the morning he mainly read – books on law, art and literature. He rested in the afternoon, much of the time gazing at Mount Fuji. In the evening, he would often listen to the radio. His days were invariably spent like this until the war ended.

On 19 May, the Prince suffered a severe spontaneous pneumothorax attack and nearly died of asphyxiation. Dr Terao, in the presence of several consultants including Dr Ryūkichi Inada, the then foremost authority on tuberculosis, inserted a hypodermic needle and extracted the air that had invaded the pleural cavity through burst tissue, and saw the Prince through the crisis. To insert a needle into a royal chest was indeed a very bold step at that time, when princes and princesses might not even be vaccinated arbitrarily.

Six days after the emergency, the Prince's condition had more or less stabilized, except that water formed in the lungs, and had to be removed and replaced by air. Once more, artificial pneumothorax was indicated. Up until then, the thickened pleura of the Prince's left lung had prevented the details of his lung from being visible in X-rays, and it was assumed that adhesion would make pneumothorax impossible. But a spontaneous pneumothorax having occurred, the lung, as well as rupturing, had effectively contracted. Now, the bacilli in the Prince's sputum were diminishing daily.

On 22 July 1944, the Tōjō cabinet withdrew, and General Kuniaki Koiso became Prime Minister. From mid-October, the Prince was able to get up, and only needed artificial pneumothorax occasionally.

By November, air raid warnings could be heard daily, as B29s flew past in formation over the Villa. Saipan having surrendered, air raids on the Japanese mainland had become a possibility. Gotemba was on the flight path of the B29s as they made for Tokyo. They would come in over Suruga Bay, and fly over Mount Fuji and Hakone, and each time they passed overhead, we would instinctively fold our hands together and pray that casualties would be light. But each day the damage got worse and worse. Trains stopped so often that finally Dr Endō, the Prince's head physician, moved to Gotemba.

In December, although the Prince donated over 223 trees from our cypress forest to the war effort, he would not allow us to obtain the necessary flour from the black market to mix with taro yams and ginger for his chest poultices. I would have gladly gone without food, clothing and shelter, for his sake, and not to be able to get this necessity for him depressed me.

But by now, the Prince's condition did not seem too bad, and the chief physician's cheerful countenance made me happier than anything.

However, the air raids continued without respite, and on 25 February 1945, fire bombs fell on the Imperial Palace in Tokyo, and part of the Emperor's residence and that of the Empress Dowager were burned. I paid a visit to Their Majesties on 6 March to enquire as to their welfare, and was happy to be able to assure those at home on my return that no one had been injured. What a relief it had been to find that the Empress Dowager was safe, and that the only damage she had sustained had been to the three-story tower of her palace, and the glass doors and sliding paper partitions. I hurried back to Gotemba to the wail of sirens.

But no sooner had I returned to Gotemba than there was an enormous air raid on Tokyo lasting from midnight on 9 March to the 10th, in which we heard that the official residence of the Imperial Household Minister had burned down. Fortunately, both my father and mother were safe. Ever since my father had been appointed to that post, realizing the gravity of his responsibilities, they had vacated the house in Shōto, and moved completely into the official residence. Being a single-minded man, devoted to duty, my father did not even consider evacuation, and therefore lost everything.

'So now I'm just an ordinary person, like everybody else', he said.

In January 1941, he had lost, to an illness, his darling youngest son Jirō, the apple of his eye, not yet quite seventeen, whom he used to call 'Ji' for short. After that, material loss meant little to him.

15 AUGUST 1945

Iwo-jima had fallen on 17 March. And as if that was not enough, still they came, night and day – the B29s in formations a hundred, and two hundred strong. It broke our hearts to think of the havoc they would be wreaking far and wide.

As for the Prince's fight against his illness, there was not much cause for optimism although the crisis was over for the time being. Dr Endō and Dr Terao were kept busy administering the difficult artificial pneumothorax treatment and the drawing out of fluid from the chest.

Because of the daily air raids, visits by members of the Imperial Family became less frequent, although the Mikasas did manage to come in between raids. Prince Takamatsu was too busy with the pressure of work at Staff Headquarters to leave Tokyo, but wrote weekly.

On 7 April, the Kantarō Suzuki cabinet was formed. A month later, on 7 May, Germany surrendered unconditionally, and although Japan's defeat seemed certain to us, the militarists were all for making a stand on the homeland. Camouflage was applied to our roof, and a strong air raid shelter was made for us by soldiers from the Tōkai Corps. It was dug in a spiral, like a snail's shell, with an escape shaft at the very end, and if necessary, the Prince would be carried to the innermost recess on a stretcher. There was also a simpler shelter built by the Imperial Household.

Meanwhile, I worked hard growing vegetables. Even if we did not become self-sufficient, it helped to have something extra. But never having grown anything but roses, I found hoeing and tilling hard work indeed. Masako Shirasu's husband made me an oven for baking bread, and I managed to make some tasty loaves out of a variety of grains and cereals.

About that time, Tokyo suffered another devastating air raid. It was on 25 May, and this time both the Emperor's Palace and that of the Empress Dowager were burned. Our residence, too, in Omote-machi, was reduced to ashes – except for part of the Japanese section – and two guards lost their lives. The Prince's Private Secretary came to see us, to apologize profoundly for having been unable to save the Prince's many prized books, among which were valuable foreign books and specialized volumes.

'Seven of us,' he said, 'did our utmost to save the books, but, alas, they all burned to a crisp.'

What could seven men – or more – with buckets, hope to do against a bombing raid by over two hundred B29s!

The Prince thanked him and urged him not to worry about it any more. 'It was something entirely beyond your control', he said.

Even after dealing such a fatal blow to Tokyo, the B29s did not stop their bombing. The Emperor and Empress moved into the library, which had escaped the fire. The Emperor's personal office was set up there too. I was finally able to get to Tokyo on 27 May, but instead of replying to my enquiries about the Palace fire, the Empress kept asking me about the Prince's health and thanking me for braving the air raids to come to see them, all she would speak about was her anxiety for all the people who had lost their homes and their loved ones.

The Ninomaru Gardens in the Palace grounds, once so lovely with azaleas and irises, were a desolate ruin, and I missed the usual sound of murmuring water in the Fukiage Gardens in the north-western part of the estate. The once limpid stream, where fireflies used to flit about on summer evenings, seemed to be silently choking back its tears with sadness.

I met the Empress Dowager in her air raid shelter. She, too, would not talk about the burning of her palace, but only spoke about the ordeal of the Japanese people.

'Take good care of Yasuhito', she said as I took leave of her, after assuring Her Majesty that her son's health was beginning to look a little better.

Lastly, I visited our Tokyo home. I was prepared for the worst, but the ruins looked even more pitiful than I had imagined. I had been instructed by the Prince not to refer to anything that was burned, but only to thank people and give them encouragement. He told me to find out the names of those soldiers who had lost their lives and arrange for someone to represent us at their funerals. In the midst of so much that was changed beyond recognition, it was comforting to find the age-old cedars and other trees still standing, albeit with their leaves somewhat singed.

On 4 June, my father, after apologizing personally to the Emperor, resigned his post as Imperial Household Minister to take responsibility for the Palace's destruction by fire. Soon after the end of the war, he sold his property in Shibuya Ward's Shōto district and moved to Senzoku. Even though not all of his property had been destroyed in the air raids and subsequent fires, the Emperor's Palace was gone, and His Majesty inconvenienced. My father felt it would not be proper to live to the same standard as before. I heard later that he let the Government of Tokyo have our old property at a price far below its value, which was so like my father, and it is now the official residence of the Governor.

By the 26th, the Prince was well enough to take walks in the grounds of our Villa, but Dr Endō and Dr Terao continued their medical supervision. Artificial pneumothorax had been suspended from the beginning of June, but there was no telling when it might become necessary again. Meanwhile, I worked in the vegetable garden every day, in my straw hat and *monpe* dungarees, ignoring the air raid warnings.

On the 30th, no sooner had the air-raid siren gone than there were some very loud booms in the direction of Gotemba Station, only three kilometres to our east. It was obviously bombs. My helpers and I ran back to the house, and with all of us gathered around the Prince, we took refuge in the shelter for the first time. We later heard that several carrier-based aircraft had strafed the area around the railway station and dropped eight 50-kilogram bombs.

The Prince had begun thinking ever since July that the constant bombing by the American forces must be in preparation for some special assault. His assumption was unfortunately correct. On 6 August the atom bomb was dropped on Hiroshima, followed by the one on

Nagasaki on the 9th. Moreover, the USSR had entered the war against Japan, and earlier, on 21 June, Okinawa had fallen. An American attack on Japan's mainland would be next, and while the Japanese Army expected a swift attack by the Americans, by this time, I think most of the Japanese people had lost their will to fight.

From Prince Takamatsu's letters and his ADC's reports, I think the Prince was pretty much aware of how the war had changed, and how its end was taking shape.

On 15 August, at the very height of the summer heat, Prince and Princess Takamatsu arrived by car from Tokyo at about 11.30 in the morning. On looking back, I think the reason they came here, leaving Tokyo so early in the morning, was because Prince Takamatsu wanted to be with his brother, and could not bear the thought of listening without him to the important, historic, unprecedented broadcast by the Emperor to the people. Or it may have simply been that he felt his bedridden brother needed his support at this time.

The Prince sat up in bed, and we all gathered around him there to listen to the noon broadcast on his bedside radio. There was a lot of static, probably because of the mountains round about Gotemba, so we could not hear His Majesty's voice very clearly. But I remember my eyes filling with tears, both with relief that the war was over, and the multitude of thoughts that welled up in my mind. I cannot remember what the brothers said after the broadcast, or what the general feeling was. The Takamatsus had said they would have to return to Tokyo at once, so all I could think of was what to give them for lunch before they left.

That day, the Prince had to have a pneumothorax treatment and lung fluid extraction for the first time in three months. He was bound to have been affected by this great turning point in history.

But he felt fine the very next day. Prince Mikasa arrived, and spent the night with us, and in spite of the Prince's invalid condition, it transpired that we would have to leave immediately for Tokyo. I went first on the 19th to make arrangements, and the Prince followed two days later.

CHAPTER ELEVEN

THE POST-WAR YEARS

◆

THE SHMOO

The reason we had to leave Gotemba so suddenly was that the GHQ of the American armed forces' occupation, to be centred on Yokohama, had issued an order that Japanese army personnel, and anyone else connected with the army, must get out of an area that included the northern part of Shizuoka Prefecture. The Higashikuni cabinet, formed on the 17th, had sent us a message saying that since Gotemba was on the edge of the area, we should move to Tokyo if at all possible. Both doctors felt it was risky, but we left Gotemba at 1 p.m., with Dr Endō and me accompanying the Prince in his car, stopping on the way for a brief rest at Marquis Nabeshima's seaside villa in Oiso.

After a hot, tiring ride, it was a great relief when we finally arrived in Tokyo without the Prince having suffered any ill effects from the drive. All that was left of our old Akasaka residence was four tatami-matted rooms of the Japanese section. The Prince had hardly ever set foot in them before, but now they represented a roof over our heads, for which we were thankful. The rooms were not elegant, and quite draughty, but that was a blessing in the humid summer weather. There was no kitchen, but Princess Takamatsu had kindly provided us with a sink and a refrigerator, which we gratefully installed in a corner of the veranda. A few chairs in one of the rooms had to suffice for the Prince to receive the Prime Minister Prince Higashikuni, Foreign Minister Yoshida, and others who came to pay their respects. Prince Takamatsu came every day, but usually just sat informally on the edge of the veranda without coming in.

The Prince got through the end of the summer heat without incident, and began to feel well enough to walk all around the burnt-out estate. On the afternoon of 15 September, I accompanied him to the Palace. His first meeting with his brother the Emperor since falling ill five years before was a deeply emotional reunion. For the last time, the Prince wore the uniform of a major-general – but without his sword, now that the war was over. The Emperor seemed delighted to see his brother looking so well, and they had so much to say to one another it was half past five before we left.

By October, I began to be worry about the effect our draughty temporary abode might have on the Prince's health as winter approached. The doctors were worried, too, and we were given permission by the Americans to move back to Gotemba on 1 November. Fuji was resplendent in early snow, the plants in the vegetable garden had been well-tended in our absence and had grown apace, and we were happy to be back. Although it was only little over a month since we had left, wondering if we would ever return, so much had happened in that short time that it seemed as if we had been away for ages. We had been an occupied country since 30 August when General MacArthur, Supreme Commander Allied Powers, landed at the former Naval Air Station at Atsugi. Everything had changed radically and bewilderingly. Only Mount Fuji remained the same, soaring aloof – nobody's captive. Rather than living a gloomy and servile life as people of an occupied country, I hoped we could just obey the army of occupation's rules and go forward in friendship, shoulder to shoulder with them.

The Prince was an optimist; a practical man with a positive outlook. While we were living in the remains of our burned-out Tokyo residence, a friend of mine from Hiroshima came to call while I was out. Her husband, the Vice-Governor, had been killed by the atom bomb, while she and her five children were saved by taking refuge in the river. She had come to thank me for the clothes and other things I had sent her. She told me the Prince said to her: 'Don't worry. You'll see. Japan will make a fine recovery. So make sure you bring up your children well. The war is over. The Japanese people are going to work hard. We're not the sort of nation and not the sort of people to go to pieces. There is nothing to worry about. Everything is going to be all right. Japan will most certainly rise again.'

My friend took the Prince's words to heart, and today her children are indeed fine members of society.

Food shortages had been severe for some time, so we dug up the gardens and the tennis court to grow more food. We tried hard to prepare nutritious meals for the Prince, but he had always been a simple 'soup and two-vegetables' man for preference, and would screw up his face if presented with anything too fancy.

One day, an American journalist came to interview the Prince. 'Your Highness, is there anything you need, or anything you would like?' he asked.To which the Prince replied, purposely looking serious: 'Yes, there is something I want badly. I have been taking the occupation newspaper and reading it every day, and in it I've been reading a comic strip in which there is something called a "Shmoo". Apparently, if one has a shmoo, one can make anything one wants. I would very much like to have a shmoo. If the Japanese had some shmoos, I'm sure they would be able to reconstruct their country and everything would be all right!'

'Wow! So Your Highness knows about shmoos!'

The journalist was delighted, and sent us the biggest shmoo you ever saw. It was folded flat and when the parcel arrived we wondered what on earth it could be. When we blew it up it was enormous. The Prince was thrilled with his shmoo, and even had his picture taken with it. The photograph appeared in the occupation newspaper, and people sent us lots and lots of shmoos.

'This is all we need for Japan's recovery', the Prince used to say.

In those days the general public still had ambivalent feelings towards the occupation and found it hard to get used to. I am quite certain the Prince's sense of humour and delight evidenced in the shmoo episode was the very first step in post Second World War Japan-American goodwill and friendship.

THE PRINCE CHICHIBU FARM

The Prince's post-war dream was to live an English-style country life, farming on a large enough scale to be completely self-sufficient as to food. We put some acreage under cultivation and grew not just kitchen-garden vegetables, as we had during the war, but crops such as potatoes, sweet potatoes, buckwheat, pumpkins, sweet corn, and finally even wheat and upland rice. Besides poultry, we kept sheep and goats. At one time we kept pigs, and later even raised milking cows. We even produced a small amount of sweet potatoes and wheat for the market, stressing quality rather than quantity. But when all was said and done, it was an amateur operation, and many were the funny happenings and episodes.

The Prince undertook some of the light work at first, such as weeding, picking off insects, treading wheat and herding sheep, but as he regained his health, he took on harvesting wheat and making compost, as well as the arduous task in summer under the scorching sun of cutting grass to make winter hay to feed the cows and goats.

At first my ladies-in-waiting and I were quite hopeless at hoeing, so the Prince asked a teacher from the Gotemba agricultural college to come and give us lessons. Oh, how difficult we found it to learn the knack of how to wield a hoe and dig a straight furrow! We tried so hard, dressed in our peasant overalls, with the sweat running down our faces, but we hardly ever got our rows straight the first time and would invariably be made to do them over again. We certainly acquired a great respect for the work of farmers.

In his eagerness for us all to experience fully the life of the English landed gentry, which he had observed first-hand while in England, the Prince got experts to come from the prefectural breeding centre to teach us how to milk our sheep and goats. The Prince loved being able to drink the fresh milk and offer it to our guests, who found our home-grown potatoes and corn a treat as well. There is nothing like freshly-picked corn. If not eaten within four hours of harvesting, corn-on-the-cob begins to dry out and the flavour deteriorates. The Prince always sent any particularly good produce of ours first to the Empress Dowager, whose obvious delight used to encourage him greatly.

The Takamatsus and the Mikasas visited us frequently, and enjoyed the freedom of life in Gotemba and the informal family gatherings impossible in Tokyo. In those desperately food-scarce post-war times, we had plenty of fresh chicken, eggs, and milk, in addition to what was provided by generous American relief agencies.

Keeping full-grown pigs had turned out not to be feasible because of our shortage of feed, so the Prince gave all our pigs away to neighbouring farms with the proviso that they give us back one piglet from each litter, which we would then raise and return when it was grown. The Prince thought up this scheme to help the farms to prosper, but alas, it did not work. In those days few farmers had the time and means to do much more than just exist from day to day. It transpired that after they received their pigs they immediately sold them! Raising pigs should have been a profitable enterprise. In reality, it was not a success. The Prince's Private Secretary, who was in charge of transferring the pigs, was upset. 'You can't very well tell them not to sell the pigs...' he used to mutter. It was quite funny, really, but rather sad at the same time.

The Prince began to be more and more ambitious in his role as English-style gentleman farmer, and put in electrically-heated beds for sprouting seeds and machines for threshing and milling, which he allowed local farmers to use. The Prince tried out tractors, as well as experimenting in various other ways. It was all rather hit or miss, and he had some real failures, learning much about the harshness of nature in the process. But the joy of a good harvest gave all of us tremendous fulfilment.

The Prince and I took lessons in spinning and weaving, and we made homespun from the wool of our sheep. We became known by our neighbours as The Prince's Experimental Farm, and the fact that it brought us into such close and friendly contact with the local people was one of the nicest results of our agricultural project.

Above all, the Prince wanted our household to be one big happy family. He loved to organize competitions. 'Fuji Prosperity', the name of the brown draught ox, was chosen this way. He also had everyone compete in making bird feeders of their own design to place wherever they wanted in the grounds, and gave a prize to the person whose feeder attracted the most birds. The Prince loved to invent things, and one of his designs was a vegetable dehydrator he set under the floor of the house.

During this time, I often made trips to Tokyo on the Prince's behalf. Following General MacArthur's occupation policy a directive was issued abolishing privilege regarding Imperial Family property, and so we had to fill out a tax return like ordinary citizens, which I then took to the Imperial Household Agency. I also represented the Prince at an Imperial Family conference when the new Constitution came into force on 3 May 1947. Its revised Imperial Family code decreed that besides the Emperor's sons, only three princes would be allowed to retain their imperial status – his brothers Prince Chichibu, Prince Takamatsu and Prince Mikasa.

We had had to give up our Hayama villa of so many memories in April 1946, after one last winter there.

On 18 October 1947, both the Prince and I went to a farewell dinner at the Akasaka Detached Palace, attended by their Majesties the Emperor and Empress and the Empress Dowager, for the former members of the Imperial Family whose Imperial status had been abolished.

'Let us always keep in touch', said the Emperor, raising his glass, and when, in reply, the now former Prince Morimasa Nashimoto raised his, saying, 'I pray for the continued prosperity of the Imperial Family,' I was choked with emotion, and at the same time, suddenly aware of the weight of responsibility now resting upon those few of us who officially remained Imperial.

'*I ENVY THE WEEDS*'

The Prince's condition improved greatly after the end of the war. Early one June, I accompanied him by car for a week's stay in Tokyo, and we stopped off in the village of Tsurukawa in Kanagawa Prefecture to see my old childhood friend Masako Shirasu.

Before going abroad to the Hartridge school at the age of fourteen in 1924 Masako had been the first woman ever to appear on the stage of a Noh theatre, and even after she married she continued her career as an essayist writing on many aspects of Japanese culture including the Noh and the classics. During the food shortage she had struggled with the unaccustomed chores of farming and rice-planting, and we wanted to see some of her crops. It was just at the season when no matter how much you weeded, the summer grasses kept springing up again. Said Masako: 'The weeds are terrible. Look at them. No matter how often you pull them up, the weeds just keep on coming.'

'I envy the weeds,' said the Prince, as if to himself. Momentarily, Masako's eyes met mine. Something about the way he said it alarmed us both. Why would he envy the weeds? Was it their life and vigour he envied? And just when the Prince seemed so very much better, too.

For a moment such thoughts ran riot in my mind, but I tried not to think about it. There was so much to talk about as we had tea in the drawing room – the Westernized *doma* of their big renovated old farmhouse. Masako's husband Jirō was not at home, and we spoke mostly about the Prince's most recent state of health.

Masako's second son Kanemasa ran in and threw his arms around the Prince from behind, saying: 'I love you, Highness, I love you!' Kanemasa was six or seven, and used to come and see us now and then in Gotemba with his parents. The Prince was very fond of him.

Nodding in reply the Prince smiled as he fondly stroked the two small hands on his shoulders. Child though he was, Kanemasa may have realized the Prince was not as well as he used to be. It was a very moving episode. On the way home the Prince said to me it was the first time he had ever experienced such a show of affection by a child.

Next day, the Prince sent Kanemasa an illustrated book about insects.

In those days in Tokyo there was a sort of hotel for royalty called the Tokiwa Matsu ('Evergreen Pines') which had been the palace of Prince Higashi-Fushimi, and is now the residence of Prince Hitachi.

When I went up to Tokyo without the Prince I always went by train. Together with my senior lady-in-waiting, Kuni Kawazu, we rode the local Gotemba Line, changing to the main Tokaido Line, and always travelled what was then known as third class, both during the war and after. I saw a lot, learned a lot, and experienced much kindness. I became so used to the Gotemba Line I called it 'my train'. And almost everyone who rode it knew me by sight. It was different on the Tokaido Line, especially during the rush hour, so I made a point of wearing my *monpe* farm overalls so as not to be conspicuous. There were a lot of tunnels on the Gotemba Line, and since the day of electric trains was still a long way off, every time we came to a tunnel one had to close the windows to keep out the smoke and then open them again for ventilation. The person by the window always did the opening and shutting. In my naivety, I was greatly impressed. Travelling by train was quite an education. The 5-something in the morning filled up with salaried men and wage earners going to work who all went to sleep but never failed to get off at their destination. So many things amazed me. And not just me. It used to be said that royalty was out of touch with reality, but I'm sure it was only because we lacked this sort of experience. There was a story going around of how I once kept the flies away from a nursing mother. She was sitting beside me in one of those wartime carriages packed with desperate foragers travelling into the country to try and find food to buy. I can't recall precisely, but I do seem to remember doing something like that.

On reaching the 'Evergreen Pines', where I kept a chest of drawers containing a complete outfit, I used to change before setting out for my destination.

In July I went to Niigata and Nagoya to represent the Prince at students' track-and-field meets.

That year was unusually hot, and the Prince worked himself to the bone mowing and reaping without taking enough nourishment. It was not only a great effort trying to obtain things like butter, it was an even greater effort getting him to eat them. One of my ladies-in-waiting once told me that while I was away in Tokyo she had given him an extra dish not on the menu, consisting of a cornflour dumpling with egg mixed in it and he had said: 'You've tricked me, haven't you?' which was hard on the serving girl! The best way to get him to eat nourishing things was to have the doctor order him to do so. Afterwards we resorted to that many times.

The heat wave continued, and on September first, the Prince's fever suddenly rose and both his chief doctors diagnosed the cause as coming from the kidneys. On Dr Endō's recommendation, Specialist Consultant Dr Haruhide Origasa came on the eleventh, and after a thorough examination decided that an operation was necessary. The Prince immediately gave his consent, expressing full trust in the consultant. The following day, I went up to Tokyo in spite of my heart being down in my boots and obtained the approval of their three Majesties. Prince Takamatsu was in Kyoto, so I informed him by letter.

The operation took place on the nineteenth in our Gotemba Villa in a medium-sized Western-style room which had to serve as the operating theatre and into which the required medical equipment was brought. A matron and three nurses were in attendance, and the day went by in an atmosphere of high tension.

Dr Origasa began operating and finished satisfactorily after one hour and twenty minutes. The Emperor had sent both his present and former chief court physicians as well as his chief chamberlain Grand Steward Tajima, all of whom were greatly relieved. The Prince was philosophic about his illness and had complete trust in the words and skill of the consultant surgeon whatever the outcome, and when I first saw him after the operation he greeted me with a tranquil smile.

His progress went well, and after attending him for ten days, Dr Origasa, together with Doctors Endō and Terao gave the Prince a final examination.

During his recuperation in Gotemba the Prince spent almost every day writing poetry, and presented the following verse at the annual New Year Poetry Party at the Imperial Palace in 1948. The subject that year was 'A Mountain in Spring'

> *Unmelted snow*
>   *Lies in deep recesses*
>   *Here and there;*
> *While amid the creeping pines*
> *Bush warblers sing.*

THE PROMISE

In February 1949, streptomycin treatment was started. 'I shall be all right now', said the Prince on receiving this new drug that had been developed in America. It arrived after his operation, and had been sent to him by the royal family of Norway as well as by the Americans. But whether the Prince's constitution was overly sensitive, or whatever the cause, the side effects were so strong that the treatment had to be stopped. It was suggested that perhaps it was just not effective in his particular case. It is my opinion, however, that it was because of the streptomycin that the Prince survived for as long as he did.

In April 1949, the Emperor and Empress attended a tree-planting ceremony in Hakone and afterwards visited the Empress Dowager who was staying at the Imperial Villa in Numazu. The following day, their majesties paid a visit to us. Although the Prince was forbidden from doing any farm work, he was allowed to spend the day in his study, except when resting, and that day he went down with me to the bottom of the paved entranceway to welcome them. Afterwards, beaming with pleasure, he showed them around, explaining everything, beginning with our view of Fuji with its lingering springtime snow. He even showed them the sheep, the hen house and the cowshed, even introducing the ox calf we had named Fuji Prosperity, born on 31 January. And there in the barley field were shoots a couple of inches high of the seedlings we had firmly trodden in that February.

Their Majesties were duly impressed, laughing out loud every now and again, looking thoroughly relaxed, and expressing kind words of appreciation to me.

It was a great joy to have them there, and such a pity that ancient custom precluded us from offering them a meal. That veto applied to the Empress Dowager as well, and even ruled out a cup of tea. Whenever she was staying at the Numazu Villa she came up to see us and used to chat away with the Prince just like any mother and son. What heartwarming times those were!

Although the Prince was still forbidden from doing farm work, he was finally well enough now to help us pack in straw bags the potatoes and taros we dug up.

That autumn I joined Prince and Princess Takamatsu in a visit to both the Koyama Hospital of Regenerative Medicine and the National Suruga Leprosy Sanatorium. It was a busy time. There were many sports events at which I represented the Prince, as well as official Imperial duties, and then on 14 November I had a message to say my father had suddenly died. He was the first Chairman of the House of Councillors (the upper house of the Diet), and had spent the morning as usual expediting the proceedings of a working committee. In the afternoon he went to the House of Representatives to confer with a Mr Williams, who had just arrived. After leaving the Diet, he stopped for some treatment at an ENT clinic, and upon his arrival home that evening he had a sudden heart attack which proved fatal. I flew like the wind to Tokyo and late that night was able to gaze on his face, peaceful in death. He and my mother had visited us in Gotemba that summer on August twentieth. That was the last time I saw him alive.

Thus ended the 24th Year of Shōwa (1949), and a new year began. Every January, people from Gotemba and villages round about used to come to the Villa to wish us a happy New Year, and it had become our custom to offer them *sake*. The Prince always made a point of attending as many of the various local events as possible, including shrine festivals and school sports days. He enjoyed mixing with the people.

Having been obliged to give up sports and his official duties on account of his illness, the Prince took up writing, on which he worked as hard as possible. 'I can't bear the thought of just going on living in idleness,' he said. 'That would be no life at all.' Hoping to encourage tuberculosis sufferers, in 1948 he wrote an article entitled 'My Convalescence' for the health magazine *Hoken Dojin*. And he persuaded me, in spite of my lack of skill, to write one too, called 'My Nursing'. Before that, he produced a book *Recollections of Britain and the United States* in which he had me do a short piece on my time in America. In September 1948, he published *Gotemba Thoughts*. After that he concentrated on essays, ten of which appeared in 1950.

That year I had so many official Imperial duties I had to stay overnight in Tokyo about once a week. Now that most of the former Imperial Family members had descended to the status of subjects, the duties had to be shared among the remaining three princely houses. And besides that, I had to represent the Prince as honorary patron of the Japan-British Society and at sporting events, as well as being myself honorary president of the Tokyo Anti-tuberculosis Association.

On the fourth of May, the Empress Dowager came up to see us from the Numazu Villa. Although as usual we were not able to give her refreshments of any sort, we had a most delightfully intimate visit, just the three of us, and she said how much she would like to stay overnight when next she came so she could hear the birds sing. We promised to arrange it.

Sometime during that summer the Prince began to complain of pains in his left chest. At the request of his chief physician, Dr Endō, Chief Surgeon Chuichi Kodama of the Kamakura Hirō Hospital – formerly Professor in Chief of medical science at Tokyo's prestigious Jikei University School of Medicine – diagnosed caries of the rib cartilege and ordered immediate surgery. The nearly two-hour operation was carried out on August twelfth. The Prince made good progress, and apart from rest periods it was not long before he was allowed back into his study.

About that time the kiln he had ordered was completed and the Prince was eager to fire up what he dubbed the '*Mitsumine kiln*' after his beloved Three Peaks in the Chichibu Mountains The first main firing took place on the sixth of September. The Prince had lessons from the potter Hajime Katō who taught him how to knead clay, turn a potter's wheel and throw a tea bowl, which gave the Prince a new joy.

But in November, he came down with jaundice. In order to cure jaundice one must cut down on fat, which is high in nutrition and indispensable in the treatment of tuberculosis. What is more, the following year, 1951, in February, the Prince had another operation, and although progress was good, it was gradually becoming apparent that his constitution was slowly being eaten away by the tubercle bacilli – a fact it was impossible any longer to turn one's eyes and mind away from. I realized it was now I, myself who had to become strong. I went up to Tokyo at once to report to His Majesty on the Prince's progress, and afterwards accepted a lift home with the Empress Dowager who was driving to Numazu, and in the car I explained to her the state of the Prince's health.

On April eleventh, General MacArthur, the Supreme Commander Allied Powers, was relieved of his post and his place was taken by General Ridgway. On the eighteenth, when I paid my respects at the Numazu Imperial Villa for the second time that spring, all the Empress Dowager spoke about was her concern for the Prince's health. After that I had to go to Tokyo on official Imperial duties and in May I attended a conference of the Kyoto chapter of the Anti-TB Association.

While I was away the Prince was examined by his four chief physicians and showed no untoward symptoms, to my great relief. Five days later, however, on a rainy seventeenth of May, something entirely unforeseen happened. The Empress Dowager died of a sudden angina attack. I hurried up to Tokyo. The Prince was not fit enough to accompany me, but insisted that I tell everyone that he was all right.

No tears came during my hasty journey for I could not yet believe that my visit just a month ago to the Numazu Villa was the last time I should see Her Majesty alive. And it had been but a year ago on the fourth of May when she visited us in Gotemba that she had expressed a desire to stay on her next visit. To keep our part of the promise we had only just that very day – the day of her death – ordered the tatami renewed in preparation for her visit.

I felt as if my main prop and stay had been pulled out from under me, and I tried desperately to pull myself together. As for the Prince, who in his weakened state had received his mother's especially deep affection, I thought how heartrending it must be for him to be the only one absent from her wake in the Omiya Palace, her Tokyo residence. I felt, therefore, that I must allow myself no tears.

Next day, the eighteenth, at two in the afternoon, Their Majesties paid their respects. After they left at 3.30 to return to their Palace, I went home to Gotemba to fetch the Prince, and we both drove back to Tokyo by car next morning, with Drs Endō and Terao in attendance. The long drive was tiring for the Prince, so we went first to the residence of the Grand Chamberlain where he could rest until the evening when just after 7 o'clock we attended the Imperial 'Ceremony of the Embarkation' (the placing of the body in the special coffin shaped like an ancient barge). The Prince looked haggard and miserable.

We stayed in Tokyo until after the Fortieth Day Ceremony. During that time the Prince underwent a great many medical examinations and it was decided to start a course of streptomycin once more.

On 8 June, the Ceremony of the Announcement of the Posthumous Name took place at the Omiya Palace. Henceforth she would be known as Empress Teimei. The Imperial Funeral was held at the Imperial Toshima-ga-oka Mausoleum on the 22nd. The Prince attended the funeral with me but I went alone to the burial rites at the tomb. Next day we both attended the first of the special ceremonies at the Omiya Palace for Her Majesty's spirit, which would be enshrined there for a year, in a small sanctuary called the 'Gonden'. The Fortieth Day Ceremony was on the 25th, and we returned to Gotemba on the 28th.

I went back up to Tokyo alone for the final Fiftieth Day Ceremony, and now that all the rites of parting had been accomplished, that night I let myself go and had my first really good cry at the loss of my beloved mentor, guide and friend.

> *In my grief, my tears*
> *Flow on and on when I think*
> *How Your Majesty*
> *Was the one who tutored me*
> *And made me what I am today.*

THE OXFORD RUGBY TEAM

At the beginning of September, a whiteness would appear each morning on the summit of Fuji. The Prince would have the whole household assemble and ask us each to guess whether it was frost or snow. After everyone had given the mountain a good stare with naked eyes, the Prince would take a look with his binoculars and determine which it was. Those who guessed correctly were rewarded with a sweet or a piece of cake.

It was fun, but we dreaded the cold winter our game presaged. Gotemba was a summer resort, and winters there were severe. When electricity restrictions were in force, the Prince would not let us apply for special permission to use electric heaters. The only alternative was a potbellied stove, which would not be good for his lungs. Eventually, a suitable house for the winter was found on a quiet south-facing hill in Kugenuma, a seaside resort near Fujisawa. The upstairs rooms were sunny, the garden large enough to put in a few of the Prince's favourite plants, and it was also within easy reach of Tokyo.

We moved there in January 1952. The Prince liked the house, which was a great relief to me, but I worried for fear the constant stream of visitors, engendered by its accessibility, would tire him. But surprisingly, he thrived so well that his team of four doctors only needed to attend about once a month. The mild climate of Kugenuma seemed to agree with the Prince. In April, we had shrubs such as red and white blossoming plum, hawthorn, kerria, laurel and juniper brought from the ruins of our Tokyo property, and the Prince supervised their replanting. He also received a mimosa and two coconut palms from his old school friend the former Viscount Hachisuka.

Having attended his coronation, the news of King George VI's death on 6 February saddened us greatly, and our hearts went out in special sympathy to the widowed Queen, of whom we had such fond memories.

The Peace Treaty, signed on 28 April, made Japan an independent country once more, which meant that someone from Japan would be invited to the coronation of Queen Elizabeth II the following year. The Prince felt strongly that it would be in the best interests of both Japan and the Crown Prince for the latter to represent the Emperor. The Anglo-Japanese political climate not being what it had been before, he felt it absolutely essential that the Crown Prince should go, and pressed the matter fervently with Imperial Household Agency Chief Tajima and Dr Shinzō Koizumi.

In a letter to the Household Agency Chief, the Prince set down his reasons as follows. 1) The Crown Prince was of the same generation as the Queen and for him to make her acquaintance now would be of benefit to the future of both nations. 2) Although the Crown Prince had only recently come of age and many people feared he lacked sufficient experience, he would only be one of many guests, and therefore could be fairly relaxed. 3) From his own experience of attending the coronation of George VI, he knew that most monarchies would be represented by a crown prince, and other countries by top-ranking people, and so he believed that it would be of great significance for him to take advantage of this matchless opportunity to meet all those people at one time. And 4), while the British had mixed feelings towards Japan, the Crown Prince was still a boy and clearly had no connection with the war, so it was very important for the future that friendly relations with other countries be forged anew, and he was the ideal one to represent the Emperor compared with the other members of the Imperial Family, who all served in the armed forces.

I am quite sure this advice from the Prince was crucial to the decision made by Imperial Household Agency Chief Tajima.

The Oxford University Rugby Team came to Japan in September, and we spent a fortnight in Tokyo so that the Prince could attend the team's matches against Japanese universities. He hosted a party for the Oxford team to which he also invited Crown Prince Akihito, and was delighted to see the latter chatting with the Oxford men. The Prince was anxious for the Crown Prince's sake that there should be at least a few people with feelings of goodwill towards him while he was a guest at Queen Elizabeth's coronation in Britain, where anti-Japanese sentiments still remained.

We returned to Gotemba once, but soon came back to Tokyo to attend the Investiture of the Crown Prince. After the ceremony on 10 November, we remained in Tokyo, and the Prince managed to maintain a full schedule in Tokyo for several days at a time, receiving ambassadors in audience, and attending embassy parties, all to make sure that the Crown Prince met and conversed with the ambassadors and dignitaries of as many countries as possible.

When the Crown Prince left for England the following year, in June 1953, the British Government issued a statement that he would receive an official welcome, and a reception was held in his honour. But by then, alas, Prince Chichibu had already departed this life.

Neither did he live to see the completion that same year of the Prince Chichibu Rugby Stadium, which commemorates for posterity his love for the game and his services to it in Japan. How it delights me to see it steadily gaining in popularity here. I have been told it is the only sports arena in this country named after a specific person. In the post-war years, while baseball stadiums proliferated and fans of the game increased rapidly, rugby lagged behind because although there were people who wanted to play it and promote it, there was no suitable ground. So a group of enthusiasts got together and made a rugby field themselves, with their own bare hands, in part of the outer gardens of the Meiji Shrine. When he heard about it, the Prince, in spite of his illness, made a point of visiting the work-site every time he was in Tokyo.

After seeing his first rugby match during his student days in England, the Prince never missed a match if he could help it, either there or in Japan. I shall never forget the first time I accompanied him to one. It was while we were in Kyoto for Emperor Shōwa's Enthronement, and took place at a prestigious high school so soon after the Ceremony that I did not have time to wash the heavy camellia grease out of my hair. It was all I could do to change out of my heavy ceremonial twelve-layered robe of ancient design into Western dress. My hair had to stay as it was, hidden by a scarf!

When the Oxford University Rugby Team played against Keio University in Tokyo, in September 1952, I was told how the Prince insisted on going all the way down to the field to greet each of the players personally, and how tremendously exhausted he was after climbing the many stairs back up to the royal box. It was evident to me then how deep was his nostalgia for the Oxford of his interrupted studies to which he was never able to return, and his love for the game of rugby.

LAST WILL AND TESTAMENT

The Prince died at Kugenuma in the early dawn of 4 January 1953. His last will and testament, written in a notebook, reads as follows:

> Looking back on the fifty years of my life, I feel nothing but gratefulness. I can only say that the life has ended of a very, very ordinary human being who just happened to be born into a position of special privilege with unlimited benefits.
> I was indeed far too favoured during my last ten years, spending a quiet life of convalescence while countless people

suffering from the same disease as I died in unspeakable privation at a time in history when my people and my country were caught between unprecedented difficult times and hardship. Therefore, not having been able to do anything for my people, nor anything for humanity at large, I would like at least to be of a little use to mankind at the end of my life. If Setsuko is not against it – I mean rather if she can stomach it – I would like my body to undergo an autopsy.

He goes on to name the parts to be dissected and examined and the doctors that he wished to have witness it, including 'others specializing in tuberculosis' and finally adding, 'subject to Setsuko's consent'. He further asks that the body be cremated, that there be no tomb, and that the final rite be very simple, 'since it only concerns Setsuko and me'. And if possible, I wish there to be no religious ceremony of any denomination.

Having obtained His Majesty's consent, an autopsy was performed on the night of 5 January. Since whatever the Prince wished would be my wish too, I raised no objections. The funeral, which took place on a rainy 12 January in the garden of the Toshimagaoka mausoleum, was basically in the Imperial Shintō tradition, but in accordance with the wishes stated in the Prince's will, was performed by those who had been closest to him. His former private secretary, Toshio Maeda, acted as chief priest, assisted by the Prince's classmate Sadao Yamaguchi, who had been his aide-de-camp. The pallbearers were representatives of various sports from the Japan Athletic Association, and musicians from the the Imperial Household Music Department performed pieces such as Beethoven's *Les Adieux* and Tchaikovsky's *Andante Cantabile*. Afterwards, his body was cremated – the first time ever for a member of the Imperial Family – and his ashes were buried in a graveyard in a corner of the mausoleum. It was all very unconventional, but I think it was more or less what the Prince would have wanted, and was made possible by the Emperor's warm understanding and Prince Takamatsu's help.

How you must have loved
Your princely elder brother,
To have helped so much!
How your kindness solaced me,
Dear Prince of Takamatsu!

For the Fortieth Day Observance on 12 February, the Emperor and Empress came over from Hayama to our villa in Kugenuma. Barely a year before, the Prince had supervised the replanting there of some of his favourite plants from our Tokyo property. Among them was a red and white plum in fragrant blossom. The Emperor sighed with deep emotion as he contemplated it, and later sent me this poem:

> *The potted plum-tree:*
>   *How fresh its fragrance fills the air!*
>   *Even though, alas,*
> *My brother is no longer there*
> *To enjoy its purity.*

When the Fiftieth Day Observance was over, visitors paying condolence calls tapered off, and I was alone most of the time, just thinking about the Prince and missing him so. There were times when I wondered if there was not some way to join him without causing too much trouble for those around me. During those times, writing poetry was a consolation.

> *The Empress Mother*
>   *Is gone, and so are you, my Prince;*
>   *What am I to do?*
> *Who am I to lean upon,*
> *How can I go on alone?*

> *Why so soon, my love,*
>   *Did you have to leave this world,*
>   *When so many here*
> *Loved you so, and needed you,*
> *And were loth to let you go?*

In spite of the cold winter rain, over fifty thousand people from the general populace thronged the road outside the mausoleum at the time of the Prince's funeral, and I noticed a great many of them wiping tears from their eyes. They included students, young people, old people, farmers, housewives, office-workers and former soldiers. Most of them were people who had only known the Prince through the newspapers and magazines, but loved and admired him. To them he was the 'Sports Prince' and the 'Mountaineering Prince'.

My mother was a tower of strength and scarcely left my side in the days after my bereavement, when I needed her most. She died in 1969, after a long illness.

> *Many were the times*
> > *I might have gone to pieces,*
> > > *In my heart's despair*
>
> *Had I not been supported*
> *By my mother's tender care.*
>
> *Even when apart,*
> > *As, perforce, most times we were,*
> > > *Knowing she was there*
>
> *Was my only underprop*
> *And my comfort and my stay.*

Just a year before, the Prince had moved a deep-red plum tree to Kugenuma from the Empress Dowager's Palace as a memento of his late mother. This red plum, blossoming later than the red-and-white variety, burst into bloom at the end of February, making me sad all over again.

> *As the evening falls,*
> > *I wonder in what garden*
> > > *They are chatting now:*
>
> *My beloved Prince and Her*
> *Late Majesty, his mother.*

As spring progressed, the trees putting forth new shoots, the flowers, the azure-winged magpie that came to our window at breakfast, for whom we used to put out bread crumbs – everything reminded me of the Prince.

> *Seeing Mount Fuji,*
> > *Always reminds me of you,*
> > > *Beside the window;*
>
> *And birdsong, too,*
> *Always reminds me of you.*
>
> *Of my memories,*
> > *None are happier than those*
> > > *Of mountains and of seas*
>
> *We visited together,*

> *And foreign lands you took me to.*
>
> *I will bear with pride*
> > *Thy name, and try to live*
> > *A life worthy of thee,*
> *Until that day arriveth*
> *When I'm summon'd to thy side.*
>
> *Although my tears*
> > *Will never bring you back to me,*
> > *As well I know,*
> *At night, when I'm all alone,*
> *Tears well up, and flow, and flow.*

THE MITSUMINE KILN

Half a year after the Prince's death, in late July, I returned to our Gotemba villa for a month's stay carrying with me part of the Prince's ashes. How nostalgic it was to return to that town where we had spent more than ten years together knowing both happiness and sadness, and myriad were the memories that came flooding back. Fuji, oh so close, blue and beautiful, manly as ever, welcomed me home.

> *We, and our household*
> > *Spent a decade of our lives*
> > > *Here in this retreat;*
> *Lo, I have brought thy spirit*
> *Back hither with me today.*
>
> *Many were the times*
> > *We trod this path together*
> > > *Which today I climb*
> *Grief-stricken, alone, clutching*
> *Thine ashes to my bosom.*
>
> *In an urn enwrapped*
> > *With silk pure and white as snow*
> > > *Thou hast returned home;*
> *And the townsfolk welcome thee*
> *In fond voices choked with tears.*

> *O house, O garden*
> > *Of fondest remembrances*
> > *If you had voices*
> *You, too, would cry welcome*
> *To his spirit that I bring!*
>
> *Coming home*
> > *To our little mountain nest*
> > *That we loved so well,*
> *May thy spirit find repose*
> *And easeful tranquilty.*
>
> *Dear familiar hut;*
> > *Every aspect of this place,*
> > *Both inside and out,*
> *Is imprinted with thy face*
> *For I see thee everywhere.*

I saw him in my mind's eye constantly. The hills and fields were just as they had always been, as was the birdsong and the chirping of the insects. Nothing had changed. The only thing that was different was the fact the Prince was no longer there in person.

Listening to the birds I thought of the Empress Dowager and our promise to have her stay so she could hear them sing. We had told her how at dawn around 4 a.m., first there is the *canna-canna-canna* of the evening cicada, and then the hoot of an owl, followed by the songs of a paradise flycatcher, Siberian meadow bunting, and great tit, before the cock begins to crow in the poultry house. And then you hear the cuckoo, the brown-eared bulbul, and the screech of the azure-winged magpie. During his long illness, the Prince waking early, learned to know the various songs and the time of day that each bird sang. Alas, I managed to learn only a few. How I regret not having got the Prince to teach me how to identify more of them.

> *Reading a letter*
> > *Here beside this window*
> > *I seem to hear*
> *The dear familiar sound of*
> *His clearing his throat to speak.*
>
> *A whiff of cologne*

> *Left on a garment he wore;*
> *Caressing it, I*
> *Gaze upon it lovingly*
> *Then soon dissolve in tears.*

> *A book he was reading*
> *And well-used pieces from a set*
> *Of Japanese chess*
> *Lie forlornly abandoned*
> *On the stand beside his bed.*

The Prince was very fond of *shōgi* (Japanese chess) and Grand Master Kimura, 8th *dan* player Katō and 7th *dan* player Izumida and others came to play shōgi with him. As he lay in bed he used to try and work out shōgi problems in the newspaper to help beguile away the hours, and whenever he managed to solve one he would send it in, in the name of one of the staff. But so many correct solutions must have been sent in that he was never lucky. He would have been so pleased if they had picked one of his.

There was a brains trust programme on NHK radio that invited questions from listeners, and he used to send those in too. His chosen field was things connected with Britain as well as with animals and plants. I used to help him a lot by looking up things in the encyclopedia. But, alas, they never used any of them. Perhaps his questions were too academic. I do so regret that not even one of the questions of his devising was ever chosen.

> *Warm tears welled up*
> *All over again as I*
> *Offered the first ears*
> *Harvested of this year's corn*
> *To thy spirit this morning.*

There was not a single thing planted by the Prince whether on the hill or in the field but brought back memories of him. The maize, or sweet corn, had become a specialty of the house of which we were proud, and we had served it to so many guests. It was an important staple during the time when food was scarce, and we had planted the variety said to be the most delicious.

> *Finally, at last,*

> *I think I have begun to*
> *Feel myself again*
> *In spite of the sadness,*
> *For 'tis here I feel at home.*

I have kept the Gotemba Villa, with all its memories, as much as possible just as it was, and I try to spend my summers there. All I have changed are things like the height of the desk and the chair in the Prince's beloved study so that I can use them now myself.

For a while I felt like an insect's cast-off skin, lost and bewildered, but I have gradually got back on my feet and found a road to follow, albeit with unsteady steps, for there is much to do. As honorary president of the Japan Anti-Tuberculosis Association I knew that I must devote myself to eradicating the disease that took the Prince's life. I seemed to hear his voice and knew I must heed that voice in addition to helping promote international friendship, too, for his sake. So my days became full with activities both inside Japan and out.

'How Your Highness has changed!' people would say. 'You used to live in the shadow of the Prince, and say so little. Now, you are so assertive.' But I had not changed. I still wept as I gazed at his photograph and I could not have gone on if I had not been able to hear his words of encouragement in my mind.

The fifth summer after his death, Prince and Princess Takamatsu and Prince and Princess Mikasa were very kind and helped me organize a cheerful pottery-making session. The first since Prince Chichibu left us.

> *We princely brothers*
> *And sisters gathered at the*
> *Mitsumine kiln*
> *For a day of memories*
> *As we fashioned pottery!*

> *After many years*
> *Smoke rising again from the*
> *Mitsumine kiln;*
> *How happy, I feel certain,*
> *My dear Prince is sure to be.*

What had led to the Prince having the kiln made in the summer of

1950 was his commissioning of a teapot by the potter Hajime Katō as a birthday present for the Empress Dowager. When the teapot was delivered, he had a good look at it and it gave him the idea of taking up pottery as a hobby, and he proceeded to take lessons from Katō. I think he also hoped it would help to make known the excellence of Gotemba clay. Mixed with fine Seto kaolin Gotemba clay gave pieces a recognizable local colour.

A long time had elapsed since I had made a pretence of making pottery, and compared with the Prince's younger brothers and their wives I was just an experimentalist, but it brought back memories of working beside the Prince, moulding clay and turning the wheel with him, and made me feel wonderfully at peace.

> *We have gathered here,*
> *All of us together,*
> *In memory of thee;*
> *Enjoying learning how*
> *And then making pottery.*
>
> *While remembering*
> *Those nostalgic days of yore*
> *We fashion the clay*
> *As rain beats on the window*
> *And a little cuckoo sings.*

The other day, when my Chief Lady-in-Waiting Shimizu was looking for something, she came across an old diary of mine. It was for the year 1951, and my eye was caught by the following entries about our pottery making:

> November 10. Saturday. Fine.
> Fuji beautiful again today.
>   Teacups etc. (the Prince's) put in second firing a few days ago finished already. Was travelling so mine not ready. So early this morning I tried planing the bases with dubious result as only learned how to use wheel day before yesterday.
> 10.30. Prince, surprisingly, accompanies me to 50th Anniversary celebrations at Gotemba High School. Speaks from the platform to everyone's joy. It is first time since recuperation. Rests in the afternoon. Just before 11, the potter, Mr Katō, comes to Villa for second time, bringing his second son Yoshiaki as assistant. From about 3 p.m. start unglazed firing. Firing stopped at 8.

November 11. Sunday. Fine.
Clear and bright. Fuji white with frost.
Busy from early morning preparing for the visit by Prince and Princess Chumbot of Thailand who are now in Japan. Decorate dining table with *ryunogiku* chrysanthemums and gentians still blooming in the outer garden, arranged in a shallow rectangular fabric-textured ceramic dish. They arrived at 10 past 12 accompanied by military and naval attachés. Entertain them after lunch by letting them decorate, with Mr Katō's help, some of the unglazed tea bowls and small cups from the kiln. Their Highnesses gleefully picked up brushes and painted delightful pictures of children and flowers. Prince Chichibu and Princess Chumbot produced a joint piece together. After 3 we took them to see the pottery workshop, where their car picked them up for their return journey.

November 12. Monday. Fine, later cloudy. Rain at night. Temperature eases.
In the morning, all the members of the staff took turns visiting the pottery workshop to decorate and glaze the pieces they had each made with such great pains. Our neighbours the Murases and the Kawanabes came to glaze theirs too. At 10 the Prince did his for half an hour, returning to receive a guest at 10.30. We have lunch with Katō and his son. (This time it was his elder son Tatsumi who came to assist.) The Katōs were busy all afternoon too with the decorating and glazing. We watched the master as he deftly painted pinetrees and other such designs on a succession of plates and *kumidashi* cups the Prince had commisisioned. It looks so easy. But you take up the brush yourself to have a go and the paint (iron) is thick and lumpy and hard to manage. Most things seem difficult when you try to do them yourself! Mr Katō absorbed in the glazing until suppertime. After supper he dealt with packing the kiln. There were so many small pieces of different shapes it took an inordinate amount of time, and while we went to see from time to time until nearly 10 o'clock, we finally went to bed before it was finished.

November 13. Tuesday. Cloudy.
Packing the kiln took until 1 a.m. After a short rest, Mr Katō got up at 4 a.m. and lit the kiln for the main firing. The first firing had gone on overnight and was extinguished the following morning, whereas this time it was kindled at dawn and designed to be completed during the daytime. I had no idea until then what back-breaking work it was!
The Prince was still feeling fine, and went down at 10 to help

check on the heat of the kiln. After observing that the heat was satisfactorily rising moment by moment the Prince stayed for some time in the workshop practising using the potter's wheel. He reached a new stage of proficiency. The heat of the kiln was increasing steadily. By just past 5 it had nearly reached 1200 degrees.

Around the clouds of black smoke scarlet flames two feet high shot heavenwards from the chimney like pillars of fire, just as the full moon rose over Otome Tōge (Maiden Pass), directly on the right, in startlingly striking contrast. The fire was extinguished at 6 o'clock. With tremendous relief, potter Katō and son called it a day and went off to an early bed.

November 14, Wednesday. Weather clear.

A rare balmy autumn day with Fuji resplendent in beauty. In the lower garden, where the ivy wove threads of scarlet in the pine woods, we saw a jay hopping from branch to branch while chirping merrily. Early in the morning Mr Katō appeared at the kiln, as eager as we, and opened up a section at the top. By around 9, the kiln temperature had dropped to 100 degrees, and at about 9.30 I attended the *kamadashi*, or kiln unpacking, alone. (The Prince had visitors coming for lunch and was obliged to rest until 11.30 as a cautionary measure.) Hearts beat fast with excitement as an amazing 200 items of tremendous variety emerged, from lustrous black tea bowls to soberly refined pieces in the style of the Korean Li dynasty. In spite of being packed in so tightly there was hardly a failure among them, to Mr Katō's great joy and my relief.

Apart from the Prince's ornament in the shape of a squirrel, his other works were his first ones turned on the wheel. Mr Katō had taken a special interest in helping with these and they turned out splendidly. The handsome glaze of the tea bowl was especially beautiful. We took them all to the sitting room to look at them, and the Prince was extremely happy with the results. As for the neighbours, their reactions alternated between joy and disappointment. It was all so much fun we almost forgot to look after our guests properly. At 11.30 the Prince went down to the workshop with us to thank Mr Katō the potter and his son for all they had done.

1 p.m. Today's guests, the new Swedish Minister Baron Lagerfelt and his wife arrived. The other guests Mr and Mrs Okamoto came by train. Needless to say, we were able to offer them the best possible welcome – unusually fine weather and Fuji at her most beautiful! After lunch we took them to see the sheep shed and the pottery workshop where we showed them what we

had taken out that morning from the kiln. While there the Prince gave the Lagerfelts a brief demonstration on the potter's wheel. After watching the process with obvious delight, the Minister and his wife left.

The second firing had ended successfully to everyone's relief, and as night came on the weather turned cold.

From the five days of this diary you not only get an idea of the sort of life we led at Gotemba but also how important pottery-making was to the Prince. After that summer of 1958 when I, together with my Imperial brothers-in-law and their wives, kneaded clay, turned the wheel, and kindled the fire in the Mitsumine kiln, we made a point of gathering at the kiln every summer if we possibly could. For we felt that it would make the Prince's spirit happy for the fire to be lit in the kiln and the smoke therefrom to billow heavenwards.

Smoke rising once more
From the keepsake you left us –
The Mitsumine kiln;
Joyfully we gathered here
To knead clay again this year.

The area on our property where the cowshed, sheep shed and hen house were is reverting to its original natural state, which does not make me sad at all. That the vestiges of our struggle to live in the immediate post-war period should disappear with the advent of prosperity would certainly make the Prince happy.

Burnet and thistle
And the fragrant lemon grass
Now begin to grow;
Gardens turning wild again:
'Twould delight the Prince, I know.

CHAPTER TWELVE

INTERNATIONAL FRIENDSHIP

◆

THE 'LITTLE HOUSE'

The Prince had been gone a year when I returned to Tokyo to live in the small part of our house that had escaped the fire-bombing. During the seventeen or eighteen years I lived there I enjoyed many happy contacts with people from other lands. One of the happiest events I experienced while there was the marriage of the present Emperor, when Crown Prince, to Michiko Shōda.

Speaking of Crown Prince Akihito, I remember meeting Mrs Vining, who had come to teach him English. Coming from America, where there was no royal family, she sought advice from my mother on Japanese court etiquette, and they became good friends. She was a lovely lady, elegant and refined, wise and intelligent.

My mother also advised Princess Michiko on court etiquette before her wedding. I think the Empress, as she is now, must have fond memories of my mother from those days, because every May 8th, the anniversary of my mother's death, she sends me flowers from her garden. Freshly picked, the flowers are sometimes wrapped in beautiful handmade *washi* paper, and sometimes artistically arranged in baskets. I appreciate Her Majesty's thoughtful kindness, and am sure my mother does too.

In November 1961, when Princess Alexandra came to Japan on an official mission to present the Emperor with a letter of goodwill greetings from the Queen, I was chosen to officially welcome Her Royal Highness because of Prince Chichibu's close connection with Britain, having studied at Oxford University and been the Honorary

Patron of the Japan-British Society, which position I now held. Afterwards, she wanted to see a social welfare organization, so I accompanied her to see some of the activities of the Japan Red Cross. She was extremely interested in everything, and although we only had a few minutes to spare, I brought her home, to see how I lived. She was immensely intrigued by my *hori-gotatsu*, the heated sunken pit in the tatami floor under the low table. She immediately tried it out, and seemed to find the idea delightful. 'You can sit here and do all sorts of things,' she said, looking as if she would have liked to stay longer. She had only just been born when I met her parents, the Duke and Duchess of Kent, at the Coronation of her uncle King George VI.

While British royal children were usually taught at home, Princess Alexandra went to an ordinary school, and then studied nursing in a hospital. Princess Alexandra was the first member of the British Royal Family to visit Japan since the Duke of Gloucester came thirty-two years earlier, and I could not help but think what a perfect goodwill ambassador she was for Queen Elizabeth's new reign.

It was Prince Charles who called my post-war Tokyo home 'The Little House'. Approaching it from across the garden of the Crown Prince's palace, it did look tiny. All the members of the British Royal Family who came to Japan have been to 'The Little House'.

Besides being Honorary Patron of the Japan-British Society, I was also Honorary Patron of the Japan-Sweden Society, and so in 1962 I paid a visit to both countries, as well as stopping over in Paris and Copenhagen.

It had been twenty-five years since the Prince and I had travelled so happily together by ship to attend King George VI's coronation in London, and now both men were no longer living, and here I was flying alone by air, bound for that nostalgic city. The intervening unfortunate war notwithstanding, nothing had changed in the warmth with which the Royal Family and friends and acquaintances welcomed me. I was greatly touched to have the Dame Grand Cross of the Order of the British Empire bestowed upon me, and felt a renewed sense of responsibility in my capacity as Honorary Patron of the Japan-British Society, and my duty to nurture good relations between our countries.

On this trip I was able to do things of personal significance I had long dreamed of. I had been unable to accompany the Prince to Oxford the time before. I shall never forget the thrill of finally being able to see for myself the place that had meant so much to him in his young days. To see the same great elms in the grounds, beneath which deer still roamed, and the minnows swimming in the same little River Cherwell. His old Magdalen College rooms were exactly the same as he had described them to me in detail so many times. As I touched the desk and the chair, it seemed as if he had only just left there. What moved me most deeply was to discover that he had replicated the arrangement of the furniture exactly in his study in both our Tokyo residence and in Gotemba.

I met scouts who remembered the Prince, and I saw the library, and the hall where he had received his degree. I also went to University College and saw the cherry tree planted by the present Emperor when he visited it as Crown Prince. How happy he would be, I thought, when I told him on my return how tall it had grown. I lunched with Dr Bouse, the President of Magdalen College, where the guests included my brother Ichirō, who was working in a bank in London, and Kazuko Asō, daughter of Prime Minister Shigeru Yoshida.

Five years later, I visited England again for an eleven-day visit to take part in the 75th anniversary celebrations of the Japan Society. As I arrived at Heathrow on 27 January 1967, I could see lots of familiar faces there to welcome me including several friends of the Prince's from Oxford days now active in politics, who later arranged for me to attend a parliamentary debate. I remember how they looked up and smiled, as I sat in the Visitor's Gallery.

Five hundred people – Japanese, British, and members of the Royal Family – came to the Anniversary Dinner at the Savoy Hotel. I said, 'To see me here, looking so happy, surrounded by all of you, must be making the Prince jealous!' My remark was greeted by warm, spontaneous laughter. I know everyone wished he could have been there with us.

I felt like the princess in the film *Roman Holiday* when friends took me to a pub – something I could never dream of doing in Japan – although the Prince had told me how people looked the other way if the Prince of Wales chose to buy sandwiches from late-night street stalls. The British, he said, feel that even royalty have a right to privacy.

It was a great thrill to find the riverside house in Walton-on-Thames where I was born and spent my first eight months. It had not changed at all. I just gazed at it from the outside for a long time. I spent my last day on the beautiful, picturesque Isle of Wight with old friends. Passing the night in their old fourteenth century stone house, I felt as if I were part of a romantic tale of long ago. We could see the white chalk cliffs of southern England as we took a walk next morning. As I left for the airport, I felt how strong the bonds were that bound me to Britain, and I hoped peace would last forever and that I would be able to come back again.

In April 1969, I received the Order of the Seraphim from the King of Sweden, and in October, I was asked to become Honorary Patron of the Traffic Accident Orphans Scholarship Society. My days were already full with activities connected with the Anti-Tuberculosis Association, my two international friendship societies, and the various cultural and sports organizations I had inherited the honorary patronage of from the Prince, but we had no children, and I no longer had to look after the Prince, and felt he would want me to do something more in the way of welfare work to benefit society, so I accepted. Time sped by for me like the proverbial arrow, which helped me cope with the grief of losing my beloved mother.

In 1971, their Majesties the Shōwa Emperor and Empress made their world tour. It was a dream the Emperor had long entertained, ever since his European tour as Prince Regent in 1921. My fervent prayers for a safe journey for them were embodied in my farewell gift to Their Majesties of a tiny ornamental tiger, an animal traditionally said to travel 'A thousand leagues there and a thousand leagues back.' From everything I heard, the Emperor's simple, unaffected sincerity, and the Empress's warm smile earned them respect and affection wherever they went. It was marvellous being able to follow Their Majesties' journey daily on television. How the Prince would have enjoyed that! He had only seen TV transmissions in their experimental stage.

I was built a lovely, comfortable new house in 1972. Although of concrete, it is a Japanese-style bungalow, designed by the architect Isoya Yoshida. It is only about half as large as the house the Prince and I lived in before the fire-bombing, but seemed enormous to me after 'The Little House'. While it was being built, I feared the wild pheasants I used to feed would forget all about me, but to my delight, they were soon back. It took us humans a little longer to get used to the new house, with its air conditioning and other modern conveniences. 'If only the Prince were here!' my servants and I would say to one another. 'What would he make of it all?'

November saw the publication of 'The Life of Prince Yasuhito' based on his diaries and papers, which I had asked the Prince's old mountaineering friend and distinguished journalist Saburō Matsukata to compile and edit. It must have been no easy task to go through the vast amount of material and sift out the facts with meticulous care and produce such a readable and complete portrait of the Prince. It was something I had wanted as a memorial to him, and the completion of the book filled me with great emotion. It had taken Saburō Matsukata fifteen years, during which time he not only led a Mount Everest expedition, but was seriously ill.

TEA WITH THE QUEEN MOTHER

In 1974, I was invited by the British Government to visit England again. Sadly, news of the Duke of Gloucester's grave illness coincided with my departure, and the invitation to spend one night with them had to be cancelled. I had rather dreaded the news conference at the Japanese Embassy on my first day, fearing some awkward questions about Japan's reaction to the oil crisis and the Labour government in Britain, but the young journalists could not have been nicer. After another nostalgic visit to Oxford, it was with a heavy heart that I visited Kensington Palace to offer my condolences on the death of the Duke of Gloucester.

That evening's dinner given for me by the Government went on as scheduled, and in the four days up to the funeral, no royal engagements were cancelled, from lunch with the Queen at Buckingham Palace to tea with the Queen Mother. The kindness and consideration of the Royal Family and the warmth of their hospitality in spite of being in mourning, touched me deeply, and was a revelation to me. Even Alice, Duchess of Gloucester, the day before the Duke's funeral, sent a message to say she would like to see me. She looked so worn and emaciated after all she had been through that I could not keep back my tears. Our mutual loss seemed to bind us together more deeply than ever. I attended the Duke's funeral next day in St George's Chapel at Windsor Castle.

I had tea with the Queen Mother at Clarence House after lunching with the Queen. She was dressed in black, and the lavender stock, arranged in a beautiful vase, gave a suggestion of mourning. The camera and Japanese vase I had brought her were already displayed on a table. I explained that the vase was the work of Yaichi Kusube, and that the camera produced the date on each photograph taken. It was then a novelty and Her Majesty seemed much intrigued.

No-one waited on us. The Queen Mother herself served me with tea, bread-and-butter, tomato sandwiches and *petit fours*. We had not met since the late King George VI's Coronation thirty-seven years before, so there was plenty to talk about. She was anxious to know whether the Emperor and Empress had really and truly enjoyed their visit to Britain the previous year. She seemed relieved when I assured her that they still spoke of it often, fondly recalling memories. She appeared to have a great affection and admiration for the Japanese Imperial Family. She gave me a little china powder box when I left. What touched me most deeply was the fact that there were no other guests, enabling us to enjoy a lovely, leisurely heart-to-heart conversation over tea. I admired the beautiful climbing roses in her garden, and was able to tell her of my visit the previous day to Hampton Court to see the hundred peonies given by our Emperor and Empress. They were doing so well I thought their colour and fragrance – unique among oriental flowers – might make them a star attraction there in years to come. I said I knew Their Majesties would be delighted to hear how the peonies were flourishing.

My full schedule of engagements included a visit to the House of Lords, where Prince Charles happened to be giving his maiden speech as Prince of Wales. Having known him since he was a child, I was impressed by his youthful dignity and boldness of argument, his spirited embracing of the cause of youth, without being in the least affected or awkward. What promise! I thought, and was moved to tears. He spoke so frankly of his ideas about sports and leisure.

After attending the funeral of the Duke of Gloucester, I spent two delightful days in Scotland as the guest of Sir William Keswick, flying there from London in an aircraft of the Queen's Flight. He and his family lived in Dumfries in a handsome white chalk manor house set in a vast green pasture where cows grazed serenely. From the moment I arrived, not only my hosts, but everyone in the village wanted to know about 'Tomo-san'. How was he? What was he doing now? By

'Tomo-san' they meant His Imperial Highness Prince Tomohito of Mikasa, my nephew, of whom I have always been very fond, and who calls me his favourite aunt. The Keswicks looked after Prince Tomohito while he was studying in England. He spent his holidays with them, and was made to feel like one of the family. He had told me how it was because of them and the people of this village that he had learned to love and appreciate Britain. I was delighted to find how fond they all were of him. The villagers put on a show of Scottish dancing with bagpipes especially for me, and I was persuaded to dance, too. It was an unforgettable evening, under a sky full of stars.

On 9 October 1978, at the British Embassy in Tokyo, I was invested with the insignia of an Honorary Dame Grand Cross of the Order of St Michael and St George by Princess Margaret acting on behalf of the Queen. It was an undeserved honour, which I consider was really bestowed on the late Prince Chichibu and the Japan-British Society he had represented, rather than on me, and symbolized the close ties between our two countries that began half a century ago.

The following year, I was invited to London again. After a busy ten days mostly filled with official engagements but which included a delightful three-day stay with the Duchess of Gloucester and her family at their country seat, I flew home via Washington, DC and a nostalgic visit to my old school and classmates. I was met at the airport by my young nephew Prince Norihito – then of Mikasa, but now Takamado – who was studying in Canada.

The old Embassy I lived in as a child had been replaced by a palatial new building, but the Friends School had not changed at all. All was just as I remembered, except that the Headmaster now was a man young enough to be my son. There was Mildred on the wisteria-enveloped veranda to welcome me with open arms. Although she had a beautiful daughter with her, the fifty-one years melted away and it seemed like yesterday that we sat with our desks side by side in the classroom. Many other old schoolmates were assembled there too for a wonderful, nostalgic party.

I was invited to England again in 1981 on the occasion of the opening of the Great Japan Exhibition at the Royal Academy, which coincided with the 90th anniversary of the Japan Society. Prince Charles and Crown Prince Naruhito – the present Emperor – were the joint patrons, and I made a great many speeches. On my way home, I paid an especially nostalgic visit to Switzerland where, after officially calling on the International Red Cross and World Health Organization in Geneva, I rode by funicular from Zermat to Gornergratt, to gaze at the Prince's beloved Matterhorn, of which I had heard so much. To see it with my own eyes was a dream come true.

Until now my travels had mostly been to Britain, and had never included Asia, but in 1985 I accepted an invitation from the Nepal Tuberculosis Prevention Association, and also visited Thailand.

'DO AS YOU PLEASE MORE'

Nowadays, I spend more time than ever in my rose garden. The Prince and I were both passionately fond of rose-growing, but had, of course, to abandon them for vegetables during the war. I learned from my British friends that in England you do not cut your roses and give them away, but invite friends to see them growing in your garden! I try to follow this custom, but do give bunches to those who are too old or infirm to come to me. Ever since the Prince died, I find growing roses keeps me from being lonely. Every morning, I gaze into their faces, and talk to my roses. They seem to appreciate your tender loving care, and will always produce fine blooms for you in return.

On account of my advanced age, I had asked to be excused from official duties, and when Crown Prince Akihito succeeded the late Shōwa Emperor in 1990, I put on my *robe décolletée* a few days before the 12 November Enthronement, and went to pay my respects to the new Emperor and Empress, but I did not attend the Enthronement ceremony or the receptions afterwards.

Although they were very busy, the Prince and Princess of Wales, who were among the representatives of sixty countries in Japan for the occasion, came to see me the day before the Enthronement. Prince Charles hugged me and greeted me with a kiss. 'Why aren't you coming to the ceremony?' he asked, urging, 'Do come! I'll look after you.' His reassuring words, so full of affection, not only encouraged me tremendously, but enabled me to know what it would be like to be gently rebuked by a son. Prince Charles always used to call me his 'Japanese grandmother'.

I decided then and there to attend one of the morning tea-parties. They were divided into two sections – heads of state at the Emperor's Palace, and crown princes and other members of royalty at the Crown

Prince's Palace. I attended the latter.

When I arrived, I found a table and chair had been provided just for me. How considerate of the young Crown Prince, I thought, and was immensely proud of the way he had grown into such a charming host. I had not expected so many people would come up and talk to me. I had a lovely time, and when Prince Charles appeared, his look of satisfaction as he watched me holding court made me suspect that he had had a hand in it, too.

The Prince and Princess of Wales were only in Japan four days, but I saw them three times. One of those times Prince Charles lectured me sternly.

'Your Highness, you should do as you please more, like our Queen Mother. You mustn't be so restrained, and so worried about what you do. Just do whatever you want. It'll be good for you.'

The Queen Mother was older than I, he told me, yet she was in fine health, and flew to France in her own aeroplane, or anywhere else she fancied. When I told him you cannot do that sort of thing in Japan – or rather I could not, he scolded me.

'Don't say you can't, just go ahead and do it!'

I smiled. But, silently, to herself, his 'Japanese grandmother' said, 'Thank you, Charles!'

The Prince of Wales had injured his right arm in a fall from his horse before coming to Japan. It was still painful, but he felt he should come, since there was no one to take his place. He kept his arm so cleverly concealed that no one noticed it during his stay in Japan. How I admired his sense of duty and responsibility!

My health has gradually improved and although I have passed my 80th birthday, I have begun to take up some of my public duties again.That same year that Akihito became Emperor, marking the end of the Shōwa reign and the beginning of the new reign called Heisei, the Japan Anti-Tuberculosis Association celebrated its fiftieth anniversary. I learned that over two hundred thousand people still suffered from the disease in this country, and eight million people each year were contracting it worldwide. How much there still was to be done! I remembered the words of Her Majesty, Empress Nagako – now the Empress Dowager – who had said to me, 'I know you will do your best.'

Mindful of her words,

I am filled with new resolve.
So much still to do.
For in their various fields,
So many have done so much.

The Poems
Romanized version of the poems in the memoir

◆

makoto koso/itsuwari ōki/yo no nami o norikiru fune no/chikara narikere	p. 106
yo no hito no/kozorite iwau/magokoro o munashiku naseso/futamoto no matsu	p. 112
mayowaji to/chikaishi kokoro/yurugu nari okiagaru hi no/ate mo nakereba	p. 164
seki no oto/kawaru ni tsukete/hito shirezu yamai susumu to/kokoro modayuru	p. 165
kanashisa ni/namida hatenashi/mioshie ni yorite kyō aru/kono mi omoeba	p. 179
animiya no/mikokoro kumite/tsukushimasu minasake ureshi/takamatsu no miya	p. 183
hachi no ume/sono ka mo kiyoku/nioedomo waga otōto no/sugata wa miezu	p. 187
hahamiya mo/kimi mo imasazu/kyō yori wa nani o tanomite/ikin kono yo o	p. 188

The Poems

kimi wa haya/yo o sarimashinu/hito mina ni
kaku shitawaretsu/oshimaretsu shite   p. 188

tomosureba/kuzuren to suru/waga kokoro
sasauru mono wa/haha no minasake   p. 188

tsune hi goro/au ni aranedo/haha imasu
sono koto nomi ga/tayori narishi o   p. 189

kono yoi wo/waga se no miya wa/hahamiya to
izuku no sono ni/katarimasuran   p. 189

fuji mitemo/kimi o zo omou/mado chikaku
kotori kiku ni mo/kimi o zo omou   p. 189

omoide wa/koyonaku tanoshi/yama ni umi ni
totsu kuni ni sae/tsuredachi shi hi no   p. 189

mina ni hajizu/ikin to zo omou/itsu no hi ka
kimi ga mimoto ni/mesaruru hi made   p. 189

nakebatote/kaeranu kimi to/shiri nagara
hitoke naki yo wa/namida ni kururu   p. 190

mikotoba ni/kokoro o shimete/tsukushi koshi
michi sorezore no/hagemi o tatau   p. 190

yuki kienu / yama no oku ni mo / ochikochi no
hai-matsu tsutai / uguisu no naku   p. 190

tomodomo ni / totose o sumishi / kono io ni
mitama sasagete / kyōshimo kaeru   p. 190

ikutabi ka / kayoishi michi o / kyōto ieba
mitama idakite / noboru kanashisa   p. 190

shiraginu no / mihako to narite / kaerimashishi
kimi o mukaete / sato wa koe nomu   pp. 190/1

omoide no / niwa yo yakata yo / koe araba
nare mo nakuramu / mitama mukaete p. 191

suminareshi / yamabe no io ni / kaeri kite
kimi ga mitama mo / yasukeku masamu p. 191

suminareshi / io no uchi soto / izuku ni mo
arishi misugata / mazamaza ukabu p. 191

kono mado ni / fumi yomi oreba / natsukashiki
on-sekibarai no / kikiyuru gotoshi pp. 191/2

utsuri-ka no / nokoru meshimono / furete mitsu
nagame mitsushite / namida ni kururu p. 192

yomisashi no / sho to tenare no / shōgi-goma
nokoru mo kanashi / beddo no soba ni p. 192

atsuki namida / mata komiageru / hatsudori no
tōmorokoshi o / kesa wa sonaete pp. 192/3

hisabisa ni / ware ni kaerishi / kokochi shite
kanashiki uchi ni / ochitsuku wa koko p. 193

harakara no / miya-uchi yorite / omoide no
kamaba ni hito hi / sue tsukurimasu p. 193

hisabisa ni / mitsumine-gama ni / tatsu kemuri
kimi mo ureshi to / misona wa suramu p. 194

kimi o shinobu / kokoro hitotsu ni / tsudoi tsutsu
suemono tsukuri / manabu tanoshisa p. 194

arishi hi o / natsukashimi tsutsu / tsuchi hineru
mado utsu ame ni / naku hototogisu p. 197

mikatami no / kama ni kotoshi mo / kemuri tate
tanoshiku tsudou / tsuchi hineri shite p. 197

waremokō, / karu-kaya, azami / medachi kite
no ni modori-yuku / niwa o tanoshimu   *pp. 206/7*

APPENDIX

INTRODUCTORY REMARKS BY DOROTHY BRITTON

◆

Written in July 1949, this essay was not published until November, 1996 in *Chuo Koron* magazine together with reminiscences of the Prince by Princess Takamatsu, who found the manuscript of this and one other essay among Princess Chichibu's papers.

Of Emperor Shōwa's three brothers, Prince Takamatsu was next in age to Prince Chichibu, and the two couples were very close. Princess Takamatsu agonized over what to do with Prince Chichibu's last two essays, and consulted the surviving brother Prince Mikasa, who said: 'By all means, publish them!'

Princess Takamatsu remembers her brother-in-law as kind and considerate, and famous for his thriftiness – often wearing old shoes and patched trousers! He was, she also writes, far more aggressive and assertive than her own shy and retiring prince; exceedingly brave and plucky too, with such courage of his convictions that led him sometimes to give way to thunderous outbursts. Regarding the 1930s coups, she relates how the rumours of his involvement gradually became the accepted theory. But she emphatically stresses that she, personally, never considered it to be the truth. She knew for a fact that her husband's phone call to Prince Chichibu that morning was the very first communication he had about the *nii/nii-roku (2/26)*, and that his decision to hurry to Tokyo was solely in order to stand by his brother the Emperor and protect him, together with the other two princes.

This essay, however, is almost certainly connected with a 'happening' of quite a different sort, which did involve the Prince, and has just come to light.

After her biography of Emperor Shōwa's chief chamberlain Grand Steward Michiji Tajima (Tokyo, 2002), Kyōko Katō published a volume entitled: *'Emperor Shōwa, Michji Tajima, and Shigeru Yoshida' (Tokyo, 2006)*. In it she describes what Tajima referred to in his diary as 'The Prince Chichibu Incident', which caused some agitation in imperial and occupation circles. On 13 July 1949, General MacArthur's aide, Colonel Bunker, summoned Tajima and showed him the text of an interview of Prince Chichibu by Ian Mutsu, the United Press correspondent, in which, he said, the Prince had criticized the occupation. The colonel ordered Tajima to undertake that the Emperor ensure that no such public criticisms be made in future by members of the Imperial Family.

Prince Chichibu maintained that Mutsu had misrepresented – or mistranslated – his words, which, he said, had in fact not been a criticism of the occupation so much as a rebuke addressed to the Japanese people to make them aware of their own shortcomings. The interview seems never to have appeared anywhere, so must have been censored. But whatever it was the prince said was very probably along the lines of this essay, judging by the date. Also, perhaps coincidentally, just around that time Ian Mutsu, who later became a successful documentary film producer (for whom, by the way, I composed many musical scores) may have been formulating his first opus, *Japan Awake*, which was a highly successful 'message to the Japanese people never again to allow dictatorial rule of their country'. What a pity Colonel Bunker did not think of arranging a meeting between General MacArthur, Prince Chichibu and Ian Mutsu. It might have been a useful colloquy.

Mutsu was the son of a distinguished Japanese count, and his British mother had once taught English to Prince Chichibu.

A Critique of the Occupation Policy
By HIH Yasuhito, Prince Chichibu

◆

I do not intend to discuss here Japan's mistaken policies or behaviour in the territories we occupied between the time of the China Incident and the Pacific War. I shall shelve that question, not because I am trying to affect ignorance, but because I have not the time to undertake the tremendous amount of research and self-criticism that would be involved.

Likewise, I shall not touch on the inevitable psychological aspect of the US army's occupation as victors, or practical factors such as military facilities and management expenditure.

There is much that we must be grateful for in the policy of the US occupation: their food policy, their sanitation policy, their policy of promoting Japan as a nation of culture and democracy. Although there is room for criticism there, we must first be grateful and not complain. That is most important.

The criticisms that follow are based on my conclusions after four years of the occupation. Naturally, there have been some wrong attitudes on the part of the Japanese; and the fact that the leaders on the Japanese side have sometimes misled the US policy-makers gives much cause for reflection and criticism.

While it is the American armed forces that are at the core of the occupation, its policies are based on fundamental American principles, and are carried out by various boards and committees in charge of dealings with Japan and the far east, but they cannot implement decisive policies on their own.

Besides that, circumstances inevitably have changed with the times, even in America itself, and with them the people's attitude towards Japan; so it is no use attacking occupation policies for wobbling. If Americans had regarded us four years ago the way they regard us today, things would be quite different now.

The intense and thorough study of Japan and the Japanese made by the Americans during the war could not have been more different from the attitude of the Japanese towards America: it was like the difference between light and darkness. I can only say how much I respect and admire them for this. But even then it was not enough; the early occupation policy of the Americans went too far in some things and guessed wrongly in others, causing much of the confusion today.

But it was probably only natural that there should be some confusion of judgement, for it was, after all, a country considered hostile up until then occupying a previously enemy country, even though it was a peaceful, orderly occupation.

Thinking that Japan was a totalitarian nation like Germany, and acting in accordance with the Potsdam Declaration, it is not surprising that the Americans started out by trying to make us a revolutionary democracy all at once.

It was said that some of the policy-makers were supporters of the New Deal, now out of favour in America, and that like we ourselves did in Manchuria they may have wanted to try in Japan what they could not achieve in America. There was also the usual extreme sectionalism, as well as a lack of unanimity of opinion. Besides all that, various things combined to cause a confusion of priorities, and wrong consequences.

Now let us take a look at the question of ideology. It probably could not have been helped, since the occupation consists of an alliance of nations, but their version of democracy, based on the principles of freedom of speech, religion and thought, tolerates communism – which absolutely denies those freedoms – and so the Americans immediately set free the communists, who had been political prisoners, giving them a tremendous break.

The Japanese general public's ignorance with regard to ideology, and the many years their freedom of thought was suppressed, had robbed the people of their power of judgement. So now that they are released from suppression and presented with a flood of ideologies the general public have no idea at all which is good and which is bad and are apt to embrace whatever appeals to mass psychology, quite unconditionally and uncritically. And it is a distinctive feature of a time of revolutionary reform to react by indiscriminately rejecting everything from the past. Recently GHQ has been emphasizing the evils of communism – but it's too late now, is all one can say!

To say the Japanese lack the power of criticism and have a tendency to follow blindly is not quite correct. It is more that the nation and the people were utterly dumbfounded by their unprecedented encounter with defeat, and when all had fallen into disorder, they found it impossible to be calm and composed even when ordered to do so.

My next point concerns freedom. After the Manchurian Incident, freedom was eroded bit by bit, and by the time of the war, none was left at all; then came the occupation, which stressed freedom in every respect, in reaction to which people rushed off in the opposite direction even to the extent of self-indulgence and debauchery. That sort of thing would be unthinkable to people like the Europeans and Americans who from birth are naturally ingrained with the fundamentals of freedom at home, at school and in society; but to the Japanese, whose freedom has been repressed for years, some seemed to have no idea that freedom has limits and there were those who caused chaos by misusing, abusing and perverting it.

The Americans were not sufficiently aware of the extreme immaturity of the Japanese in regard to community living. Japanese people grossly lack training and education – both in school and in the home – in how to behave as members of society. We've heard for years about the need for more public spiritedness and social morality, but the situation has never got any better.

I am inclined to think that not enough importance is given in Japan to the idea of standing on one's own feet. Children abroad are taught from an early age that they must study towards a trade or profession in order to be able to fend for themselves. Parents have a tendency to do too much for children here in Japan, so they grow up lacking in self-reliance and independence.

If a well-regulated revolutionary reform had been planned in defeated Japan, positive measures regarding such things as the politics and economy should have been more strongly promoted. Leaving the government in place and giving it considerable authority no doubt lightened the burden of the occupying forces, but it allowed the Japanese to forget their defeat in the war and let them off too easily. They were allowed to lose their determination to prepare for greater hardship than the execution of the war in their reconstruction of defeated Japan. But rather than attempting, with national and racial solidarity, to surmount the difficulties resulting from the aforementioned ideological confusion and misunderstanding of the concept of freedom, it led to rampant inter-factional struggles for power and self-centred black-marketing.

In party government, where the people are the constituency, you must woo the short-sighted general public, so you cannot decisively carry out bold policies. It is especially so in times like present-day Japan when there are no outstanding politicians. It is safe to say that no constructive, earnest efforts have been expended. That is why I think strong, forceful leadership by the occupation forces was necessary, with the cabinet left as merely an executive machine. The post-war cabinets will probably shirk responsibility by telling you that with the 'house on top of the roof' (GHQ above them) they could not form any consistent policy. The occupation's acceptance of this sort of excuse was a great mistake.

I must also severely criticize the direct importation of American systems that do not fit Japanese conditions. For instance, I have a feeling we are rushing too quickly into things like the 6-3 school education system and the autonomous police system. Whether it is the weak attitude of the Japanese authorities, or their irresponsibility, or a lack of sufficient effort by the Americans to understand the real state of affairs in Japan, I cannot help but think that the way the occupation authorities do things shows a tendency to push things through indiscriminately according to theoretical *kijō keikaku*, or 'desk-plans', formulated at a central office in the USA!

INDEX

Air-raids, 166-9
Aizu, 33-8, 40, 44, 46, 54, 58-61, 83, 89, 91, 97, 100-105, 115, 126, 136
Aizu spirit, 40, 44, 46, 58-61, 91
Andō, Teruzō, 11, 13, 17
Anglo-Japanese Alliance, 5, 31
Anti-Tubersulosis Society, 150, 152-3, 164, 181, 193, 201, 206
Apology, 18
Asō, Kazuko, 200
Asō, Takeji, 131
Atom, 169, 172
Autopsy, 187

B29s, 166-8
Baelz, Dr Erwin von, 6, 9, 20
Bean-bags, 48-50
Beijing (formerly Peking), 26, 43-4, 146
Birds, 145, 156, 175, 181, 189, 191
Blunders, 32, 41, 124
Bouse, Dr, 200
Brazil, 33
British monarchy, 13-16, 19
British Royal Family, 14-15, 19, 144, 158, 179, 198-200, 202
Buckingham Palace, 144-5, 150, 202
Bungei Shunjū, 21
Bunker, Colonel Lawrence, 214
Byakkotai, 34

Chamberlain, Neville, 13
Chichibu mountain range, 133, 181
Chōshū, 34, 60
Chrysanthemum, 29, 30, 114
Chumbot, Prince & Princess, 195
Chuō Kōron, 213

Comfit, 122, 157
Communism, 216
Coronation of King George VI, 5, 130, 141-4, 184-5, 199, 203
Coronation of Queen Elizabeth II, 184-5, 199
Coups, 3, 17, 213
Craigie, Sir Robert, 159, 160
Crown Prince Akihito, 136, 185, 198, 205-206
Crown Prince Naruhito, 204
Czechoslovakia, 12

Daijōsai, 119
Democracy, 215-16
Divine Wind, 142
Divinity, 19
Drum, 122
Drummond, Major General Laurence, 13-14, 117, 142-3

Earthquake, Great Kantō, 55-8
Eden, Anthony, 144
Edward, Prince of Wales, 1, 141, 144
Emperor Meiji, Mutsuhito, 5-6, 8-10, 13, 16, 35, 39, 43, 63, 87, 107, 110, 118, 217
Emperor Shōwa, Hirohito, 3-5, 9, 12, 13, 15-17, 19-21, 81, 87
Emperor Taishō, Yoshihito, 4, 6, 8-9, 11, 19, 31, 62, 77, 81, 118, 157
Empress Dowager, 19, 28, 77, 80, 88-91, 97, 101-102, 104, 107, 110-12, 114-15, 117, 119, 122-4, 127, 130, 132-4, 136-8, 142, 146, 157, 162, 166, 168, 174, 176, 179-82

219

Empress Haruko (Shōken) consort of Emperor Meiji, 33
Empress Nagako, consort of Emperor Shōwa, 188, 191, 193, 206, 219
Empress Sadako (Teimei) consort of Emperor Taishō, 28, 30, 61, 63, 183
Endō, Dr, 154, 162, 166-7, 169, *passim*
Enthronement of Emperor Heisei, 205
Enthronement of Emperor Shōwa, 101, 103, 119-20, 124, 186
Essays, 13, 15, 18, 20, 21, 26, 181, 213

Farming, 176, 211, 233
February 26 uprising (see 2/26 Incident), 3, 20, 21, 139
First World War, 53
Flood, 47
Friends School, 68-9, 71, 74-5, 79, 93, 96, 204
Fuji, Mt, 4, 25-6, 28, 129, 149, 153, 155-63, 165-6, 172, 175, 179, 183-4, 189-90, 194, 196, 209

Gakushūin (Peers' School), 25, 36, 39, 53, 60, 62, 65, 71, 74, 90, 126
Germany, 38, 47, 144, 146, 149, 167, 215
Gloucester, Duchess of, 202, 204
Gloucester, Duke of, 142, 144, 199, 202-203
Golf, 83, 85
Grand Shrine, Ise, 118-19
Grew, Joseph, 159
Grindelwald, 146

Hair, 41, 51-2, 63, 102-103, 107- 108, 110, 162, 186
Hakkoda, Mt, 137
Hakone, 149, 153-4, 156, 166, 179
Hampton Court, 203
Hartridge School, 66-7
Hata, Ikuhiko, 3, 20, 21
Hayama, 7, 9, 15, 131, 148-50, 154-5, 176, 186
Hirosaki, 136-41, 151, 160
Hiroshima, 101, 169, 172
Hitler, Adolf, 147
Hokkaidō, 136, 141
Honjō, General Shigeru, 16
Honma, General Masaharu, 81, 122, 125, 129-30, 133, 161-2
Hosaka, Masayasu, 3, 20, 21
Hove, 142
Howard, Ethel, 5

Ichijō, Count, 40, 41
Ideology, 216
Imperial Family Social Club, 132, 138
Italy, 38, 41, 47

Japan Society, 200, 204
Japan-British Society, 117, 148, 181, 198-9, 204
Japanese Alps, 131, 155

Kabayama, Count Aisuke, 25-8, 55, 66, 86-92, 95, 99, 155
Kabayama, Masako (later Mrs Shirasu), 26, 28, 55, 61, 66, 70, 86
Kaga, 37
Kaiser Wilhelm, 8
Kanroji, Chamberlain Osanaga, 17, 20, 21
Kase, Shun'ichi, 159, 160
Katō, Hajime, 193-6
Katō, Kyōko (author), 18, 21, 214
Katō, Takaki, 42

Katsura cabinet, 31
Kawamura, Admiral Count, 5-6, 87
Kawazu, Kuni, 177
Kent, Duke and Duchess, 199
Keswick, Sir William, 203-204
Kido, Marquis Kōichi, 17
King Edward VII, 5
King Edward VIII, 141, 145
King George V and Queen Mary, 141, 143-4
King George VI, 13, 130, 141, 143-4, 184-5, 199, 203
Kita, Ikki, 16
Komura, Jutarō, 29, 31-3, 40-2
Komura, Kin'ichi, 32
Korea, 8, 30, 31, 56, 196
Kotoku Incident, 13
Kugenuma, 184, 186, 187, 189
Kyoto, 10, 33-4, 101, 118-20, 182, 186

Lagerfelt, Baron, 196
Lindbergh, Charles, 75-7, 85, 142

MacArthur, General Douglas, 172, 175, 182, 214
Maeda, Marquis Kagatsugu, 37
Makino, Viscount, 116
Makino, Viscountess, 37
Matsudaira, Ichiro (elder brother), 29-32, 38, 41, 44, 100, 122, 138, 144, 151, 200
Matsudaira, Jirō (younger brother), 30, 31, 48, 83, 167
Matsudaira, Kataharu (uncle), 35, 54
Matsudaira, Katamori (grandfather), 33-8, 44, 60, 107
Matsudaira, Masako (sister), 30, 31, 43-4, 47, 50, 55, 57, 61-2
Matsudaira, Morio (uncle), 35-6, 54, 59, 93, 97, 102, 104-105,
107, 109, 116
Matsudaira, Nobuko (née Nabeshima) (mother), 27, 29, 32-3, 38-41, 43 *passim*
Matsudaira, Tsunekazu (nephew), 31
Matsudaira, Tsunenari (younger brother), 31
Matsudaira, Tsuneo (father), 33, 35, 38, 46, *passim* 89, 104
Matsudaira, Tsunetada (nephew), 31
Matsukata, Saburō, 202
Matterhorn, 131, 205
May 15 Incident, 16, 17, 134
McVeigh, US Ambassador and Mrs, 121
Meiji Constitution, 12, 16, 120
Meiji Restoration, 4, 34, 89
Memory game, 54-5
Ministry of Education, 45
Ministry of Foreign Affairs, 30, 38, 43-4, 53, 56-7, 78, 87, 116, 159
Mitsumine (Chichibu Range's '3 Peaks'), 136
Mitsumine Kiln, 181, 190, 193, 197, 210
Mitsumine Shrine, 134
Morita, Toshihachi, 11, 13
Mountaineering, 10, 12, 131, 163, 188, 202
Mutsu, Yōnosuke Ian, 214

Nabeshima, Marchioness Eiko, 38, 55, 95
Nabeshima, Marquis Naohiro, 37, 39, 95, 114, 171
Nagoya, 119, 178
Nanking (now Nanjing), 148
Nara, 118
Neputa festival, 140
New Deal, 216

New Year, 83, 94, 110, 126, 132, 139, 148, 179-80
New York, 75, 78, 84, 142
Nikko, 7, 60-2, 77, 91, 112, 131
Noh, 68, 126-7, 176
Norway, 146, 179
Numazu, 162-3, 179-82

Occupation, 171-3, 175, 213-18
Okinawa, 170
Omiya Palace, 182-3
Operations, 154, 178-9, 181
Otani, Masao, 10
Oxford, 12-3, 15-6, 19, 80-1, 142-4, 198-200, 202
Oxford Rugby Team, 183, 185-6

Pacific War, 130, 215
Paris, 13, 15, 40-1, 75-6, 120, 199
Philippines, 81, 130, 161-2
Poem-card games, 126-7, 132
Poetry, 101, 128-9, 134, 137, 179, 188
Police, 15, 121, 124, 134, 145, 218
Potsdam Declaration, 216
Pottery, 193-7
Pound, Admiral of the Fleet Sir Dudley, 142
President Coolidge, 80, 120
President of the United States, 75, 80, 104
Prince Charles, 75, 199, 203-206
Prince Chichibu, Yasuhito
  2/26 Incident, 3, 50-1, 139-40 *passim*
  Birth, 4
  Death, 186
  Falls ill, 153
  Gakushin, 6
  Gotemba, 155 *passim*
  Kugenuma, 184, 186, 187, 189
  London, 5, 130 *passim*
  Marriage, 107-14
  Military Academy, 9
  Popularity, 10
  Staff college, 125-6 *passim*
Prince Chichibu Rugby Stadium, 185
Prince Higashi-Fushimi, 177
Prince Higashi-Kuni, 164, 171
Prince Hitachi, Masahito, 177
Prince Li, 56, 184
Prince Mikasa, Takahito
  (childhood title: Sumi), 62, 127, 156-8, 161, 167, 170, 174-5, 193, 213
Prince Nashimoto, 37, 57, 176
Prince Takamado, 204
Prince and Princess Takamatsu, 4, 17, 21, 116, 123, 127, 133, 139, 140, 144, 154, 157, 161, 167, 170 *passim*
Prince Tomohito of Mikasa, 203-204
Prince Yamato-Takeru, 10
Princess Alexandra, 198-9
Princess Asaka, Nobuko, 110
Princess Chichibu, Setsuko
  Birth, 29
  Death, x, xv
  Friends School, 69
  Gotemba, 155 *passim*
  Heatstroke, 45
  JBS patron, 198
  Kugenuma, 184 *passim*
  London, 5, 130 *passim*
  Marriage, 107-14
  Prince's visit, the, 77-80
  Trips to UK, 199, 200, 202, 204
Princess Kan'in, 27, 55, 60
Princess Kitashirakawa, Fusako, 110
Princess Takamatsu, Kikuko, 213
Princess Takeda, Masako, 110
Pu Yi, 136

Index 223

Queen Elizabeth II, 14, 142, 145, 184-5, 198-9
Queen Mother, 144, 184, 202-204, 206

Red Cross, 44, 59, 154, 199, 205
Regent, 9, 12-13, 19, 143, 201
Ridgway, General Matthew B., 182
Roses, 96, 168, 203, 205
Rugby, 132, 142, 183, 185-6
Russian revolution, 43
Russo-Japanese War, 31, 38-9, 44

Saga, 37, 39
San Francisco, 65-6, 80, 98
Satsuma, 5, 34, 60, 61
Scull, 15, 131
Second World War, 3, 17-8, 81, 122, 123, 173
Shillony, Ben-Ami, 8-9, 20, 21
Shimizu (lady-in-waiting), 71, 194
Shintō, 12, 45, 104, 187
Shirasu, Jirō, 168
Shirasu, Kanemasa, 177
Shirasu, Masako (see Kabayama), 25-6, 68, 92, 176
Shmoo, 171, 173
Shōda, Michiko (later Empress), 198
Shōgi, 8, 160, 192
Shōgun, 34
Shōwa, 3
Sidwell, Dr Thomas, 66
Sino-Japanese War, 38, 144, 146, 148
Skiing, 138-9
Squash, 130-1
Staff College, 121, 125-7, 129, 131, 133-4, 149
Streptomycin, 155, 179, 183
Suzuki, Kantarō, 167
Sweden, 146, 199, 201
Switzerland, 80, 146, 204

Tajima, Grand Steward Michiji, 18, 178, 184-5, 214
Taka, 43 *passim*, 112, 115, 121-2, 153
Takahashi, Korekiyo, 3
Tennis, 28, 47, 73-5, 84-5, 99, 130, 173
Terao, Dr, 164-5, 167, 169, 179, 182
Tianjin (formerly Tientsin), 25-6, 44-7, 50-1
Tilley, Sir John, 117
Tōjō, Hideki, 156, 166
Tokugawa, 33, 119, 133
Tonami, 35, 42, 44, 54
Trousseau, 104, 138
Tsuda, Umeko, 59
Tuberculosis, 4, 151-3, 155, 165, 180-1, 187, 205
Two-two-six (2/26) Incident, 3, 50-1, 139-40, 172, 213, 219

USSR, 170

Vassar, 59
Vining, Mrs, 198

Waka, 101, 106, 127, 129
Wakamatsu Castle, 34-5, 44, 58
Walton-on-Thames, 29, 200
Washington, 19, 28, 53, 64-9, 74-5 *passim*, 98, 105
Weismuller, Johnny, 117

Yamakawa, Sutematsu, 59, 60-1
Yamamoto, Isoroku, 83-4, 163
Yamaza, Enjirō, 29, 30, 44
Yamaza, Mrs, 108, 110, 113-14, 126, 141
Yokoyama, Taikan, 162
Yoshida, Shigeru, 142, 171, 200, 214